HANDBOOK IN RESEARCH AND EVALUATION

A Collection of Principles, Methods, and Strategies Useful in the Planning, Design, and Evaluation of Studies in Education and the Behavioral Sciences

THIRD EDITION

Stephen Isaac
Department of Evaluation Services
San Diego Unified School District
San Diego, California (Ret.)

and

William B. Michael
University of Southern California
Los Angeles, California

EdITS/Educational and Industrial Testing Services
P.O. Box 7234, San Diego, California 92167

FIRST PRINTING MARCH, 1995
SECOND PRINTING MARCH, 1997

Cover Design: Terri R. Thompson

THIRD EDITION
LIBRARY OF CONGRESS CATALOG CARD NUMBER (95-60160)
ISBN (0-912736-32-1)
MANUFACTURED IN THE UNITED STATES OF AMERICA

FOREWORD TO THE THIRD EDITION

From its original appearance in 1971, which was well received, the Handbook has continued to thrive. The attribute underscoring its usefulness across the years is its selection of key topics in the research and evaluation domains and the compressed manner in which it captures the essence of these topics, often in an outline or checklist format. Although the downside of this feature is lack of depth and detail, such treatment is amply available in the standard textbooks dealing with these subjects.

The need filled by this Handbook is that of providing an overview and a summation of often complex topics, as well as a synopsis of essential concepts or techniques. This benefits both individuals at a graduate student level who are just beginning research and evaluation activities, as well as more experienced practitioners who need to refresh their familiarity with topics or techniques not used on a regular basis.

The research and evaluation needs in the decade of the nineties and beyond reflect the increased demands for efficiency and accountability that exist in a time of limited resources for their execution. This circumstance suggests that much of the work will be carried out by enterprising graduate students and organizational staff members who recognize areas of need and who find the incentive to pursue their fulfillment. Certainly, the behavioral disciplines are considerably more informed and equipped to accomplish such a grassroots thrust today than in previous decades: Witness, in particular, the microcomputer revolution. In recognition of new approaches, this Third Edition has added the important dimension of naturalistic and qualitative methodologies, useful in their own right or as adjuncts to more traditional quantitative alternatives.

The authors welcome suggestions and comments from users of this Handbook that future revisions will continue to reflect state-of-the-art methods and techniques.

WHY RESEARCH AND EVALUATION IN EDUCATION IS TIMELY AND IMPORTANT

1. In educational assessment and decision-making, it is the only way to make rational choices between alternative practices, to validate educational improvements, and to build a stable foundation of effective practices as a safeguard against faddish but inferior innovations.
2. Policies of private and government agencies currently make approval of research grants contingent upon evidence of good planning and sound evaluation procedures.
3. The influence of behavioristic viewpoints on education which emphasize observable behaviors and objective evaluation.
4. The impact of computer technology and the systems approach which necessitate quantifiable input information, mathematically and logically defined concepts and relationships, and a systems operation based on terminal objectives.
5. The overall power and facility of computers to order, store, and process information rapidly and economically, analyzing large volumes of data with complex statistical programs.
6. The advent of cost effectiveness accounting procedures to evaluate educational programs using behaviorally defined objectives and tangible evaluation criteria which, often, are scores on standardized tests.
7. The recent upswing of interest by industry to develop new educational materials, equipment, and programs with built-in features for feedback and evaluation.
8. The availability of people, techniques, and funds to meet the challenge of research and evaluation needs in the applied educational setting.
9. The persistence of negative or inconclusive findings in the literature of educational research which raise serious questions about the validity of many current programs, both established and innovative, and the viewpoints underlying them.

WHO SHOULD DO RESEARCH AND EVALUATION

Research and evaluation is most relevant when it builds upon and involves the people directly affected. Too often research in education is done by outsiders for their own purposes using the schools as a source of data: departments of universities or colleges, graduate students doing projects, theses, or dissertations, and publishers or industrial firms field testing new publications, products, and programs. While this may eventually benefit education, the local school's needs are often neglected. The classroom teacher and the guidance consultant, along with the director or administrator, should have the opportunity to identify problems, set goals, formulate plans, gather data, analyze outcomes, and reach conclusions.

HOW THE HANDBOOK WILL HELP IN RESEARCH AND EVALUATION

Few people in education have opportunities to apply whatever training they received in research and evaluation. Furthermore, most of the textbooks on this subject are detailed and technical, making their occasional use impractical. A helpful aid should be a handbook summarizing basic information drawn from several key sources. It should be useful in several ways:

1. As a pool of guidelines, methods, and techniques selected from various references on research design, measurement, and statistics and ordinarily not available in a single document.

2. As a refresher to the individual who has not kept current on methods and techniques in this area.

3. As a checking and comparing aid for the researcher to insure that important considerations are taken into account, that advantages and limitations among alternatives are correctly weighed and that the researcher has been placed in the strongest position to reach useful and defensible conclusions.

WHAT THE HANDBOOK DOES NOT DO: A CALCULATED RISK

The Handbook presents only highlights, outlines, and essentials to achieve emphasis, clarity, and brevity. The risk involved in gaining these advantages is *oversimplification*. Each user is expected to supplement this document with more complete information from the standard texts or qualified consultants in this field, once they have their bearings.

BACKGROUND AND ACKNOWLEDGMENTS

The need for such a handbook initially occurred to the first author while working on an R&D team in industry, but it was not until his return to education that serious work began. Essential to the quality and scope of the original handbook was the invaluable assistance of the first author's teacher and friend, Bill Michael. The present volume is a significant revision and extension of both the first and second editions. It is worth noting that the first edition itself became a reality only after the appearance of two preliminary versions with limited circulation. Particular appreciation remains due to Mr. J. Richard Harsh of the Educational Testing Service, Los Angeles office, and Mrs. Isabel H. Beck and staff members of the Southwest Regional Laboratory (SWRL) who carefully reviewed the early manuscripts, making many valuable suggestions.

Finally, the first edition, on which the second and third editions build, became a reality in 1971 through the support of the Superintendent and Governing Board of the Department of Education, San Diego County – a debt of gratitude that time and this revision must not overlook.

TABLE OF CONTENTS

CHARTS, FIGURES, ILLUSTRATIONS AND TABLES

CHAPTER ONE

EDUCATIONAL INQUIRY

CHARACTERISTICS OF SCIENTIFIC INQUIRY

Most of educational inquiry has been based upon the use of the scientific method which has as one of its major goals the collection of information based upon the objective and systematic observation of natural phenomena with a frequent effort to achieve possible cause and effect relationships. The system of philosophy underlying the scientific method has been often referred to as *logical positivism* of which one major principle has been that of *verifiability* of relationships among natural phenomena. Customarily, these observations have manifested themselves in the form of a quantitative presentation of data that have been subjected to various forms of statistical analysis to facilitate interpretation. Typically, interrelated hypotheses (tentative statements of possible relationships between two or more variables) derived from a theory are tested and evaluated for their tenability. If the hypotheses are shown to be tenable, the theory is judged to be supported; if the hypotheses cannot be verified, the investigator may be led to revise or modify the theory or to check whether the measures employed have been reliable and valid indicators of the variables entering into the hypotheses.

During the past several years positivistic science has been criticized on the grounds that observation cannot be completely objective or neutral, for in a societal context such as education or psychology values are likely to be introduced in the observation process. Such criticisms have led to an increasing emphasis upon the use of qualitative, naturalistic, ethnographic, and case study approaches in which the observer may be an important part of the event itself that is being observed, rather than a neutral or detached recorder of the event. As Borg and Gall (1989)[1] have pointed out, a *postpositivistic philosophy* of science has emerged alongside positivism with an increasing emphasis upon value-laden and theory-laden principles that direct the acquisition of knowledge about phenomena that are not directly observable through the senses. From a pragmatic standpoint, the educational researcher probably finds it most helpful to keep an open mind and to endeavor to determine whether a convergence of findings can arise from use of a variety of philosophical orientations and from employment of alternative methodologies (known as triangulation) that are appropriate to those differing orientations.

---

[1]Borg, W. R., & Gall, M. D. (1989). *Educational research: An introduction* (5th ed.) (Chapter 1). White Plains, NY: Longman.

THREE MODES OF EDUCATIONAL INQUIRY

The area of educational inquiry may be thought of as consisting of three major components: research, evaluation, and development (or design). In the following paragraphs an effort is made briefly to describe each of these three components.

Research

In a simplistic manner, educational research may be defined as a systematic approach to (a) identifying relationships of variables representing concepts (constructs) and/or (b) determining differences between or among groups in their standing on one or more variables of interest (i.e., the relationship of membership in two or more groups to their standing on one or more variables). Educational research constitutes an endeavor to generate new knowledge or to resolve contradictions of inconsistencies in given bodies of knowledge. In educational practice, it is customary to test a number of hypotheses that have been deduced from a theory in order to verify, modify, or reject the major propositions, axioms, or assumptions on which the theory is based. Several of the terms just mentioned and others need to be defined to clarify some of the underlying aspects of educational research.

Variable. A variable is an entity or factor or characteristic that can assume several values along a continuum or can represent two or more classifications or categories, often qualitatively different. A continuous variable is one that typically comprises numbers that have been assigned to objects along a scale from low to high with many gradations of intensity or amount. Examples of continuous variables include such characteristics as height, weight, reaction time, blood pressure, test scores, and time. A discrete variable consists of two or more categories to which objects or individuals have been assigned. Often called classificatory variables, discrete variables may be illustrated in terms of categories such as gender (male or female), marital status, (e.g., never married, married, divorced, separated, or widowed), make of automobile, religious affiliation, or ethnic identity. In the instance of discrete variables, frequencies are often reported of the number of objects or individuals associated with each of the categories or classifications.

Construct. A construct, which is analogous to a concept, is a nonobservable hypothesized characteristic that is inferred to be present within the organism on the basis of a linkage of observed events or activities in a stimulus context to the observed behavior of an individual in response to the stimulus situation. Examples of constructs would include such concepts as anxiety, verbal aptitude, mathematics aptitude, school achievement, level of aspiration, leadership, ego strength, need achievement, self-concept, and reenforcement. An example which would lead one to conclude that a person possessed a high level of verbal aptitude (the construct) would be that a score placed him or her in the top 5% of a norm group (the score representing an indication of an individual's behavior or response to a set of well constructed items on a standardized test administered under controlled conditions–the stimulus context). One could infer that an individual manifested a high level of anxiety (the construct) if he or she turned pale and perspired profusely (the response component) to harsh and threatening remarks from his or her obnoxious employer (the stimulus situation).

Operational definition. In most scientific inquiry, an effort is made to define a construct in terms of some form of objective procedure or measure that will yield a quantitative (numerical) designation of standing on a variable reflecting that construct. For many years a mentally gifted minor (MGM) was defined as one who placed at a score two standard deviations or more above the mean (roughly in the top 2% of scores) on a standardized test that had been administered to a representative norm group of the same age as that of the child. In an experiment involving two subgroups identified as high or low in anxiety, an operational definition would be that individuals would be classified as high or low in anxiety in terms of earning scores on a standardized anxiety scale, respectively, at or above the 75th percentile (high anxiety) or at or below the 25th percentile (low anxiety). Operational definitions afford the opportunity for a second or third researcher to replicate the work of another by using the same experimental procedure or instrument so that an equivalent basis is provided for a meaningful comparison of data across studies.

Hypothesis. An hypothesis may be viewed as being a declarative statement of a relationship between two variables often recast from a corresponding research question. One definition of an hypothesis is that of a tentative relationship that has been suggested to exist between two constructs. Another form of stating an hypothesis would be that of posing a possible difference between two groups or among three or more groups on a given variable which represents an operational definition of a construct. In a well-formulated theory (a term to be defined subsequently) from which an hypothesis has been derived or deduced, the hypothesis almost always will be a directional one in which either only a positive or only a negative relationship or in which either only a positive or only a negative difference has been indicated.

Hypotheses may be presented at three levels: (a) a *substantive or conceptual* formulation involving the constructs directly, (b) an *operational* statement describing the relationship in terms of the actual measures employed or precise experimental procedures performed, and (c) a translation into a *statistical hypothesis* which can assume two forms–first, an alternative hypothesis followed by a null hypothesis.

An example of an hypothesis at each of these three levels would be the following:

Substantive Statement

There would be a positive relationship between college achievement and verbal aptitude.

Operational Formulation

There would be a positive association between college achievement as indicated by the grade point average earned during the freshman year in 24 or more academic units and scores on the Verbal portion of the *Scholastic Aptitude Test* (SAT) of the College Entrance Examination Board.

Statistical Expression

In a population from which a sample was selected, the alternative hypothesis would be that a positive correlation would exist between grade point average and verbal test scores.

Null Hypothesis

In the population from which the sample was selected, the null hypothesis would be that the correlation between grade point average and verbal test scores would be negative or at most zero.

Theory. A theory is basically a set of interrelated hypotheses that have been derived from one or more definitional statements–super hypotheses (axioms, postulates, or conceptual assumptions that define the major given features of the theory). A theory constitutes a tentative explanation of a complex phenomenon such as the nature of learning, or that of intelligence. The derived hypotheses serve to amplify upon the postulates and to give body to the theory itself. For example, most learning theories have basic definitional statements concerning the role of practice or repetition, sequencing of material, reenforcement or reward, transfer of information, and possibly memory or retention. Within the framework of these major definitional components (postulates of the learning process), several hypotheses may be derived that serve to describe how each of these components can be manifested in a number of different interrelated ways depending upon the characteristics of the groups involved and the nature of the tasks presented.

Another example adapted from the text by Wilson, Robeck, and Michael (1974)[1] would be in the area of a very simplistic theory of achievement motivation in which students manifest a need to achieve. Two basic postulates (axioms, conceptual assumptions, or simply definitional statements) may be posed that students who exhibit a need to achieve are those that (a) would identify with role models who value achievement and (b) receive reward or recognition from significant others such as teachers, parents, or valued peers for their achievement. For the first postulate, two derivable hypotheses (predictions) would be that in two groups of children of the same ability level those with high achievement motivation in contrast to those with low achievement motivation would volunteer more frequently in class when a question was asked by the teacher and (b) would spend more time discussing with parents activities that had taken place at school. For the second postulate, two derivable hypotheses would be that with ability level controlled those students high in achievement motivation in contrast to those low in achievement motivation (a) would receive more encouragement and praise from their parents and teachers for their academic efforts at school and (b) would exert more effort in trying to receive an "A" grade irrespective of how difficult or interesting an assignment might be. These hypotheses which imply that a directional difference between two groups would exist also could be restated in the form of a relationship such that membership in the high or low group with respect to achievement motivation would be related to the greater or lesser amount of behavior represented in each of the four activities previously stated. If confirmatory evidence should be found for each of these hypotheses and for several other related ones derived from the same postulates, then support would be realized for the theory. If affirmative evidence for the hypotheses did not occur, modifications in the theory might be required or changes in the indicators of the constructs might need to be made.

Model. A model is a representation or replica of a complex phenomenon typically communicated in a visual format. Toys such as airplanes, automobiles, and boats constitute models as do maps in an atlas or the drawn plans of an architect for a physical structure. In educational and psychological research, a model may be equated to a theory when the major elements of the model are constructs that are being related to one another in different ways. Frequently, in a diagram intended to portray the model, circles or squares or rectangles may reflect constructs, and the arrows joining these geometric figures reflect how one construct impacts upon another construct or interacts with it.

Paradigm. In many of the social sciences a paradigm often has been used almost synonymously with the term model. Many educational researchers, however, tend to view the paradigm as a procedural diagram indicating steps that need to be followed in

---

[1]Wilson, J. A. R., Robeck, M. C., & Michael, W. B. (1974). *Psychological foundations of learning and teaching* (2nd ed.) (Chapter 17, pp. 457-459). New York: McGraw-Hill Co.

completing a task or in reaching a particular goal. Many of the charts describing steps to be taken in programmed learning, as in branching, or diagramed steps to be followed in a complex registration process could be referred to as paradigms. In a subsequent chapter, various experimental designs are set forth in the form of paradigms indicating the sequence of administration of a pretest, the introduction of an intervention (or lack of intervention), and administration of a posttest to two or more groups.

Evaluation

As a second form of educational inquiry, evaluation involves primarily a determination of the effectiveness or worth of an educational program or of some other form of intervention such as a recently completed instructional unit or counseling activity. It is important that criteria of effectiveness be established so that judgments can be made in a relatively objective manner. Evaluation is highly dependent upon the interpretation of outcomes of a program or intervention that have been expressed in the form of either quantitative or qualitative language. The next chapter is devoted almost entirely to differing features of the evaluation process.

As is to be noted later, evaluation is a precursor to making statements regarding accountability. In the following chapter, distinctions are made between (a) formative evaluation, which is concerned largely with determining the effectiveness of steps taken in the intervention process during the developmental phases of a project or program, and (b) summative or terminal evaluation, which is concerned with ascertaining how effective a program has been once refined and then initiated.

Development

Whereas in educational research an effort is made to generate new knowledge or to resolve existing conflicts or inconsistencies in existing bodies of knowledge, methodology in the area of development or design is directed toward achieving a reasonably well defined product of functional utility such as computer software, a programmed learning exercise, a computerized instructional unit, or a standardized psychological test. In the area of education, development may rely heavily on what research has revealed concerning the characteristics of the teaching-learning-evaluation process. Nevertheless, the goal is the creation of a particular product that is expected to meet a given set of established needs.

In engineering and the applied sciences, invention, for example, is a process that makes great use of the developmental approach. Such creativity extends to all disciplines. Development typically involves (a) a clear-cut identification of the problem area for which the product or system comprising it is to serve, (b) a conceptualization of the problem area in terms of its components, (c) a detailed analysis of the various interrelated components within what may be considered a system in order to pinpoint any new features of the problem area that might modify design-related specifications, and (d) an insightful perception of how the components can be transformed or combined in new ways to achieve a useful and workable product, such as an instructional package, a system of carefully delineated procedures to be followed in a variety of problem-solving activities, or even a piece of apparatus. It is important that the effectiveness of the product be evaluated in field tests and in pilot studies before its adoption. The developmental aspect of educational inquiry requires a great deal of innovation and ongoing decision-making that will allow the creation of the most functional or workable product.

In this text, relatively little emphasis is placed upon developmental research, although its importance should not be discounted. It is the one methodology that is highly dependent upon both the research and evaluation components previously described. It is well known to the reader that many large business organizations have research and development units (called R&D). For example, a pharmaceutical firm would integrate the findings of both basic and applied research in the medical sciences to develop an important drug or medication that would need to be evaluated periodically for its effectiveness in a number of laboratory or field settings prior to its being accepted by the Federal Drug Administration for marketing. Thus, the three forms of inquiry–namely, research, evaluation, and development–often interact in a mutually reenforcing manner in a variety of disciplines.

REFERENCES

Best, J. W., & Kahn, J. V. (1993). *Research in education* (7th ed.). Needham Heights, MA: Allyn and Bacon.

Borg, W. R., & Gall, M. D. (1989). *Educational research: An introduction* (5th ed.). White Plains, NY: Longman.

Borg, W. R., Gall, J. P., & Gall, M. D. (1993). *Applying educational research: A practical guide* (3rd ed.). White Plains, NY: Longman.

Bogdan, R. C., & Biklen, S. K. (1992). *Qualitative research for education: An introduction to theory and methods* (2nd ed.). Boston: Allyn & Bacon.

Creswell, J. W. (1994). *Research design: Qualitative and quantitative approaches.* Thousand Oaks, CA: Sage Publications.

Crowl, T. K. (1993). *Fundamentals of educational research.* Madison, WI: WCB Brown and Benchmark.

Fraenkel, J. R., & Wallen, N. E. (1993). *How to design and evaluate research in education.* New York: McGraw-Hill.

Kerlinger, F. N. (1986). *Foundations of behavioral research* (3rd ed.). New York: Holt, Rinehart, and Winston.

Krathwohl, D. R. (1991). *Methods of educational and social science research: An integrated approach.* White Plains, NY: Longman.

McMillan, J. H., & Schumacher, S. (1989). *Research in education: A conceptual introduction.* (2nd ed.). Glenview, IL: Scott, Foresman.

Miles, M. B. & Huberman, A. M. (1994). *An expanded sourcebook: Qualitative data analysis* (2nd ed.). Thousand Oaks, CA: Sage Publications.

Pedhazur, E. J., & Schmelken, L. P. (1991). *Measurement, design, and analysis: An integrated approach.* Hillsdale, NJ: Erlbaum.

Rosenberg, R. (1993). *Foundations of behavioral research.* New York: Holt, Rinehart & Winston.

Vockell, E. L., & Asher J. W. (1995). *Educational research* (2nd ed.). Englewood Cliffs, NJ: Merrill.

The purpose of evaluation is to improve, not to prove.

Daniel L. Stufflebeam

CHAPTER TWO

PLANNING EVALUATION STUDIES

Research and evaluation studies stand or fall according to how well they measure up to established scientific standards of excellence. Pitfalls, sources of contamination, and invalidating factors by many names abound to challenge the findings and interpretations reported in any given study.

The most effective insurance against unwitting errors is sound and thorough planning which foresees problems and makes acceptable allowances where unavoidable difficulties exist. A critic is always impressed by a study anticipating its own limitations and choosing the most nearly appropriate and powerful solution to a given problem.

After a distinction is made between research and evaluation studies on the next page of this chapter, attention is given to the topic of evaluation as a form of educational inquiry. Much of the material to be found in subsequent chapters has relevance to the completion of evaluation studies just as it does to that of research investigations. In particular, a great deal of the information about instrumentation and measurement in Chapter Five and many of the criteria and guidelines set forth for planning, preparing, writing, and evaluating research proposals, reports, theses, dissertations, and articles in Chapter Nine are just as relevant to evaluation studies as to the more traditional endeavors in basic and applied research. In short, the interrelationships among the nine chapters are substantial indeed and largely mutually reinforcing.

RESEARCH AND EVALUATION - TWO DISCIPLINES

Historically, research in the behavioral sciences goes back to the emergence of psychology as a scientific discipline in the 1800's. As psychology matured, it evolved a collection of methodologies and techniques borrowed from the physical and biological sciences, including principles of scientific inquiry, measurement, and data analysis–the latter incorporating statistical models many of which were developed for agricultural applications. Anthropology, sociology, education, and other behavior-oriented fields added further adaptations to research methodology in these new areas.

Research, having its origin in science, is oriented toward the development of theories and its most familiar paradigm is the experimental method, in which hypotheses are logically derived from theory and put to a test under controlled conditions. Evaluation, on the other hand, has come the way of technology rather than science. Its accent is not on theory building but on product delivery or mission accomplishment. Its essence is to provide feedback leading to a successful outcome defined in practical, concrete terms. Such a process has functioned informally since the beginning of time, although its more formal version coincided with the advent of the computer to give rise in the 1950's to the "man-machine systems" movement, and currently, to the "systems approach." Its general steps are: (1) setting objectives; (2) designing the means to achieve these objectives; and (3) constructing a feedback mechanism to determine progress toward, and attainment of, the objectives. Its basic paradigm, in computer language, is:

$$\text{input} \longrightarrow \text{processing} \longrightarrow \text{output}$$

Paradoxically, this is a sequence that actually is designed in reverse order. First, it is determined what the system must accomplish (output); second, all the intermediate steps to accomplish this outcome must be programmed (processing); and, lastly, all the necessary ingredients to be fed into the system must be determined (input).

In distinguishing evaluation from research, Stufflebeam has said, "The purpose of evaluation is to improve, not to prove."

The statement *to improve* suggests that a judgment must be made regarding what constitutes worth or *value*. In other words, the term evaluation typically is associated with how effective or ineffective, how adequate or inadequate, how good or bad, how valuable or invaluable, and how appropriate or inappropriate a given action, process, or product is in terms of the perceptions of the individual who makes use of information provided by an evaluator.

The figure on the next page furnishes a distinction between research and evaluation with respect to each of ten criteria. The similarities and differences noted should help clarify variations and emphases accompanying these two forms of inquiry. Incidental mention should probably be made of the fact that a third component of educational inquiry entitled *development* (as in the preparation of curricular materials, program learning exercises, and certain forms of so-called software in educational technology) is not a central topic of consideration in this volume.

TWO TYPES OF DISCIPLINED INQUIRY

CHARACTERISTIC:	Research	Evaluation
Purpose	New Knowledge, Truth	Mission Achievement, Product Delivery
Outcome	Generalizable Conclusions	Specific Decisions
Value	Explanatory and Predictive Power	Determining Worth and Social Utility
Impetus	Curiosity and Ignorance	Needs and Goals
Conceptual Basis	Cause and Effect Relationships	Means-Ends Processes
Key Event	Hypothesis Testing	Assessing Attainment of an Objective
Classic Paradigms	1. Experimental Method $\begin{array}{ccc} E & T_1 & X & T_2 \\ C & T_1 & & T_2 \end{array}$ 2. Correlational Method r_{xy}	1. Systems Approach input → processing → output 2. Objectives Approach objectives → means → measures
Discipline	Control and Manipulation of Variance	Program Planning and Management
Criteria	Internal and External Validity	Isomorphism (fit between the expected and the obtained) and Credibility
Functional Types	Pure and Applied True Experimental Quasi-experimental	Formative - Summative Process - Product

*Originally presented by Stephen Isaac at the first annual conference of the California Society for Educational Program Auditors & Evaluators, San Diego, May, 1975. The authors are indebted to discussions by Worthen, B. R., & Sanders, J. R. (1973). *Educational evaluation: Theory and practice,* Worthington, OH: Charles A. Jones Publishing Co.; and Stufflebeam, D. L., et al. (1971). *Educational evaluation and decision making,* Itasca, IL: F. E. Peacock Publishers, Inc.; and Worthen, B. R., & Sanders, J. R. (1987). *Educational evaluation: Alternative approaches and practical guidelines.* New York: Longman.

PROGRAM EVALUATION IN A NUTSHELL

Though program evaluation is often a complex process involving many components and considerations, at its heart lies a simple three-step sequence:

OBJECTIVES	MEANS	MEASURES
State clearly and specifically each objective in measurable or observable terms.	Plan the various strategies and activities which will be implemented to attain each objective.	Select or develop the measure(s) by which attainment of each objective will be determined.

Simply stated, decide what objectives are to be accomplished; determine how they will be accomplished; then find out whether, in fact, they were accomplished.

In actuality, program evaluation most often manifests in one of two guises: (1) *accountability*, analogous to the bank auditor checking the books to determine whether or not there is an acceptable balance across the original expectations, final accomplishments, and associated cost-effectiveness considerations; and (2) *feedback*, analogous to the athletic coach skillfully shaping and refining the performance of an individual or team toward continuing improvement.

A Salient Point

Although great care should be taken to insure that the objectives are substantive and worthwhile, that the means of achieving the objectives are among the most promising and effective available, and that the measures themselves are sound and valid, once the program design is complete, one fact acquires paramount significance. The measures on which the successful attainment will be based have now become the operational definition of the objectives. Regardless of the wording of the objective, a particular measuring instrument only will give back what was built into it – that, and nothing more. Program materials, activities, or content that lie outside the sensitivity of the instrument, however meritorious or valued in the eyes of the program staff, are likely to contribute nothing to the *measured success* of the program. This circumstance does not mean the program should slavishly focus on what the instruments measure or that it should abandon activities unrelated to them. It does mean that the staff should clearly recognize what has a direct bearing on the outcome measures and what does not and that an optimum effort should address those things which contribute to this measurement.

A corollary to this observation is to select or to develop measures that have the best possible fit with the program objectives to minimize any lack of correspondence between them. In the area of educational achievement this goal is the principal rationale behind the criterion-referenced testing movement, in contrast to the widespread use of norm-referenced tests which tend to have only a modest overlap with instructional content.

As program evaluation increases in complexity, additional components are added to the three basic steps. One widely used model is the following:[1]

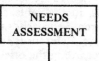

NEEDS ASSESSMENT

A need has been defined as the discrepancy between *what is* and *what ought to be*. Once identified, needs are placed in order of priority. They are the basis for setting program goals.

PROGRAM PLANNING

From program goals, specific, measurable objectives are derived and a plan containing the means to attain these objectives — the program procedures, strategies, and activities — is formulated.

These two components comprise the *formative* or *process* phase of evaluation.

IMPLEMENTATION EVALUATION

Seeks out discrepancies between the plan and reality; keeps the program true to its design or modifies it appropriately.

PROGRESS EVALUATION

Monitors indicators of progress toward the objectives; makes mid-course corrections, as appropriate.

OUTCOME EVALUATION

This step is the *summative* or *product* phase of the evaluation; it determines whether or not the objectives have been attained. This phase often includes an analysis of program strengths and weaknesses, with recommendations for future modifications, if appropriate.

---

[1]Based on a monograph by Alkin, M. C. (1971, August). *A Theory of Evaluation.* Center for the Study of Evaluation, UCLA Graduate School of Education, Los Angeles, CA; subsequently adapted for workshop presentations by CTB McGraw-Hill, Monterey, CA. Notations added.

MODELS FOR PROGRAM EVALUATION

In the pages to follow tables and figures are set forth that highlight various models of program evaluation. Specifically, in the table entitled "Some Models of Program Evaluation" on page 13, six different approaches to evaluation are examined from the standpoint of what they emphasize. References are furnished for the reader to consult if more information is desired regarding the orientation to evaluation identified. The detailed table on page 14 affords a descriptive summary of two models that have been intended to serve as frameworks for planning evaluation studies. With respect to each of twelve characteristics, brief statements are made for each of two different models. This table provides a basis for examining similarities and differences among two of the better known models for program evaluation.

In the pages following this table, three models are considered in detail. Perhaps the best known one–and certainly the one that has received the greatest amount of attention--is the model formulated by Stufflebeam and his associates. Several pages are devoted to both the presentation of a narrative and the inclusion of diagrams to illustrate the major features of this important model, which is called the context-input-process-product (CIPP) evaluation model. Following this important formulation is a brief presentation of the eight-step Metfessel-Michael paradigm that allows the specification of a series of steps to be pursued in carrying out an evaluation of the outcomes or products of educational programs relative to specified objectives. Next, a teaching-learning-evaluation model that represents an expansion by the second author of this volume of work done by other psychologists is summarized in diagrammatic form for ease of interpretation.

THE CIPP MODEL

Intended to provide a basis for making decisions within a system analysis of planned change, the CIPP model constitutes the culmination of almost four years of work by the Phi Delta Kappa National Study Committee of Evaluation under the chairmanship of Daniel Stufflebeam with the assistance of six coworkers–Walter J. Foley, William J. Gephart, Egon G. Guba, Robert L. Hammond, Howard A. Merriman, and Malcolm M. Provus. This model is consistent with the definition of educational program evaluation proposed by the Committee as being "the process of delineating, obtaining, and providing useful information for judging decision alternatives." This definition, in effect, incorporates three basic points. First, evaluation is a continuous, systematic process. Second, this process includes three pivotal steps: (1) stating questions requiring answers and specifying information to be obtained, (2) acquiring relevant data, and (3) providing the resulting information as it becomes available to potential decision-makers who can consider and interpret it in relation to its impact upon decision alternatives that can modify or improve existing educational programs. Third, evaluation supports the process of decision-making by allowing the selection of an alternative and by following up on the consequences of a decision.

EARLY MODELS OF PROGRAM EVALUATION

Model	Emphasis	Selected References
Goal-Oriented Evaluation	Evaluation should assess student progress and the effectiveness of educational innovations.	Bloom, B. S., Hastings, J. T., & Madaus, G. F. *Handbook on formative and summative evaluation of student learning.* New York: McGraw-Hill, 1971. Provus, M. *Discrepancy evaluation for educational program improvement and assessment.* Berkeley, CA: McCutchan, 1971.
Decision-Oriented Evaluation	Evaluation should facilitate intelligent judgments by decision-makers.	Stufflebeam, D. L., Foley, W. J., Gephart, W. J., Guba, E. G., Hammond, R. L., Merriman, H. O., and Provus, M. M. *Educational evaluation and decision-making.* Itasca, IL: F. E. Peacock, 1971.
Transactional Evaluation	Evaluation should depict program processes and the value perspectives of key people.	Rippey, R. M. (Ed.). *Studies in transactional evaluation.* Berkeley, CA: McCutchan, 1973. Stake, R. E., et al. *Evaluating the arts in education: A responsive approach.* Columbus, OH: Charles E. Merrill, 1975.
Evaluation Research	Evaluation should focus on explaining educational effects and devising instructional strategies.	Campbell, D. Reforms as experiments. *American Psychologist,* 1969, *24,* 409-429. Cooley, W. W., & Lohnes, P. R. *Evaluation research in education.* New York: Irvington Publishers, 1976.
Goal-Free Evaluation	Evaluation should assess program effects based on criteria apart from the program's own conceptual framework.	Scriven, M. Pros and cons about goal-free evaluation. In W. J. Popham (Ed.), *Evaluation in education: Current applications.* Berkeley, CA: McCutchan, 1974.
Adversary Evaluation	Evaluation should present the best case for each of two competing alternative interpretations of the program's value with both sides having access to the same information about the program.	Levine, M. Scientific method and the adversary model: Some preliminary suggestions. *Evaluation Comment,* 1973, *4*(2), 1-3. Owens, T. R. Educational evaluation by adversary proceedings. In E. R. House (Ed.), *School evaluation: The politics and process.* Berkeley, CA: McCutchan, 1973.

Source: Morris, L. L., & Fitz-Gibbon, C. T. (1978). *Evaluator's Handbook* (p. 7). Beverly Hills, CA: Sage Publications. Adapted and produced with permission. [See also: Herman, J. L., Morris, L. L., & Fitz-Gibbon, C. T. (1987). *Evaluators handbook.* In J. L. Herman (Ed.), Program Evaluation Kit (2nd Ed.). Thousand Oaks, CA: Sage Publications].

A DESCRIPTIVE SUMMARY OF FRAMEWORKS
FOR PLANNING EVALUATION STUDIES

Chart adapted and reprinted with permission of the authors and publisher, from Worthen, B. R., & Sanders J. R. (1973). *Educational evaluation: Theory and practice*, (Chapter 3). Worthington, OH: Charles A. Jones. (Original version appeared in *SRIS Quarterly*, Spring, 1972, Vol. 5, No.1. Phi Delta Kappa, Bloomington, IN, pp 10-13.)

STUFFLEBEAM	METFESSEL-MICHAEL
Definition	
Defining, obtaining & using information for decision-making.	Tylerian; comparing measured performance with behavioral standards.
Purpose	
To provide relevant information to decision-makers.	To formulate recommendations that furnish a basis for further implementation, for modifications & for revisions in broad goals & specific objectives.
Key Emphasis	
Evaluation reports used for decision-making.	Specification of objectives & using multiple criterion measures to assess outcomes, involvement of many different audiences.
Role of Evaluator	
Specialist who provides evaluation information to decision-makers.	Measurement specialist who involves lay individuals, school personnel and students in developing a set of recommendations.
Relationship to Objectives	
Terminal stage in context evaluation is setting objectives; input evaluation produces ways to reach objectives; product evaluation determines whether objectives are reached.	Evaluation entails measurement of congruency of outcome behaviors with objectives.
Relationship to Decision-making	
Evaluation provides information for use in decision-making.	Suggestions are made concerning revisions in objectives or program strategies. Feedback is given to all individuals involved in the school program.
Types of Evaluation	
(1) Context (2) Input (3) Process (4) Product.	Eight-stage evaluation process.
Constructs Proposed	
(1) Context-evaluation for planning decisions, (2) Input-evaluation for programming decisions, (3) Process-evaluation for implementing decisions, (4) product-evaluation for recycling decisions.	Multiple criterion measurement.
Criteria for Judging Evaluation	
(1) Internal validity, (2) External validity, (3) Reliability, (4) Objectivity, (5) Relevance, (6) Importance, (7) Scope, (8) Credibility, (9) Timeliness, (10) Pervasiveness, (11) Efficiency.	Involvement of diverse audiences, specification of objectives required, use of valid, reliable and objective measures, use of multiple criterion measures.
Implications for Design	
(1) Experimental design not applicable, (2) Use of systems approach for evaluation studies, (3) Directed by administrator.	Eight-stage evaluation process; involve various audiences, specify objectives, make periodic observations using multiple criterion measures; make recommendations to various audiences.
Contributions	
(1) Provides a service function by supplying data to administrators & decision-makers charged with conduct of program, (2) Is sensitive to feedback, (3) Allows for evaluation to take place at any stage of the program, (4) Wholistic.	Involvement of various audiences, forces specifications of objectives, continuous feedback and periodic observations, appendix of multiple criterion measures, reporting to various audiences, based on measurement technology, easy to apply.
Limitations	
(1) Avoidance of value concerns, (2) Decision-making process is unclear; methodology undefined, (3) May be costly & complex if used entirely, (4) Not all activities are clearly evaluative.	Focus on available instrumentation, testing can become excessive, focus only on outcome behaviors (little process or antecedent concern), lack of methodology for establishing standards or evaluating objectives.

In the CIPP model evaluation serves four types of decisions: (1) *planning decisions,* which influence selection of goals and objectives, (2) *structuring decisions,* which ascertain optimal strategies and procedural designs for achieving the objectives that have been derived from planning decisions, (3) *implementing decisions,* which afford the means for carrying out and improving upon the execution of already selected designs, methods, or strategies; and (4) *recycling decisions,* which determine whether to continue, change, or terminate an activity or even the program itself. To serve these four types of decisions are four respective kinds of evaluation. *Context* evaluation yields information regarding needs (the extent to which discrepancies exist between what is and what is desired relative to certain value expectations, areas of concern, difficulties, and opportunities) in order that goals and objectives may be formulated. *Input* evaluation furnishes information about strong points and weak points of alternative strategies and designs for the realization of specified objectives. *Process* evaluation provides information for monitoring a chosen procedure or strategy as it is being implemented so that its strong points can be preserved and its weak points eliminated. *Product* evaluation affords information to ascertain to what extent the objectives are being achieved and to determine whether the strategies, procedures, or methods being implemented to attain these objectives should be terminated, modified, or continued in their present form.

Central to most evaluations is an ongoing simultaneous interplay between product and process evaluation in which the feedback derived from the level or quality of products achieved can be employed in process evaluation to improve future products by overcoming deficiencies and by making refinements in ongoing activities based on implementing decisions. Moreover, feedback can also be used in input evaluation to redesign strategies so as to achieve more nearly suitable products. Thus, the CIPP model allows four questions to be answered: (1) Which objectives should be obtained? (2) Which strategies or procedures should be tried? (3) How adequately are these strategies or procedures working? and (4) How effectively are the goals and objectives being accomplished?

Supplementary information concerning the CIPP model is set forth in the figure on page 16 and an elaboration of the dynamic activities within the CIPP model is given in the figure on page 17. An additional insight about the model may be noted in the figure on page 16 in terms of these facts: (1) planning and recycling decisions are aimed toward the realization of *ends* (goals or objectives), (2) structuring and implementing decisions are directed toward the *means* of reaching these ends, (3) planning decisions and structuring decisions portray *intentions,* and (4) implementing and recycling decisions relate to *actualities.* Examination of the figure on page 17 reveals how each of the four kinds of evaluations interacts in a dynamic manner to serve each of four types of decisions. The use of lines and arrows to designate feedback functions shows the continual interplay between an immediately supportive or servicing type of evaluation and a given type of decision as well as the feedback activities that take place from decisions of any kind or from evaluation of any type to another kind of decision and its respective type of evaluation. In short, information can be communicated from any stage of the decision-making activity to an earlier stage so that modifications can be introduced in the type of evaluation performed and in the resulting decisions arrived at from these modified evaluations. Finally, it might be mentioned that the model has application not only to a large program setting, but also to the ongoing activities within a classroom environment. (Additional information regarding the CIPP model is summarized in the table on page 18.)

EDUCATIONAL ACCOUNTABILITY AND THE CIPP MODEL

Educational accountability represents the designation or assignment of responsibility to personnel in the educational environment for the realization or lack of realization of educational outcomes that are expected by members of the educational community–not only teachers and administrators, but also parents, taxpayers, and other concerned citizens. The CIPP model affords one framework within which accountability can be defined in terms of a past orientation or retroactive view in which records of prior actions, realized achievements, and visible products are examined in relation to educational decisions previously initiated. This retrospective perception of the CIPP model in the context of accountability is in contrast to one of proactive or future orientation of decision-making activities in evaluation.

FOUR TYPES OF DECISIONS IN RELATION TO FOUR TYPES OF EVALUATION: A TYPOLOGY IN A GIVEN EDUCATIONAL SYSTEM OR FRAMEWORK.

	Intentions *Phase 1*	Actualities *Phase 4*
	Intended ends (objectives)	Actual ends (attainments)
Ends (consequential goals or objectives)	*Planning decisions*–choice of alternative change-oriented objectives (existing, modified, or new improvement-oriented objectives) in an educational system represented by a project or program served by *Context evaluation*–provides information to develop systematic rationale for objectives largely through analysis of unrealized needs and unused opportunities and through diagnosis of those difficulties preventing needs being met and contributing to discrepancies between intentions and actualities	*Recycling decisions*–choice of alternative interpretations of how well objectives have been attained in relation to context, input, and process information and the judging of alternatives to continue, terminate, develop, or modify activities intended to solve problems posed by an educational system served by *Product evaluation*–provides information from which reactions and judgments of program or project attainments (products) can be made regarding extent to which objectives (change efforts) have been met either at the end or at any temporal point in a project cycle
	Phase 2	*Phase 3*
	Intended means (procedural designs)	Actual means (procedures in use)
Means (instrumental objectives)	*Structuring decisions*–choice of alternative designs, strategies, and procedures arising from planning decisions served by *Input evaluation*–provides information for identifying and assessing relevance and capabilities of designs, strategies, and procedures in light of human and material resources for achieving those objectives arising from planning decisions	*Implementing decisions*–choice of alternative courses of action involved in operationalizing, carrying out, controlling, and refining a previously chosen project design or strategy of known specifications served by *Process evaluation*–provides information (feedback) for monitoring by personnel responsible in implementing previously chosen procedures–information that allows (1) detection of existing or potential defects, (2) data generation for programmed decisions, and (3) record keeping of activities as they occur

From Wilson, J. A. R., Robeck, M. C., & Michael, W. B. (1974). *Psychological foundations of learning and teaching* (2nd ed., p. 446). New York: McGraw-Hill. (Reproduced with permission.)

Information set forth in the figure at the top of page 19 helps to clarify the distinction between decision-making activities for various types of evaluation and the corresponding ones associated with accountability. Additional insights regarding data requirements for accountability relative to certain key questions are explicated for each of four evaluation types in the figure at the bottom of page 19.

DYNAMIC ACTION IN CIPP EVALUATION MODEL

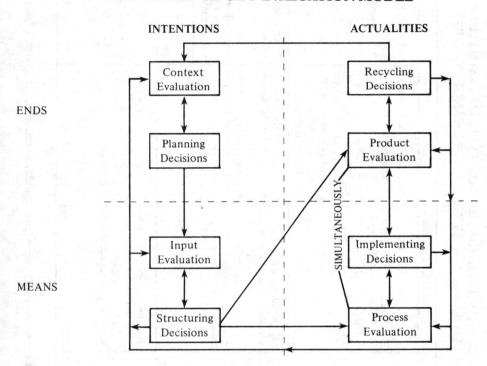

From Wilson, J. A. R., Robeck, M. C., & Michael, W. B. (1974). *Psychological foundations of learning and teaching* (2nd ed., p. 447). New York: McGraw-Hill. (Reproduced with permission.)

THE OBJECTIVES AND METHODS OF FOUR TYPES OF EVALUATION IN RELATION TO DECISION-MAKING IN THE CHANGE PROCESS

| | Four Types of Evaluation | | | |
	CONTEXT EVALUATION	INPUT EVALUATION	PROCESS EVALUATION	PRODUCT EVALUATION
Objectives	To define the *operating context*, to identify and assess *needs* and *opportunities* in the context, and to diagnose *problems* underlying the *needs and opportunities*.	To identify and assess *system capabilities*, available input *strategies*, and *designs* for implementing the strategies.	To identify or predict, in process, *defects* in the procedural design or its implementation, to provide information for the preprogrammed decisions, and to maintain a record of *procedural events and activities*.	To relate *outcome information* to objectives and to context, input, and process information.
Methods	By describing the context; by comparing actual and intended inputs and outputs; by comparing probable and possible system performance; and by analyzing possible causes of discrepancies between actualities and intentions.	By describing and analyzing available human and material resources, solution strategies, and procedural designs for relevance, feasibility and economy in the course of action to be taken.	By monitoring the activity's potential procedural barriers and remaining alert to unanticipated ones, by obtaining specified information for programmed decisions, and describing the actual process.	By defining operationally and measuring criteria associated with the objectives, by comparing these measurements with predetermined standards or comparative bases, and by interpreting the outcomes in terms of recorded context, input and process information.
Relation to Decision-Making in the Change Process	For deciding upon the *setting* to be served, the *goals* associated with meeting needs or using opportunities, and the *objectives* associated with solving problems, i.e., for *planning* needed changes.	For selecting *sources of support*, solution *strategies*, and procedural designs, i.e., for *structuring* change activities.	For *implementing and refining the program design and procedure*, i.e., for effecting process control.	For deciding to *continue, terminate, modify,* or *refocus* a change activity, and for linking the activity to other major phases of the change process, i.e., for recycling change activities.

From Worthen, B. R., & Sanders, J. R. (1973). *Educational evaluation: Theory and practice* (p. 139). Worthington, OH: Charles A. Jones. (Reproduced with permission.)

THE RELEVANCE OF THE CIPP MODEL TO DECISION-MAKING AND ACCOUNTABILITY

| | EVALUATION TYPES | | | |
	CONTEXT	INPUT	PROCESS	PRODUCT
DECISION MAKING **U S E S**	Objectives	Solution strategy Procedural design	Implementation	Termination, continuation, modification, or installation
ACCOUNTABILITY	Record of objectives and bases for their choice	Record of chosen strategy and design and reasons for their choice	Record of the actual process	Record of attainments and recycling decisions

DATA REQUIREMENTS FOR ACCOUNTABILITY THAT CAN BE MET BY THE CIPP EVALUATION MODEL

| Data Requirements for Accountability | EVALUATION TYPES | | | |
	Context	Input	Process	Product
What objectives were chosen?	√			
Why?	√			
Were they adopted?		√	√	
Were they achieved?				√
What designs were chosen?		√		
Why?	√	√		
Were they implemented?			√	
What were their effects?				√

From Stufflebeam, D. L. (1971). The relevance of the CIPP evaluation model for educational accountability, *Journal of Research and Development in Education, 5*, 19-25. (Reproduced with permission.)

THE METFESSEL-MICHAEL PARADIGM INVOLVING MULTIPLE CRITERION MEASURES FOR THE EVALUATION OF THE EFFECTIVENESS OF SCHOOL PROGRAMS[1]

Eight major steps in the evaluation process:

1. Involve both directly and indirectly members of the total school community as participants, or facilitators, in the evaluation of programs–lay individuals and lay groups, professional personnel of the schools and their organizations, and students and student-body groups.

2. Construct a cohesive paradigm of broad goals and specific objectives (desired behavioral changes) arranged in a hierarchical order from general to specific outcomes (both cognitive and noncognitive) in a form, for example, that might resemble one or both of the taxonomies set forth by Bloom *et al.* (1956) and Krathwohl *et al.* (1964). Substeps involved in this second phase include (a) setting broad goals that embrace the philosophical, societal, and institutional expectations of the culture; (b) stating specific objectives in operational terms permitting relatively objective measurement whenever possible and/or empirical determination of current status or of changes in behaviors associated with these objectives; and (c) developing judgmental criteria that permit the definition of relevant and significant outcomes as well as the establishment of realistic priorities in terms of societal needs, of pupil readiness, of opportunities for pupil-teacher feedback necessary in motivating and directing learning, and of the availability of staff and material resources.

3. Translate the specific behavioral objectives into a form that is both communicable and applicable to facilitating learning in the school's environment.

4. Develop the instrumentation necessary for furnishing criterion measures from which inferences can be formulated concerning program effectiveness in terms of the objective set forth.

[1]Metfessel, N. S., & Michael, W. B. (1967). A paradigm involving multiple criterion measures for the evaluation of the effectiveness of school programs. *Educational and Psychological Measurement, 27,* 931-943.

Eight major phases of process of evaluating school programs in approximate temporal sequence numbered (1) through (8). The facilitating role of lay individuals (L), professional personnel (P), and students (S) is indicated in lower right hand corner of boxes. The parentheses around L, P, and S in lower right corner of boxes indicate a secondary or indirect role and the absence of parentheses a primary role.

(4) Instrumentation Necessary for Furnishing Measures Allowing Inferences about Program Effectiveness	(5) Periodic Observations of Behaviors	(6) Analysis of Data Given by Status and Change Measures	(7) Interpretation of Data Relative to Specific Objectives and Broad Goals	(8) Recommendations Culminating in Further Implementation, Modifications, and in Revisions of Broad Goals and Specific Objectives
Selection and/or construction of a variety of relatively objective tests, scales, and indices furnishing measures from which inferences can be drawn concerning the degree to which cognitive and non-cognitive objectives have been attained Standardized aptitude, ability and achievement tests Standardized self-inventories concerned with adjustment, appreciations, attitudes, interests, and temperament Standardized observational devices such as rating scales and check lists concerned with achievement, affectivity, and products Informal teacher-made tests and scales concerned with knowledge, skills, problem solving, attitudes, and appreciations Interviews and questionnaires Miscellaneous indicators of the behaviors of students, school personnel, or community members such as GPA or numbers of awards, absences, days in attendance, withdrawals, transfers, referrals, telephone calls, books and magazines read, peer nominations, elective offices held, service points earned, frequency and types of disciplinary actions, requests for information, articles published, conferences held, concerts attended, memberships in professional or social organizations, time spent in community activities, and many others P(S)	Periodic administration of tests and scales and use of other indicators over sufficient period of time to furnish reliable and valid indices of the status at a given moment and of changes in behaviors sampled relative to specific objectives P	Data analysis preparatory to drawing conclusions about the effectiveness of the school program *Typical statistical methods:* 1. Comparing obtained measures (corresponding to objectives) with those of norm groups 2. Significance of differences between means and proportions 3. Intercorrelations of measures including multiple regression and factor analysis P	Setting judgmental standards and values concerning what are considered desirable levels of performance on the totality of measures collated and summarized through comprehensive measurement, observation, and other samplings of behaviors—standards that permit interpretations concerning how adequately (meaningfully and significantly) measures of performance, standing, or change on each of several outcomes (objectives) considered to be important approximate the minimal acceptable levels within the expectations of the evaluation model; a basis for drawing conclusions about the direction of growth, the progress of students, and the effectiveness of the total school program and for validating hypotheses which both lay and professional individuals have had concerning the relative effectiveness of various administrative, counseling, and instructional strategies P(S)	On the basis of the inferences and interpretations made concerning the nature and degree of the relationship of program outcomes to antecedent instructional, counseling, and administrative strategies, suggestions are made concerning either how certain specific as well as broad objectives which are unrealistic or unattainable in present form can be modified or how changes can be made in the strategies employed. Feedback in the form of information communicated to all individuals involved in the school program is essential if the evaluation efforts are to result in substantial improvements in the school program. Once the outcomes are made known to all individuals concerned, the cycle of the evaluation process starts once again P(S)(L)

5. Carry out periodic observations through use of the tests, scales, and other indices of behavioral change that are considered valid with respect to the objectives sampled.
6. Analyze data furnished by the status and change measures through use of appropriate statistical methods.
7. Interpret the data in terms of certain judgmental standards and values concerning what are considered desirable levels of performance on the totality of collated measures—the drawing of conclusions which furnish information about the direction of growth, the progress of students, and the effectiveness of the total program.
8. Formulate recommendations that furnish a basis for further implementation, for modifications, and for revisions in the broad goals and specific objectives so that improvements can be realized—recommendations which for their effectiveness depend upon adequate feedback of information to all individuals involved in the school program and upon repeated cycles of the evaluation process.

A few cautions: It should also be emphasized that judgmental decisions are involved throughout all phases of the evaluation process, as the participants at each stage may be expected to make adjustments in their activities in terms of the amount and kinds of feedback received. The alert evaluator needs also to be aware that measures may yield indications of false gains or false losses that are correlated with (1) experiences in the school environment as well as outside the school environment that go beyond the intent of the specific behavioral objectives, (2) uncontrolled differences in the facilitating effects of teachers and other school personnel (usually motivational in origin), (3) inaccuracies in collecting, reading, analyzing, collating, and reporting of data, and (4) errors in research design and statistical methodology. In such situations, the wisdom and seasoned judgment of the trained evaluator are particularly helpful and necessary if meaningful, honest, and realistic conclusions are to be derived from the data obtained in the evaluation process.

A. FORMULATION OF A COMPREHENSIVE AND CONSISTENT SET OF BROAD GOALS AND SPECIFIC INSTRUCTIONAL OBJECTIVES

Development of a cohesive and comprehensive framework of broad goals and specific behavioral objectives (intended behavioral changes or outcomes) frequently arranged in a hierarchical order or taxonomy from general to specific outcomes (cognitive, affective, and psychomotor)

A-1 *Broad educational objectives or goals,* the social, institutional, and philosophical significance of which is determined by lay individuals and groups, professional individuals and groups (in education), and students and student groups

A-2 *Specific behavioral (performance) objectives* customarily stated by professional personnel in operational form to permit relatively objective measurement and/or empirical determination of the degree to which desired behavioral changes, or outcomes, have been attained in terminal performance

A-3 *Developing judgmental criteria* for defining relevance, significance, and appropriateness of objectives and for determining acceptable levels of measurable outcomes (behaviors) of these objectives within a framework of realistic priorities in relation to societal needs and expectations; learner–teacher readiness and capabilities; opportunity for student-teacher interaction and feedback to motivate and guide learning; availability of staff, financial, and physical resources; and opportunity to obtain or devise appropriate evaluative instruments

B. ENTERING BEHAVIORS (INTERNAL CONDITIONS) IN STUDENTS AND TEACHERS

Characteristics of students and teachers prior to instructional-learning activities and potentially interacting with one another

B-1 *Students*

Information customarily available from pretests, cumulative folders, or preliminary observations allowing teachers to modify instructional procedures relative to individual differences in abilities and aptitudes, readiness-maturation, previous relevant knowledge, existing cognitive and psychomotor skills, motivational patterns (attitudes, interests, values, needs, energy levels), learning sets and styles, social and cultural determinants, physical-physiological status, and specific disabilities (sensory, perceptual, intellectual, or psychomotor), if any

B-2 *Teachers*

Information not too readily available though obtainable regarding such characteristics as abilities and aptitudes, competencies in subject matter, motivational patterns, capabilities in learning diagnosis, teaching-style preferences, temperament patterns, empathy, physical-physiological status, and specific disabilities, if any

A four-stage teaching-learning-evaluation (TLE) model derived in part from the basic teaching model proposed by Glaser, R. (1962). Psychology and instructional technology in R. Glaser (Ed.), *Training research and education.* (pp. 1-30). Pittsburgh, PA: University of Pittsburgh Press; and elaborated upon by DeCecco, J. P. (1968). *The psychology of learning and instruction: Educational psychology.* Englewood Cliffs, NJ: Prentice Hall; and in part from the evaluation paradigm prepared by Metfessel & Michael (1967). (p. 174). Prepared by William B. Michael. (1969). San Marino, CA.

C⸻INSTRUCTIONAL PROCEDURES
(TEACHER INFORMATION, PROCESSING)

Implementation of teaching process-learning activities intended to result in relatively permanent changes in behavioral tendencies (capabilities or dispositions as inferred from performance measures and observable outcomes) in the following: simple association (stimulus-response) learning, verbal knowledge and skills, concept and principle acquisition (including discrimination and generalization), problem-solving capabilities necessitating positive transfer of learning (involving meaningful reception learning and expository teaching, discovery learning, and inquiry training), creative endeavor, social and affective learning (modifications in attitudes, interests, values, and perceptions of human relationships), and psychomotor skills

Manipulative conditions in Stimulus Situation for
Modifying Learning Subject to Teacher Control and Decision-Making Capabilities

C–1 Content Components

Selection and organization of content involving projected use of instructional materials: books, manuals, periodicals, films, film strips, tapes, programmed learning packages, laboratory-field exercises, lesson plans, independent study and research plans, and special equipment

C–2 Process Components

Selection, organization, and execution of teacher-behaviors (teaching acts) to facilitate student learning activities, and interaction or two-way feedback of teacher-learner behaviors as manifested, e.g., in lectures, question-and-answer periods, discussions, report writing, and direct and guided use of films, tapes, and programmed materials

C–3 External Conditions in Learning Situation which Teacher Takes into Account and Manipulates in Attaining Instructional Objectives

External conditions, which mediate between content and process components in C and which interact with internal conditions of the learner and teacher in B, being functionally related to characteristics of instructional materials and to teachers' planning students' meaningful exposure to and use of efficient activities with materials through the skillful application of principles of learning theory: contiguity, redintegration, amount and kind of practice (e.g., frequency; part vs. whole, massed vs. spaced practice), reinforcement, feedback, and arrangement of degree of similarity in stimuli (associated with positive transfer or interference as in retroactive and proactive inhibition)

D. EVALUATION OF PERFORMANCE WITH FEEDBACK LOOPS TO STEPS C, B, AND A

Determination of extent to which intended behavioral outcomes have been realized in terms of data furnished by tests, scales, observations, and other samplings of behaviors once judgmental standards have been set concerning what are considered desirable changes in levels of performance or desirable standings on criterion variables in the absence of pretest data needed to determine change—the effectiveness of the teaching-learning process (a) being judged in terms of the degree of congruence or correspondence between intended and observed levels of performance on specific objectives with some provision made for unexpected or creative outcomes and (b) being interpreted in relation to entering behaviors (step B) and instructional procedures including content and process components (step C); a judgment resulting in new decisions being made regarding possible alterations in nature and priorities of objectives, in revisions of or modifications in instructional materials and teaching behaviors, and in possible changes in expected levels of student performance

NEEDS ASSESSMENT

In the chart on page 11 the first step in a comprehensive evaluation model is to undertake a needs assessment, a process which determines the key needs to be addressed by the program. Once identified, these needs are translated into program goals that are eventually spelled out in the behavioral language of specific and attainable objectives. Pages 24 through 31 present selected outlines and checklists to illustrate both the different viewpoints regarding the definition of need and sample instruments that are available to assist in the needs assessment task.

ADVANTAGES AND DISADVANTAGES ACCRUING FROM DIFFERENT DEFINITIONS OF NEED[1]

Definitions	Advantages	Disadvantages
Discrepancy View A need is a discrepancy between desired performance and observed or predicted performance.	o is highly amenable to the use of norm-referenced and criterion-referenced tests as well as certification checklists o is generally accepted by school districts and state education departments	o tends to concentrate needs assessment studies on those variables for which tests and norms are available o oversimplifies the criterion problem by attributing more validity than is deserved to norms, arbitrary standards and pronouncements by accrediting agencies o tends to reduce needs assessment to a simplistic mechanical process
Democratic View A need is a change desired by a majority of some reference group.	o is easy to apply o has high public relations value o is democratic o tends to consider a wide range of variables o involves many people in the goal-setting process o provides useful information for determining the relative importance of potential need	o confuses needs with preferences o depends heavily on the extent that the reference group is informed o tends to confound needs determinations with cost and comfort considerations o admits very real possibilities of forming invalid goals
Diagnostic View A need is something whose absense or deficiency proves harmful.	o assumes that survival needs will not be overlooked o provides for the identification of met and unmet needs o uses logic and available research evidence to ascertain what deficiencies would be harmful o is amenable to the checklist approach	o concentrates on basic survival needs to the exclusion of higher order needs o concentrates on removing the harmful effects of deprivation to the exclusion of seeking ways to improve on practice and performance that are already satisfactory o is highly subjective in practice, since research in education provides little evidence about the effects of various kinds of educational deprivation o is based on the questionable assumption that some needs are absolute
Analytic View A need is the direction improvement is predicted, given information about current status.	o exhalts informed judgment and systematic problem solving o seeks full and complete description o focuses on improvement as opposed to remediation o does not depend on a prior statements of standards	o is an abstraction that may be difficult to operationalize o requires highly skilled personnel

---

[1]Stufflebeam, D. L. (1977, September) *Needs assessment in evaluation.* Paper presented at the AERA Evaluation Conference, San Francisco, CA. Reproduced with permission of Daniel Stufflebeam.

SAMPLE CHECKLIST FOR A NEEDS ASSESSMENT[1]

Check one: **Parent**
Staff
Other (indicate role)

DIRECTIONS:

Below are listed sixteen areas of student growth to consider in planning next year's program. Select which four of the 16 you think are the most important *for a school to concentrate on,* and which are the four least important. Please place checks in the columns provided. There should be four checks in "most important," four checks in "least important," and eight areas which will have no checks. Obviously all 16 are important and plans will be made in each area. By completing this form *you are not suggesting that cuts should be made;* you are helping set priorities. The items are placed in this order so that later on responses can be easily tallied. DO NOT assume they are already in some order.

	Among 4 Most Important	Among 4 Least Important
1. A child is able to sound out words and understand what he or she has read.		
2. A child puts reading skills into practice; for example, reading books from a library and reading during leisure time.		
3. A child listens well and responds to others.		
4. A child uses speech in clear and accurate communication with others.		
5. A child writes, spells and punctuates using complete sentences.		
6. A child knows the basic math concepts and performs computation skills.		
7. A child puts mathematical facts and ideas into everyday life; for example, making change, telling time.		
8. A child knows how to think through a situation in order to understand it better and can apply scientific principles to better understand the environment.		
9. A child behaves in a way that shows that he or she is becoming a good citizen.		
10. A child knows about his or her own culture and about other cultures.		
11. A child shows pride in his or her own culture and shows awareness, understanding of, and respect for other people.		
12. A child understands and appreciates the value that art, music, dance, and drama have on our life style.		
13. A child knows the significance of the consumer in society and is aware of how one's career affects a life style.		
14. A child is physically healthy.		
15. A child feels positive about himself or herself and others.		
16. A child feels good about school in general.		

> Place completed form in the enclosed envelope and return with your child.

PRACTICAL GUIDELINES TO NEEDS ASSESSMENT[1]

The steps proposed for conducting a school's needs assessment are:

1. Identify the student-oriented goals.
2. Rank the importance of these goals without regard to performance levels.
3. Assess the level of performance for each of the goals.
4. Establish a priority for each student goal, considering both importance and performance.

Step 1: Identify the student-oriented goals

Student needs in any particular school are based upon the goals the school has for its students. Thus, the first step of a needs assessment is to identify these student-oriented goals.

Step 2: Rank the importance of the goals

Each group of people deemed significant to the planning process ranks the student goals in order of importance. It is not likely that equal attention will be needed or can be given to all areas. To keep the process simple, yet moving steadily toward the desired outcome, the importance of each goal is considered *without regard to current performance level;* e.g., a school might have very high reading achievement but still consider mastery of basic reading skills a high importance goal. Goals are categorized as high, moderate, or low importance.

Step 3: Assess the level of performance for each of the goals

Data are collected to identify how well students are performing in each goal area. The data should come from the best available source. For example, a profile of each student in reading or math, including a record of skill mastery, provides a far better source of information than does a questionnaire calling for teacher estimates of mastery. A general rule of thumb is to use those available data which stand the best chance of being accurate. The performance level for each goal is categorized as high, moderate, or low.

Step 4: Establish a priority for each student goal, considering both importance and performance

The goals are placed into one of the nine cells provided in the figure on page 27. Priorities are established, high to low, from upper left to lower right with cell number 1 being top priority. Cells numbered 2 have second-level priority; cells numbered 3 are third level; and cells 4 and 5 have least priority.

---

[1]Cox, J. (1979, July). *The needs assessment: A guide for school level activities* (pp. 2-3). Downey, CA: Office of the Los Angeles County Superintendent of Schools. Reproduced with permission.
The rationale for the procedure described is based in large measure upon procedures that Dr. Cox reports having learned in the early 1970's in interactive discussions with professional personnel at the Center for the Study of Evaluation, University of California, Los Angeles.

PERFORMANCE

IMPORTANCE	LOW	MODERATE	HIGH
HIGH	[1]	[2]	[3]
MODERATE	[2]	[3]	[4]
LOW	[3]	[4]	[5]

The technique used for displaying the data is based on the following premises:

1. Findings of a needs assessment, in order to be useful, *must* establish priorities.
2. Importance of the goal and the performance level share equally in determining priorities.
3. Data are not useful unless the users understand, accept, and can *act* upon the information.

A CHECKLIST FOR DESIGNING NEEDS ASSESSMENT STUDIES[1]

A. *Preparation*

1. Determine the *key elements* of the proposed needs assessment.
   _____Identify the *purpose* to be served by the needs assessment.
   _____Before proceeding, insure that this is *defensible,*
   i.e., ethical and potentially viable.
   _____Define the *client* and other *audiences.*

2. Clarify the *reasons* for the study.
   _____What are the *stated reasons* (e.g., selection of persons or groups to participate in a program, allocation of funds, modification of the curriculum, interpretation of program outcomes, or public relations)?
   _____What possible *unstated reasons* exist (e.g., to justify a previous decision to cancel a program or to discharge certain personnel)?
   _____Before proceeding, insure that the reasons for the study are *honorable.*

---

[1]Stufflebeam, D. L. (1977, September). *Needs assessment in evaluation.* Paper presented at the AERA Evaluation Conference, San Francisco, CA. Reproduced with permission of Daniel Stufflebeam.

3. Make an initial approximation of the client's and audiences' *information needs.*
   _____What are their *questions* (e.g., which students or schools most need assistance)?
   _____What areas of the curriculum are most deficient? What knowledge and skills will students need after they graduate from a particular program?
   _____What *information* do they think they need (e.g., teacher judgments, analysis of anecdotal records, test scores, and employer judgments)?
4. Secure and maintain *political viability.*
   _____*Involve* members of key groups (such as school board members, administrators, teachers, students, and parents) in the design of the study.
   _____Maintain *communication* with these groups throughout the study (through such means as a newsletter, news releases, public meetings, and an open door policy).
   _____Determine and honor appropriate *protocol* (concerning such matters as entering and leaving school buildings, involving school personnel, obtaining clearance for data collection forms and procedures, and reviewing records).
5. Characterize the *subject(s)* of interest.
   _____Decide on a definition of the *population* of interest.
   _____*Describe* this population (in terms of such variables as number, age, sex, S.E.S., location, relevant experiences, and past achievements).
6. Identify other *variables* of interest.
   _____What needs to be learned about the *setting* (e.g., its urban, rural, political, economic, and geographic character)?
   _____What *program* variables are of particular interest (e.g., goals, procedures, budget, staff, and facilities)?
   _____What *outcome* variables should be monitored (e.g., achievements in intellectual, emotional, physical, aesthetic, vocational, social, and moral areas)?
   _____Are there any expected *negative side effects* of the program that should be monitored (e.g., potential lawsuits brought on by due process difficulties or reduced public support because of the revelation that students' needs have not been met)?
   _____How about possible *positive side effects* (e.g., increased community understanding and parental involvement)?
   _____Whose *judgments* about the existence and importance of needs should be obtained (e.g., those of program, staff, parents, students, and site visitors)?
   _____What information should be obtained about *costs* of the program (e.g., developmental, maintenance, and opportunity costs)?
   _____What about the *intrinsic qualifications* of the program (regarding especially its philosophical and conceptual adequacy)?
7. Formulate a general *design* for the study.
   _____Define *key terms* (especially need and needs assessment).
   _____State the primary and secondary *objectives* of the study (e.g., to assess and assign priorities to program goals, to select

persons and institutions for compensatory service, to involve a broad reference group in goal setting, and/or to establish criteria for use in interpreting goal-free observations).

_____Provide a *logical structure* for the study (e.g., present a list of concerns and issues drawn from prior investigations, or lists of possible learner and treatment needs given an analysis of the program under study).

_____Describe the *procedures* to be used (such as surveys, document reviews, testing forecasts, and case studies).

_____Summarize the *standards* that are viewed as appropriate for judging the study (e.g., *technical adequacy, use* by the client, *probity*, and *practicality*).

8. Develop a *management plan.*

_____Present a detailed *schedule* of procedures (including the data gathering, analysis and reporting activities).

_____Specify the *support* that will be needed to carry out the procedures (including staff, facilities, and finances).

_____Describe any ways in which the study will contribute to *improved needs assessment practice* (especially in regard to training, development, and research).

9. Summarize the *formal agreements* that will govern the needs assessment.

_____Clearly identify the *parties to the agreement* (including who will finance, conduct, and utilize the study).

_____Delineate each participant's *responsibility and authority* for carrying out or facilitating the various parts of the study (especially in the data collection area).

_____Specify the *reports and other products* that are to be produced (including their format, contents, and timing).

_____Define the provisions covering *access to data* (such as a restriction against the review of personnel records or a provision for interviewing certain persons).

_____Specify who will have *final editorial authority.*

_____Specify who will have *authority to release the final report* including the conditions under which it may be released (e.g., the client may be assigned to release the report to the public, but only in an unedited form).

_____Present the established *budget* (to include the schedule of payments and specified accounting and billing procedures).

_____Define procedures for *reviewing and renegotiating* the formal agreements (e.g., if there are cost overruns in certain budget categories or if unforeseen factors make it desirable to modify the study design).

B. *Implementation*
    1. Acquire the needed *instrumentation.*

_____Specify the *sources* of information (e.g., relevant files, the professional literature, the subjects, experts, policy groups, administrators, staff, the client, parents, and members of the community).

_____ *Operationalize* the variables of interest (using techniques such as literature search, position papers, observation scales, rating scales, content analysis format, questionnaires, interview schedules, norm-referenced tests, criterion-referenced tests, and applied performance tests).

_____ Decide what to do about *critical levels* for each test (e.g., it may be appropriate to decide that no advance designations are possible or desirable, or past practice or research may give direction for identifying useable cutting scores).

_____ Select *critical comparisons* (such as the past or current performance of a local norm group, the past or current performance of an external norm group, or an accrediting agency's specifications).

2. Collect the *data*.

_____ Use appropriate *sampling techniques* (such as random, stratified random, matrix or systematic sampling).

_____ Have *key groups* rate the *importance of* the variables of interest (e.g., teachers and parents might assign ratings of essential, desirable, neutral, and dysfunctional).

_____ Obtain the *basic data* (which may include background, current status, and predicted status).

_____ *Process* the obtained data (by verifying, coding, and storing it).

3. *Analyze* and *synthesize* the obtained data.

_____ *Describe the program* of interest as completely as the data permit (noting especially the program's goals, design, process, costs and results).

_____ *Describe the subjects* of interests as completely as the data permit (especially in terms of their developmental levels and their attitudes toward the program).

_____ List the *issues and concerns* that are revealed in the program and student data (e.g., weak administration, unrealistic goals, lackluster teaching, poor parental support, unmotivated students, inadequate finances, and unsafe conditions).

_____ Search out *evidence* that would either *support* or *refute* the identified issues and concerns (such evidence may be in interview and observation protocols previously not scrutinized or in other data that have not been analyzed in detail; or it may be necessary to collect additional data on the questions of interest).

_____ Perform *discrepancy analyses* if they are called for in the needs assessment design (e.g., such analyses may identify the percentages of students that performed above some critical level on a given instrument).

_____ Perform *comparative analyses* if they are specified in the design (these may identify the percentages of students that are observed in each decile or quartile or a norm group distribution; they may give the position of a score, mean, or median in a percentile or standard score distribution for a norm group; or they may show the relative heights of a cumulative bar graph for each subject or group of subjects).

_____Perform a *strengths analysis* (e.g., by searching out funding opportunities, and qualified persons that are available and may be applied to the validated issues and concerns).

_____Formulate *conclusions* and *projections* (e.g., these may concern realized versus unrealized objectives, met and unmet needs, treatment sufficiencies and deficiencies, desirable or undesirable side effects, used, unused and misused opportunities, problems and tradeoffs, and possible alternative futures.

4. *Report* the findings.

_____Establish appropriate *reporting levels* (e.g., summary, main and technical reports).

_____Decide on report *contents* (such as purpose and design of the study, predilections of investigators, description of the program and subjects, identification and investigation of issues, discrepancy analysis, comparative analysis, strengths analysis, conclusions and projections, recommendations, limitations of the study, and the content that governed the study).

_____Report the findings through some appropriate *media* (e.g., printed reports, newspaper accounts, oral presentations, public hearings, TV and radio presentations, and sociodramas).

C. *Application*

1. Assess the *merit of the study.*

_____Check its *technical adequacy* (on such counts as defined object, defined setting, validity, reliability, and objectivity).

_____Assess its *probity* (in terms of its full and open disclosure, contract fulfillment, and conflict of interest possibilities).

_____Assess its *utility* (especially in regard to its timeliness, scope, relevance, dissemination, credibility, and importance).

_____Assess its *practicality* (in regard to realistic design and cost considerations).

2. *Apply* the conclusions and projections.

_____Assist the client and other audiences to *apply* the findings to their particular questions (focus on the preestablished questions but also help the audiences use the data to discover and address additional concerns).

_____Help the audiences to make *full use* of the findings (e.g., to clarify objectives, set priorities, appropriate funds for development, write specifications for developmental efforts, assess program plans, assess outcome data, provide accountability reports, and to recycle the needs assessment process).

_____Promote the use of the needs assessment study for purposes in addition to those for which the study was done (e.g., to provide *instruction* in needs assessment or to assist in generating and validating *new tools and strategies* for needs assessment work).

REFERENCES

Berk, R. A., & Rossi, P. H. (1990). *Thinking about program evaluation*. Thousand Oaks, CA: Sage Publications.

Bloom, B. S., Hastings, J. T., & Madaus, G. F. (1971). *Handbook in formative and summative evaluation of student learning*. New York: McGraw-Hill.

Boruch, R. F. (1991). The President's mandate: Discovering what works and what works better. In M. W. McLaughlin, & D. C. Phillips (Eds.), *Ninetieth yearbook of the National Society for the Study of Education: Pt. II. Evaluation and education at quarter century*. Chicago, IL: National Society for the Study of Education.

Boruch, R. F., & Wothke, W. (Eds.). (1985). *Randomization and field experimentation*. New directions for program evaluation: No. 28. San Francisco, CA: Jossey-Bass.

Erlandson, D. A., Harris, E. L., Skipper, B. L., & Allen, S. D. (1993). *Doing naturalistic inquiry: A guide to methods*. Thousand Oaks, CA: Sage Publications.

Guba, E. G., & Lincoln, Y. S. (1992). *Effective evaluation*. San Francisco, CA: Jossey-Bass.

Guba, E. G., & Lincoln, Y. S. (1989). *Fourth generation evaluation*. Thousand Oaks, CA: Sage Publications.

Joint Committee on Standards for Educational Evaluation. (1994). *The program evaluation standards*. Thousand Oaks, CA: Sage Publications.

Lincoln, Y. S., & Guba, E. G. (1985). *Naturalistic inquiry*. Thousand Oaks, CA: Sage Publications.

Michael, W. B., & Benson, J. (1994). *Evolution of evaluation design*. In T. Husen, & T. H. Postlethwaite (Eds.). *International encyclopedia of education* (2nd ed.). (Vol. 4, pp. 2079-2089). Oxford, England: Elsevier Science, Ltd.

Patton, M. Q. (1986). *Utilization-focused evaluation* (2nd ed.). Newbury Park, CA: Sage Publications.

Patton, M. Q. (1990). *Qualitative evaluation and research methods*. Thousand Oaks, CA: Sage Publications.

Reichardt, C., & Cook, T. (1979). Beyond qualitative versus quantitative methods. In T. Cook, & C. Reichardt (Eds.), *Qualitative and quantitative methods in evaluation research*. Research Progress Series in Evaluation: Vol. 1. Thousand Oaks, CA: Sage Publications.

Rossi, P. H., & Freemen, H. E. (1993). *Evaluation* (5th ed.). Thousand Oaks, CA: Sage Publications.

Shadish, W. R., Jr., Cook, T. D., & Leviton, L. C. (1991). *Foundations of program evaluation*. Thousand Oaks, CA: Sage Publications.

Stufflebeam, D. L. (1971). The use of experimental design in educational evaluation. *Journal of Educational Measurement, 8*, 267-274.

Stufflebeam, D. L., & Shinkfield, A. J. (1985). *Systematic evaluation: A self-instructional guide to theory and practice*. Hingham, MA: Kluwer-Nijoff.

Tyler, R. W. (1991). General statement on program evaluation. In M. W. McLaughlin, & D. C. Phillips (Eds.), *Ninetieth yearbook of the National Society for the Study of Education: Pt. II. Evaluation and education at quarter century*. Chicago, IL: National Society for the Study of Education.

Wolf, R. M. (1984). *Evaluation in education: Foundations of competency assessment and program review* (2nd ed.). New York: Praeger.

Worthen, B. R., & Sanders, J. R. (1987). *Educational evaluation*. White Plains, NY: Longman.

Program Evaluation
(CSE Source)

The following set of nine books constitutes the *Program Evaluation Kit* (Second Edition) that was prepared under the editorship of Joan L. Herman and contributed to by members of the professional staff of the Center for the Study of Evaluation (CSE), University of California at Los Angeles. The kit was subsequently printed by Sage Publications in Thousand Oaks, California. The references to be presented are in order of the volume listing rather than in alphabetical sequence by author.

1. Herman, J. L., Morris, L. L., & Fitz-Gibbon, C. T. (1987). Evaluator's handbook. In J. L. Herman (Ed.), *Program Evaluation Kit* (2nd Ed.). Thousand Oaks, CA: Sage Publications.
2. Stecher, B. M., & Davis, W. A. (1987). How to focus on evaluation. In J. L. Herman (Ed.), *Program Evaluation Kit* (2nd Ed.). Thousand Oaks, CA: Sage Publications.
3. Fitz-Gibbon, C. T., & Morris, L. L. (1987). How to design a program evaluation. In J. L. Herman (Ed.), *Program Evaluation Kit* (2nd Ed.). Thousand Oaks, CA: Sage Publications.
4. Patton, M. Q. (1987). How to use qualitative methods in evaluation. In J. L. Herman (Ed.), *Program Evaluation Kit* (2nd Ed.). Thousand Oaks, CA: Sage Publications.
5. King, J. A., Morris, L. L., & Fitz-Gibbon, C. T. (1987). How to assess program implementation. In J. L. Herman (Ed.), *Program Evaluation Kit* (2nd Ed.). Thousand Oaks, CA: Sage Publications.
6. Henerson, M. E., Morris, L. L., & Fitz-Gibbon, C. T. (1987). How to measure attitudes. In J. L. Herman (Ed.), *Program Evaluation Kit* (2nd Ed.). Thousand Oaks, CA: Sage Publications.
7. Morris, L. L., Lindheim, E., & Fitz-Gibbon, C. T. (1987). How to measure performance and use tests. In J. L. Herman (Ed.), *Program Evaluation Kit* (2nd Ed.). Thousand Oaks, CA: Sage Publications.
8. Fitz-Gibbon, C. T., & Morris, L. L. (1987). How to analyze data. In J. L. Herman (Ed.), *Program Evaluation Kit* (2nd Ed.). Thousand Oaks, CA: Sage Publications.
9. Morris, L. L., Fitz-Gibbon, C. T., & Freeman, M. E. (1987). How to communicate evaluation findings. In J. L. Herman (Ed.), *Program Evaluation Kit* (2nd Ed.). Thousand Oaks, CA: Sage Publications.

Program Evaluation
(Other Sources)

Anderson, S. B. (Ed.). (1978). *New directions in program evaluation*. San Francisco, CA: Jossey-Bass.

Borich, G. D. (Ed.). (1974). *Evaluating educational programs and products*. Englewood Cliffs, NJ: Educational Technology.

Cronbach, L. J., & Associates (1981). *Toward reform of program evaluation: Aims, methods, and institutional arrangements*. San Francisco, CA: Jossey-Bass.

Rutman, L. (1980). *Planning useful evaluations: Evaluability assessment*. Thousand Oaks, CA: Sage Publications.

Thompson, M. (1980). *Benefit-Cost analysis for program evaluation*. Thousand Oaks, CA: Sage Publications.

The Joint Committee on Standards for Educational Evaluation. (1994). *The program evaluation standards* (2nd ed.). Thousand Oaks: Sage Publications.

Walberg, H. J. (Ed.). (1974). *Evaluating educational performance: A sourcebook of methods, instruments, and examples*. Berkeley, CA: McCutchan.

Reference Works

Anderson, S. B., Ball, S., Murphy, R. T., & Associates. (1975). *Encyclopedia of educational evaluation*. San Francisco, CA: Jossey-Bass.

Struening, E. L., & Guttentag, M. (Eds.). (1975). *Handbook of evaluation research* (Vols. 1, 2). Thousand Oaks, CA: Sage Publications.

Periodicals

AERA. *Educational Evaluation and Policy Analysis*. [Quarterly Journal]. Washington, D.C. American Educational Research Association.

JAI Press Inc. *Evaluation Practice*. [Quarterly]. Greenwich, CT: JAI Press. [Sponsored by the American Evaluation Association].

Jossey-Bass Publisher. *New Directions for Program Evaluation*. [Ongoing series somewhat intermittent]. San Francisco: Jossey-Bass Publisher.

Sage Publications. *Evaluation* [Bi-monthly: February, May, August, November]. Thousand Oaks, CA: Sage Publications.

The formulation of a problem is far more often essential than its solution, which may be merely a matter of mathematical or experimental skill. To raise new questions, new possibilities, to regard old problems from a new angle requires creative imagination and marks real advance in science.

A. Einstein and L. Infeld
THE EVOLUTION OF PHYSICS
Simon and Schuster, 1938

CHAPTER THREE

PLANNING RESEARCH STUDIES

Carrying out research investigations requires careful planning similar to that found in evaluation studies. Central to a research investigation is a clear-cut statement of the research problem. In this chapter attention is given to (a) steps to be taken in analyzing a problem situation and in formulating the problem statement, (b) citation of the advantages of completing the pilot study, (c) an enumeration of common mistakes often made by graduate students in research endeavors, and (d) planning stages to be undertaken by a computer in processing and analyzing data.

FORMULATION OF THE PROBLEM

"A question well-stated is a question half-answered."

Some common mistakes in problem-formulation:

1. Collecting data without a well-defined plan or purpose, hoping to make some sense of it afterward.
2. Taking a "batch of data" that already exists and attempting to fit meaningful research questions to it.
3. Defining objectives in such general or ambiguous terms that your interpretations and conclusions will be arbitrary and invalid.
4. Undertaking a research project without reviewing the existing professional literature on the subject.
5. *Ad hoc* research, unique to a given situation, permitting no generalizations beyond the situation itself and making no contribution to the general body of educational research.
6. Failure to base research on a sound theoretical or conceptual framework, which would tie together the divergent masses of research into a systematic and comparative scheme, providing feedback and evaluation for educational theory.
7. Failure to make explicit and clear the underlying assumptions within your research so that it can be evaluated in terms of these foundations.
8. Failure to recognize the limitations in your approach, implied or explicit, that place restrictions on the conclusions and how they apply to other situations.
9. Failure to anticipate alternative rival hypotheses that would also account for a given set of findings and which challenge the interpretations and conclusions reached by the investigator.

STEPS IN PREPARING A RESEARCH INVESTIGATION[1]

A. PROBLEM-ANALYSIS PROCEDURES:

1. Select a problem that engages your attention and begs for a solution.
2. Accumulate the facts that might be related to the problem.
3. Settle by observation whether the facts are relevant.
4. Trace any relationships between facts that might reveal the key to the difficulty.
5. Propose various explanations (hypotheses) for the cause of the difficulty.
6. Ascertain through observation and analysis whether they are relevant to the problem.
7. Trace relationships between explanations that may give an insight into the problem solution.
8. Trace relationships between facts and explanations.
9. Question assumptions underlying the analysis of the problem.

---

[1]Van Dalen, D. B. (1979). *Understanding educational research* (4th ed., Chapter 7). New York: McGraw-Hill.

B. EVALUATION OF A PROBLEM:

Personal Considerations
1. Is the problem in line with my goal expectations and the expectations of others?
2. Am I genuinely interested in this problem but free from strong biases?
3. Do I possess or can I acquire the necessary skills, abilities, and background knowledge to study this problem?
4. Do I have access to the tools, equipment, laboratories, and subjects necessary to conduct the investigation?
5. Do I have the time and money to complete it?
6. Can I obtain adequate data?
7. Does the problem meet the scope, significance, and topical requirements of the institution or periodical to which I will submit my report?
8. Can I obtain administrative support, guidance, and cooperation for the conduct of the study?

Social Considerations
1. Will the solution of this problem advance knowledge in the field appreciably?
2. Will the findings be of practical value to educators, parents, social workers, or others?
3. What will be the breadth of the application of the findings in terms of range of individuals, years of applicability, and areas of coverage?
4. Will the investigation duplicate the work that has been or is being done adequately by someone else?
5. If this topic has been covered, does it need to be extended beyond its present limits?
6. Is the topic sufficiently delimited to permit an exhaustive treatment yet sufficiently significant to warrant investigating it?
7. Will the conclusions of the study be of doubtful value because the tools and techniques available to conduct the inquiry are not adequately refined and sufficiently reliable?
8. Will the study lead to the development of other investigations?

TEN STEPS IN PLANNING GOOD RESEARCH[1]

1. *Basic difficulty*—What is it that has caught your interest or raised a question in your mind?
2. *Rationale and theoretical base*—Can this be fitted into a conceptual framework that gives a structured point-of-view? In other words, can you begin from a position of logical concepts, relationships, and expectations based on current thinking in this area? Can you build a conceptual framework into which your ideas can be placed, giving definition, orientation, and direction to your thinking?
3. *Statement of the purpose or problem*—What is it that you plan to investigate? What are the general goals of the study? Define the problem.
4. *Questions to be answered*—When the research is finished, what are the questions to which reasonable answers can be expected?
5. *Statement of hypotheses or objectives*—Spell out the particular research hypotheses you will test or the specific objectives at which the research is aimed. Be concrete and clear, making sure that each hypothesis or objective is stated in terms of *observable behavior* allowing objective evaluation of the results.

---

[1]Lefever, D. W. Criteria taken from seminar in research methods at University of Southern California.

6. *Design and procedure*—State who your subjects will be, how they will be selected, the conditions under which the data will be collected, treatment variables to be manipulated, what measuring instruments or data-gathering techniques will be used, and how the data will be analyzed and interpreted.
7. *Assumptions*—What assumptions have you made about the nature of the behavior you are investigating, about the conditions under which the behavior occurs, about your methods and measurements, or about the relationship of this study to other persons and situations?
8. *Limitations*—What are the limitations surrounding your study and within which conclusions must be confined? What limitations exist in your methods or approach—sampling restrictions, uncontrolled variables, faulty instrumentation, and other compromises to internal and external validity?
9. *Delimitations*—How have you arbitrarily narrowed the scope of the study? Did you focus only on selected aspects of the problem, certain areas of interest, a limited range of subjects, and level of sophistication involved?
10. *Definition of terms*—List and define the principal terms you will use, particularly where terms have different meanings to different people. Emphasis should be placed on operational or behavioral definitions.

ADVANTAGES OF A PILOT STUDY[1]

1. It permits a preliminary testing of the hypotheses that leads to testing more precise hypotheses in the main study. It may lead to changing some hypotheses, dropping some, and developing new hypotheses when called for.
2. It often provides the research worker with ideas, approaches, and clues not foreseen prior to the pilot study. Such ideas and clues greatly increase the chances of obtaining clear-cut findings in the main study.
3. It permits a thorough check of the planned statistical and analytical procedures, thus allowing an appraisal of their adequacy in treating the data. Needed alterations also may be made in the data-collecting methods, so that data in the main study may be analyzed more efficiently.
4. It greatly reduces the number of treatment errors, because unforeseen problems revealed in the pilot study may be overcome in redesigning the main study.
5. It may save the research worker a major expenditure of time and money on a research project that will yield nothing. Unfortunately, many research ideas that seem to show great promise are unproductive when carried out in the field or laboratory. The pilot study almost always provides enough data for the research worker to make a sound decision on the advisability of going ahead with the main study.
6. In many pilot studies it is possible to get feedback from research subjects and other persons involved that leads to important improvements in the main study although the pilot study should follow the main study procedure for the most part, variations such as trying alternative instruments and procedures and seeking feedback from subjects on the treatment, measures, and other aspects of research are usually desirable.[2]

---

[1]Borg, W. R. (1963). *Educational research: An introduction* (p. 185). New York: David McKay Company, Inc. By permission, (Items 1-5 and 7). [See also Borg, W. R., & Gall, M. D. (1989). *Educational research: An introduction* (5th ed.) (p. 78-79). White Plains, NY: Longman.]

[2]Borg, W. R., & Gall, M. D. (1979). *Educational research* (3rd ed.). Copyright © by Longman, Inc.

7. In the pilot study, the research worker may try out a number of alternative measures, and then select those that produce the best results for the main study without some tentative evidence that they would be productive. If the student plans to continue beyond the Master's degree, Master's research may sometimes serve as a pilot study for later research to be carried out as part of the student's doctoral program. The less research experience the student has, the more likely he or she is to profit from the pilot study. Because of this, the student should attempt a pilot study whenever possible, even if it must be limited to only a dozen or so cases.

COMMON MISTAKES MADE BY GRADUATE STUDENTS

A. COMMON ERRORS IN FORMULATING A RESEARCH STUDY[1]

1. Puts off selection of a problem until all or most course work has been finished.
2. Uncritically accepts the first research idea that is thought of or suggested.
3. Selects a problem that is too vast or too vague to investigate meaningfully.
4. Prepares fuzzy or untestable hypotheses.
5. Fails to consider methods or analysis procedures in developing a tentative research plan.

B. COMMON ERRORS IN REVIEWING THE LITERATURE[2]

1. Carries out a hurried review of the literature in order to get started on the research project. This usually results in overlooking previous studies containing ideas that would have improved the student's project.
2. Relies too heavily upon secondary sources.
3. Concentrates on research findings when reading research articles, thus overlooking valuable information on methods, measures, and so forth.
4. Overlooks sources other than education journals, such as newspapers and popular magazines which often contain articles on educational topics.
5. Fails to define satisfactorily the topic limits of the review of the literature. Searching too broad an area often leads to the student becoming discouraged or doing a slipshod job. Searching too narrow an area can cause the student to overlook many articles that are peripheral to the research topic but contain information that would help design a better study.
6. Copies bibliographic data incorrectly and is then unable to locate the reference needed.
7. Copies far too much material onto note cards. This often indicates that the student does not have a clear understanding of the project and thus cannot separate important from unimportant information.

---

[1]Borg, W. R. (1963). *Educational research: An introduction* (p. 38). New York: David McKay Company, Inc. By permission. [See also Borg, W. R., & Gall, M. D. (1989). *Educational research: An introduction* (5th ed.) (p. 78). White Plains, NY: Longman.]
[2]Ibid, p. 67. [See also Borg, W. R., & Gall, M. D. (1989). *Educational research: An introduction* (5th ed.) (p. 161). White Plains, NY: Longman.]

C. COMMON ERRORS IN GATHERING RESEARCH DATA[1]

1. Pays insufficient attention to establishing and maintaining rapport with subjects. This often leads to refusals to cooperate or to a negative attitude that can reduce the validity of tests and other measures.
2. Weakens research design by making changes for the administrative convenience or the schools from which the subjects are drawn.
3. Fails to explain the purposes of measures used in the research to teachers and administrators. If a teacher thinks a test or measure is silly or worthless, her or his attitude is quickly sensed by pupils and leads to poor cooperation.
4. Fails to evaluate available measures thoroughly before selecting those to be used in research. This often leads to the use of invalid or inappropriate measures.
5. Selects measures to use in research of such low reliability that true differences are hidden by the errors of the measure.
6. Selects measures to use in research without being qualified to administer and score.

D. COMMON ERRORS IN USE OF STANDARD MEASURING INSTRUMENTS[2]

1. Fails to check the content validity of achievement measures in the situation in which the research is to be carried out.
2. Fails to standardize or control the teacher's role in the data collection situation, therefore introducing bias resulting from nonstandard instructions, coaching of some of the pupils involved in the study, and variations in degree of assistance given pupils during test.
3. Checks overall validity and reliability of measures selected but fails to check validity and reliability data on subtest scores even though these scores are to be employed in the research analysis.
4. Uses personality inventories and other self-reporting devices in situations in which the subject might be expected to fake replies in order to create a desired impression.
5. Assumes that standard tests measure what they claim to measure without making a thorough evaluation of validity data available.
6. Attempts to use measures without sufficient training to administer, analyze, or interpret.
7. Fails to make optimum use of the testing time available by administering long tests when shorter ones are available that meet the requirements of the research project equally well.
8. Does not carry out a pretrial of measuring instruments and, as a result, makes blunders in the administration procedures during the collection of first data, thus introducing bias.

---

[1]Borg, W. R. (1963). *Educational research: An introduction* (p. 94). New York,: David McKay Company, Inc. By permission. [See also Borg, W. R., & Gall, M. D. (1989). *Educational research: An introduction* (5th ed.) (pp. 241, 285). White Plains, NY: Longman.]

[2]Ibid, p. 94. [See also Borg, W. R., & Gall, M. D. (1989). *Educational research: An introduction* (5th ed.) (pp. 285, 313). White Plains, NY: Longman.]

E. COMMON ERRORS IN USE OF STATISTICAL TOOLS[1]

1. Selects a statistical tool that is not appropriate or correct for proposed analysis.
2. Collects research data, and then tries to find a statistical technique that can be used in analysis.
3. Uses only one statistical procedure when several can be applied to the data. This often leads to overlooking results that could have made a significant contribution to the thesis.
4. Uses statistical tools in situations in which the data grossly fail to meet the assumptions upon which the tools are based. Most statistical tools will give reasonably accurate results unless assumptions are seriously violated.
5. Overstates the importance of small differences that are statistically significant.
6. Avoids correlational analysis if the standard product-moment correlation cannot be applied.
7. Uses the incorrect correlation technique–such as, using the biserial correlation when the widespread biserial correlation is called for.
8. Uses the product-moment correlation significance tables to interpret non-Pearsonian correlations. Because most non-Pearsonian correlations have a larger standard error than the product-moment correlation, this mistake leads to over-estimating the significance of coefficients so interpreted.
9. Uses correction for attenuation in situations where it is not appropriate in order to make the results appear more significant.

F. COMMON ERRORS IN RESEARCH DESIGN AND METHODOLOGY[2]

1. Student fails to define the research population.
2. Uses a sample too small to permit analysis of the performance of interesting subgroups.
3. Attempts to conduct research using volunteer subjects.
4. Changes design in ways that weaken the research in order to make data collection more convenient for the schools involved.
5. Attempts to collect as much data as possible, then makes excessive demands upon subjects that lead to their refusal to cooperate.
6. Attempts to carry out a study in one semester that would require two/three years to do satisfactorily.
7. Fails to plan data collection in sufficient detail to avoid excessive treatment errors.
8. Starts collecting research data without carrying out a pilot study or adequately testing measures and procedures.

---

[1]Borg, W. R. (1963). *Educational research: An introduction* (pp. 145, 164). New York: David McKay Company, Inc. By permission. [See also Borg, W. R., & Gall, M. D. (1989). *Educational research: An introduction* (5th ed.) (p. 374). White Plains, NY: Longman.]

[2]Ibid, p. 186. [See also Borg, W. R., & Gall, M. D. (1989). *Educational research: An introduction* (5th ed.) (pp. 78, 241). White Plains, NY: Longman.]

G. COMMON ERRORS IN HISTORICAL RESEARCH[1, *]

1. A research area is selected in which sufficient evidence is not available to conduct a worthwhile study or to test the hypotheses adequately.
2. Excessive use of secondary sources of information is frequently found in studies not dealing with recent events.
3. Attempts to work on a broad and poorly-defined problem.
4. Fails to evaluate historical data adequately.
5. Allows personal bias to influence research procedures.
6. The student's report recites facts but does not synthesize or integrate these facts into meaningful generalizations.

H. COMMON ERRORS IN DESCRIPTIVE RESEARCH[2, *]

1. Student does not formulate clear and specific objectives.
2. Relates data-gathering procedure to objectives in only a general way and thereby fails to get quantitative data specific to problem.
3. Selects sample on the basis of convenience rather than attempting to obtain a random sample.
4. Does not plan analysis until after data are collected.
5. Structures data-collecting devices (questionnaires, interview guides, observation forms, and so on) so that biased results are obtained.

I. COMMON ERRORS IN QUESTIONNAIRE STUDIES[3, *]

1. Student uses a questionnaire in working with problems that can be better studied with other research techniques.
2. Gives insufficient attention to the development of the questionnaire and fails to pretest it.
3. Asks too many questions, thus making unreasonable demands on the respondent's time.
4. Overlooks details of format, grammar, printing, and so on that, if observed, give the respondent a favorable first impression.
5. Fails to check a sample of nonresponding subjects for possible bias.

J. COMMON ERRORS IN INTERVIEW STUDIES[4, *]

1. Student does not adequately plan the interview or develop a detailed interview guide.
2. Does not conduct sufficient practice interviews to acquire needed skills.
3. Fails to establish safeguards against interviewer bias.
4. Does not make provisions for calculating the reliability of interview data.
5. Uses language in the interview that is not understood by the respondents.
6. Asks for information that the respondent cannot be expected to have.

[1]Borg, W. R. (1963). *Educational research: An introduction* (pp. 196-198). New York: David McKay Company, Inc. By permission.
[2]Ibid, p. 233.
[3]Ibid, pp. 233-234.
[4]Ibid, p. 234.
*[See also Borg, W. R., & Gall, M. D. (1989). *Educational research: An introduction* (5th ed.) (pp. 465, 836). White Plains, NY: Longman.]

K. COMMON ERRORS IN OBSERVATIONAL STUDIES[1, *]

1. Student does not sufficiently train observers and thus obtains unreliable data.
2. Uses an observation form that demands too much of the observer.
3. Fails to take adequate safeguards against the observer disturbing or changing the situation to be observed.
4. Attempts to evaluate behavior that occurs so infrequently that reliable data cannot be obtained through observations.

L. COMMON ERRORS IN CONTENT ANALYSIS[2, *]

1. Student selects content that is easily available but does not represent an unbiased sample of all content related to the research objectives.
2. Fails to determine the reliability of content-analysis procedures.
3. Uses classification categories that are not sufficiently specific and comprehensive.

M. COMMON ERRORS IN THE STUDY OF RELATIONSHIPS[3, *]

1. Student assumes the results of causal-comparative or correlational research to be proof of a cause-and-effect relationship.
2. Uses sample in causal-comparative research that differs on so many pertinent variables that comparisons of groups can yield no interpretable results.
3. Attempts to study possible causes of a broadly-defined behavior pattern that actually includes a number of unlike subgroups. This usually leads to a jumble of confused and contradictory results with no clear relationships emerging.
4. Tries to build a correlational study around conveniently available data instead of collecting the data needed to do a worthwhile study.
5. Selects variables for correlation that have been found unproductive in previous studies.
6. Fails to make use of educational and psychological theory in selecting variables for study in correlation research.
7. Uses simple correlation techniques in studies where partial correlation or multiple correlation is needed to obtain a clear picture of the way the variables are operating.
8. Applies tables giving significance levels of Pearsonian correlation coefficients to non-Pearsonian correlations, which often leads to reporting nonsignificant relationships as being significant.
9. Uses the "shotgun" approach in exploratory relationship studies.
10. Fails to develop satisfactory criterion measures for use in correlation studies of complex skills or behavior patterns.

---

[1]Borg, W. R. (1963). *Educational research: An introduction* (p. 260). New York: David McKay Company, Inc. By permission.
[2]Ibid, p. 260.
[3]Ibid, pp. 286-287.
*[See also Borg, W. R., & Gall, M. D. (1989). *Educational research: An introduction* (5th ed.) (pp. 529, 567, 634). White Plains, NY: Longman.]

PLANNING FOR COMPUTER ANALYSIS
AND DATA PROCESSING

The role of the computer in processing and analyzing research data is a major consideration in studies involving complex calculations and large amounts of data. The advantages of a computer are speed and volume. As a result, the actual cost of computer time is quite reasonable, since seconds or minutes are involved to process data that would require weeks or months to perform with a standard desk calculator.

The economy and efficiency of the computer, however, depends upon some practical contingencies: (1) The data must be coded to meet computer input requirements. Someone must then enter the raw data correctly in an ASCII or text-only format. (2) The data are analyzed by a computer program. You should check to make sure that your data are compatible with the *hardware* (type of computer) and *software* (program to be used). If you can match your own design and analysis requirements to *existing* software, you will not incur additional costs involved in having new programs written or old ones modified; therefore it is important to investigate the availability of both computer facilities and computer programs specific to your particular needs before including plans for analysis of your data.

Suggestions for recording data —Final advice for the collection and recording of data with computer processing in mind should always be obtained from the staff of the computer facility with which you will be dealing. It would be wise to do a pilot run of your data recording and processing procedures to work out any difficulties.

Some cautions about computer analysis of research data—The power and prestige of computers can easily mislead the inexperienced researcher. Two cautions are worth listing:

1. *Errors*—While the actual mechanism and circuitry of an operational computer tend to be highly reliable, human errors can be introduced in a number of ways: An error can be made in data entry; an error can exist in the computer program itself (program errors can be extremely obscure—appearing irregularly or only under certain conditions); and floppy disks and magnetic tapes on which the computer programs are stored can be mishandled.

2. *The "Black Box" problem*—To the typical researcher, the technicalities of computers, computer programs, and their statistical manipulations amount to a "black box"—the researcher cannot see the inside workings and must take on faith what the computer printouts yield as well as what the computer experts say about the whole mysterious process. For many research purposes, this presents no problem but in exploratory research it is important to keep close to the data—to "have a feel for it" that can only come through processing the data by hand. One of the consultants to this handbook reported the he always parallels computer analysis of his data with the hand analysis of a small subsample. In this way, he stays closer to his data and frequently uncovers errors in the particular analysis program.

REFERENCES

Borg, W. R., & Gall, M. D. (1989). *Educational research: An introduction* (5th ed.). White Plains, NY: Longman.

Krathwohl, D. R. (1993). *Methods of educational and social science research: An integrated approach.* White Plains, NY: Longman.

Wiersma, W. (1995). *Research methods in education: An introduction* (6th ed.). Boston: Allyn & Bacon.

The tragedies of science are the slayings of beautiful hypotheses by ugly facts.

T. H. Huxley

CHAPTER FOUR

GUIDE TO TRADITIONAL RESEARCH DESIGNS, METHODS, AND STRATEGIES

When the research study has been formulated, the next step is to construct the research design. This is the plan of attack: What approach to the problem will be taken? What methods will be used? What strategies will be most effective?

Design decisions depend on the purposes of the study, the nature of the problem, and the alternatives appropriate for its investigation. Once the purposes have been specified, the study should have explicit scope and direction, and attention can be focused on a delimited target area. The nature of the problem then plays the major role in determining what approaches are suitable. Design alternatives can be organized into nine functional categories based on these differing problem characteristics:[1]

1. Historical
2. Descriptive
3. Developmental
4. Case or Field
5. Correlational
6. Causal-comparative
7. True experimental
8. Quasi-experimental
9. Action

The most obvious characteristics of each of these categories are summarized in the chart on the next two pages. Each category, then, is individually presented in the series of pages following the chart (pages 48-59).

---

[1]Because authorities differ in their classification criteria, the above scheme is arbitrary and overlapping. "Descriptive" research, for instance, is commonly used in a much broader sense encompassing everything except "historical" and "experimental" research. To avoid the complication of subcategories under main categories, "descriptive" research is used here in its more literal and narrow sense. This makes possible a list of single categories as if each was separate and distinct. Actually, there are as many similarities as differences and the categories are not always mutually exclusive, crossing over under many conditions. The reader is urged to examine the more complete information within this section and to compare the scheme presented here with others in current textbooks on research.

NINE BASIC METHODS OF RESEARCH

METHOD	PURPOSE
HISTORICAL	To reconstruct the past objectively and accurately, often in relation to the tenability of an hypothesis.
DESCRIPTIVE	To describe systematically a situation or area of interest factually and accurately.
DEVELOP-MENTAL	To investigate patterns and sequences of growth and/or change as a function of time.
CASE AND FIELD	To study intensively the background, current status, and environmental interactions of a given social unit: an individual, group, institution, or community.
CORRE-LATIONAL	To investigate the extent to which variations in one factor correspond with variations in one or more other factors based on correlation coefficients.
CAUSAL-COMPARATIVE or "EX POST FACTO"	To investigate possible cause-and-effect relationships by observing some existing consequence and searching back through the data for plausible causal factors.
TRUE EXPERIMENTAL	To investigate possible cause-and-effect relationships by exposing one or more experimental groups to one or more treatment conditions and comparing the results to one or more control groups not receiving the treatment (random assignment being essential).
QUASI-EXPERIMENTAL	To approximate the conditions of the true experiment in a setting which does not allow the control and/or manipulation of all relevant variables. The researcher must clearly understand what compromises exist in the internal and external validity of his design and proceed within these limitations.[1]
ACTION	To develop new skills or new approaches and to solve problems with direct application to the classroom or other applied setting.

[1]For a discussion of the concept of "control" see page 86; "internal and external validity" are discussed on pages 66-70.

EXAMPLES

A study reconstructing practices in the teaching of spelling in the United States during the past fifty years; tracing the history of civil rights in the United States education since the civil war; testing the hypothesis that Francis Bacon is the real author of the "works of William Shakespeare."

Population census studies, public opinion surveys, fact-finding surveys, status studies, task analysis studies, questionnaire and interview studies, observation studies, job descriptions, surveys of the literature, documentary analyses, anecdotal records, critical incident reports, test score analyses, and normative data.

A longitudinal growth study following an initial sample of 200 children from six months of age to adulthood; a cross-sectional growth study investigating changing patterns of intelligence by sampling groups of children at ten different age levels; a trend study projecting the future growth and educational needs of a community from past trends and recent building estimates.

The case history of a child with an above average IQ but with severe learning disabilities; an intensive study of a group of teenage youngsters on probation for drug abuse; an intensive study of a typical suburban community in the Midwest in terms of its socio-economic characteristics.

To investigate relationships between reading achievement scores and one or more other variables of interest; a factor-analytic study of several intelligence tests; a study to predict success in college based on intercorrelation patterns between college grades and selected high school variables.

To identify factors related to the "drop-out" problem in a particular high school using data from records over the past ten years; to investigate similarities and differences between such groups as smokers and nonsmokers, readers and nonreaders, or delinquents and nondeliquents, using data on file.

To investigate the effectiveness of three methods of teaching reading to first grade children using random assignments of children and teachers to groups and methods; to investigate the effects of a specific tranquilizing drug on learning behavior of boys identified as "hyperactive" using random assignment to groups receiving three different levels of the drug and two control groups with and without a placebo, respectively.

Most so-called field experiments, operational research, and even the more sophisticated forms of action research which attempt to get at causal factors in real life settings where only partial control is possible; e.g., an investigation of the effectiveness of any method or treatment condition where random assignment of subjects to methods or conditions is not possible.

An inservice training program to help teachers develop new skills in facilitating class discussions; to experiment with new approaches to teaching reading to bilingual children; to develop more effective counseling techniques for underachievers.

BASIC STEPS IN THE PLANNING
AND CONDUCT OF RESEARCH

1. Identify the problem area.
2. Survey the literature relating to it.
3. Define the actual problem for investigation in clear, specific terms.
4. Formulate testable hypotheses and define the basic concepts and variables.[1]
5. State the underlying assumptions which govern the interpretation of results.
6. Construct the research design to maximize internal and external validity.[2]
    a. Selection of subjects.
    b. Control and/or manipulation of relevant variables.
    c. Establishment of criteria to evaluate outcomes.
    d. Instrumentation–selection or development of the criterion measures.
7. Specify the data collection procedures.
8. Select the data analysis methodology.
9. Execute the research plan.
10. Evaluate the results and draw conclusions.

HISTORICAL RESEARCH

Purpose:

To reconstruct the past systematically and objectively by collecting, evaluating, verifying, and synthesizing evidence to establish facts and reach defensible conclusions, often in relation to particular hypotheses.

---

[1]Variables can be classified into three categories:
   a. *Independent (input, manipulated, treatment,* or *stimulus) variables,* so-called because they are "independent" of the outcome itself; instead, they are presumed to cause, effect, or influence the outcome.
   b. *Dependent (output, outcome,* or *response) variables,* so-called because they are "dependent" on the independent variables: the outcome presumably depends on how these input variables are managed or manipulated.
   c. *Control (background, classificatory,* or *organismic) variables,* so-called because they need to be controlled, held constant, or randomized so that their effects are neutralized, canceled out, or equated for all conditions. Typically included are such factors as age, sex, IQ, SES (socio-economic status), educational level, and motivational level; it is often possible to redefine these particular examples as either independent or dependent variables, according to the intent of the research.

   A fourth category often is cited having to do with conceptual states within the organism: *intervening variables (higher order constructs).* These cannot be directly observed or measured and are hypothetical conceptions intended to explain processes between the stimulus and response. Such concepts as learning, intelligence, perception, motivation, need, self, personality, trait, and feeling illustrate this category.
[2]See pages 67-70.

Examples:

A study of the origins of grouping practices in elementary schools in the United States to understand their basis in the past and relevance to the present; to test the hypothesis that Francis Bacon was the real author of "the works of William Shakespeare."

Characteristics:

1. Historical research depends upon data observed by others rather than by the investigator. Good data result from painstaking detective work which analyzes the authenticity, accuracy, and significance of source material.
2. Contrary to popular notions, historical research must be rigorous, systematic, and exhaustive; much "research" claiming to be historical is an undisciplined collection of inappropriate, unreliable, or biased information.
3. Historical research depends upon two kinds of data: *primary sources* where the author was a direct observer of the recorded event, and *secondary sources* where the author is reporting the observations of others and is one or more times removed from the original event. Of the two, primary sources carry the authority of firsthand evidence and have priority in data collection.
4. Two basic forms of criticism weigh the value of the data: *external criticism* which asks, "Is the document or relic authentic?" and *internal criticism* which asks, "If authentic, are the data accurate and relevant?" Internal criticism must examine the motives, biases, and limitations of the author which might cause exaggeration, distortion, or overlooking information. This critical evaluation of the data is what makes true historical research so rigorous–in many ways, more demanding than experimental methods.
5. While historical research is similar to the "reviews of the literature" which precede other forms of research, the historical approach is more exhaustive, seeking out information from a larger array of sources. It also tracks down information that is much older than required by most reviews and hunts for unpublished material not cited in the standard references.

Steps:

1. Define the problem. Ask yourself these questions: Is the historical approach best suited for this problem? Are pertinent data available? Will the findings be educationally significant?
2. State the research objectives and, if possible, the hypotheses that will give direction and focus to the research.
3. Collect the data, keeping in mind the distinction between primary and secondary sources. An important skill in historical research is note-taking–small file cards (3 x 5, 4 x 6), each containing one item of information and coded by topic, are easy to rearrange and convenient to file.
4. Evaluate the data, applying both internal and external criticism.
5. Report the findings, including a statement of the problem, a review of source material, a statement of underlying assumptions, basic hypotheses, and methods used to test the hypotheses, the findings obtained, the interpretations and conclusions reached, and a bibliography.

DESCRIPTIVE RESEARCH

Purpose:

To describe systematically the facts and characteristics of a given population or area of interest, factually and accurately.

Examples:

1. A public opinion survey to assess the pre-election status of voter attitudes toward a school bond election.
2. A community survey to establish the needs for a vocational education program.
3. A study and definition of all personnel positions in an education center.
4. A report of test score results in a school district.

Characteristics:

1. Descriptive research is used in the literal sense of describing situations or events. It is the accumulation of a data base that is solely descriptive—it does not necessarily seek or explain relationships, test hypotheses, make predictions, or get at meanings and implications, although research aimed at these more powerful purposes may incorporate descriptive methods. Research authorities, however, are not in agreement on what constitutes "descriptive research" and often broaden the term to include all forms of research except historical and experimental. In this broader context, the term *survey studies* is often used to cover the examples listed above.

2. Purpose of Survey Studies:[1]
   a. To collect detailed factual information that describes existing phenomena.
   b. To identify problems or justify current conditions and practices.
   c. To make comparisons and evaluations.
   d. To determine what others are doing with similar problems or situations and benefit from their experience in making future plans and decisions.

Steps:

1. Define the objectives in clear, specific terms. What facts and characteristics are to be uncovered?
2. Design the approach. How will the data be collected? How will the subjects be selected to insure they represent the population to be described? What instruments or observation techniques are available or will need to be developed? Will the data collection methods need to be field-tested and will data gatherers need to be trained?
3. Collect the data.
4. Report the results.

---

[1]Based in part on Van Dalen, D. B. (1979). *Understanding educational research* (4th ed.). New York: McGraw-Hill.

DEVELOPMENTAL RESEARCH

Purpose:
To investigate patterns and sequences of growth and/or change as a function of time.

Examples:
1. Longitudinal growth studies directly measuring the nature and rate of changes in a sample of the same children at different stages of development.
2. Cross-sectional growth studies indirectly measuring the nature and rate of these same changes by drawing samples of different children from representative age levels.
3. Trend studies designed to establish patterns of change in the past in order to predict future patterns or conditions.

Characteristics:
1. Developmental research focuses on the study of variables and their development over a period of months or years. It asks, "What are the patterns of growth, their rates, their directions, their sequences, and the interrelated factors affecting these characteristics?"
2. The sampling problem in the longitudinal method is complicated by the limited number of subjects it can follow over the years; any selective factor affecting attrition biases the longitudinal study. If the threat of attrition is avoided by sampling from a stable population, this introduces unknown biases associated with such populations. Furthermore, once underway, the longitudinal method does not lend itself to improvements in techniques without losing the continuity of the procedures. Finally, this method requires the continuity of staff and financial support over an extended period of time and typically is confined to university or foundation centers that can maintain such an effort.
3. Cross-sectional studies usually include more subjects, but describe fewer growth factors than longitudinal studies. While the latter is the only direct method of studying human development, the cross-sectional approach is less expensive and faster since the actual passage of time is eliminated by sampling different subjects across age ranges. Sampling in the cross-sectional method is complicated because the same children are not involved at each age level and may not be comparable. To generalize intrinsic developmental patterns from these sequential samples of children runs the risk of confusing differences due to development with other differences between the groups that are artifacts of the sampling process.
4. Trend studies are vulnerable to unpredictable factors that modify or invalidate trends based on the past. In general, long-range prediction is an educated guess while short-range prediction is more reliable and valid.

Steps:
1. Define the problem or state the objectives.
2. Review the literature to establish a baseline of existing information and to compare research methodologies including available instruments and data collection techniques.
3. Design the approach.
4. Collect the data.
5. Evaluate the data and report the results.

CASE AND FIELD STUDY RESEARCH

Purpose:
To study intensively the background, current status, and environmental interactions of a given social unit: an individual, group, institution, or community.

Examples:
1. Piaget's studies of cognitive growth in children.
2. An in-depth study of a pupil with a learning disability by a school psychologist or a student on probation by a social worker.
3. An intensive study of the "inner city" culture and living conditions in a large metropolitan environment.
4. An anthropologist's exhaustive field study of cultural life on a remote Indian reservation in the Southwest.

Characteristics:
1. Case studies are in-depth investigations of a given social unit resulting in a complete, well-organized picture of that unit. Depending upon the purpose, the scope of the study may encompass an entire life cycle or only a selected segment; it may concentrate upon specific factors or take in the totality of elements and events.
2. Compared to a survey study which tends to examine a small number of variables across a large sample of units, the case study tends to examine a small number of units across a large number of variables and conditions.

Strengths:
1. Case studies are particularly useful as background information for planning major investigations in the social sciences. Because they are intensive, they bring to light the important variables, processes, and interactions that deserve more extensive attention. They pioneer new ground and often are the source of fruitful hypotheses for further study.
2. Case study data provide useful anecdotes or examples to illustrate more generalized statistical findings.

Weaknesses:
1. Because of their narrow focus on a few units, case studies are limited in their representativeness. They do not allow valid generalizations to the population from which their units came until the appropriate follow-up research is accomplished, focusing on specific hypotheses and using proper sampling methods.
2. Case studies are particularly vulnerable to subjective biases. The case itself may be selected because of its dramatic, rather than typical, attributes; or because it neatly fits the researchers preconceptions. To the extent selective judgments rule certain data in or out, or assign a high or low value to their significance, or place them in one context rather than another, subjective interpretation is influencing the outcome.

Steps:
1. State the objectives. What is the unit of study and what characteristics, relationships, and processes will direct the investigation?
2. Design the approach. How will the units be selected? What sources of data are available? What data collection methods will be used?

3. Collect the data.
4. Organize the information to form a coherent, well-integrated reconstruction of the unit of study.
5. Report the results and discuss their significance.

CORRELATIONAL RESEARCH

Purpose:
   To investigate the extent to which variations in one factor correspond with variations in one or more other factors based on correlation coefficients.

Examples:
1. A study investigating the relationship between grade point average as the criterion variable and a number of the variables of interest.
2. A factor-analytic study of several personality tests.
3. A study to predict success in graduate school based on intercorrelation patterns for undergraduate variables.

Characteristics:
1. Appropriate where variables are very complex and/or do not lend themselves to the experimental method and controlled manipulation.
2. Permits the measurement of several variables and their interrelationships simultaneously and in a realistic setting.
3. Gets at the degrees of relationship rather than the all-or-nothing question posed by experimental design: "Is an effect present or absent?"
4. Among its limitations are the following:
   a. It only identifies what goes with what–it does not necessarily identify cause-and-effect relationships.
   b. It is less rigorous than the experimental approach because it exercises less control over the independent variables.
   c. It is prone to identify spurious relational patterns or elements which have little or no reliability or validity.
   d. The relational patterns are often arbitrary and ambiguous.
   e. It encourages a "shot-gun" approach to research, indiscriminately throwing in data from miscellaneous sources and defying any meaningful or useful interpretation.

Steps:
1. Define the problem.
2. Review the literature.
3. Design the approach:
   a. Identify the relevant variables.
   b. Select appropriate subjects.
   c. Select or develop appropriate measuring instruments.
   d. Select the correlational approach that fits the problem.
4. Collect the data.
5. Analyze and interpret the results.

CAUSAL-COMPARATIVE RESEARCH[1]

Purpose:

To investigate possible cause-and-effect relationships by observing some existing consequence and searching back through the data for plausible causal factors. This is in contrast to the experimental method which collects its data under controlled conditions in the present.

Examples:

1. To identify factors characterizing persons having either high or low accident rates, using data in insurance company records.
2. To determine the attributes of effective teachers as defined, for example, by their performance evaluations and other data in the personal files. Teacher records over the past ten years are then examined, comparing these data to the amount of summer school attendance or to each of several other factors.
3. To look for patterns of behavior and achievement associated with age differences at the time of school entrance, using descriptive data on behavior and achievement test scores in the cumulative pupil records of children currently in the sixth grade.

Principal Characteristics:

Causal-comparative research is "ex post facto" in nature, which means the data are collected after all the events of interest have occurred. The investigator then takes one or more effects (dependent variables) and examines the data by going back through time, seeking out causes, relationships, and their meanings.

Strengths:

1. The causal-comparative method is appropriate in many circumstances where the more powerful experimental method is not possible:
   a. When it is not always possible to select, control, and manipulate the facts necessary to study cause-and-effect relations directly.
   b. When the control of all variations except a single independent variable may be highly unrealistic and artificial, preventing the normal interaction with other influential variables.
   c. When laboratory controls for many research purposes would be impractical, costly, or ethically questionable.
   Note: The *experimental method* involves both an experimental and a control group. Some treatment "A" is given the experimental group, and the result "B" is observed. The control group is not exposed to "A" and their condition is compared to the experimental group to see what effects "A" might have had in producing "B." In the *causal-comparative method*, the investigator reverses this process, observing a result "B" which already exists and searches back through several possible causes ("A" type of events) that are related to "B."
2. It yields useful information concerning the nature of phenomena: what goes with what, under what conditions, in what sequences and patterns, and the like.
3. Improvements in techniques, statistical methods, and designs with partial control features, in recent years, have made these studies more defensible.

---

[1]The authors are indebted to Van Dalen, D. B. (1979). *Understanding educational research* (4th ed.). New York: McGraw-Hill, for much of this material.

Weaknesses:

1. The main weakness of any ex post facto design is the lack of control over independent variables. Within the limits of selection, the investigator must take the facts as they are found with no opportunity to arrange the conditions or manipulate the variables that influenced the facts in the first place. To reach sound conclusions, the investigator must consider all the other possible reasons or *plausible rival hypotheses* which might account for the results obtained. To the extent that the conclusions can be successfully justified against these other alternatives puts the investigator in a position of relative strength.
2. The difficulty in being certain that the relevant causative factor is actually included among the many factors under study.
3. The complication that no single factor is the cause of an outcome but some combination and interaction of factors go together under certain conditions to yield a given outcome.
4. A phenomenon may result not only from multiple causes but also from one cause in one instance and from another cause in another instance.
5. When a relationship between two variables is discovered, determining which is the cause and which the effect may be difficult.
6. The fact that two, or more, factors are related does not necessarily imply a cause-and-effect relationship. They all simply may be related to an additional factor not recognized or observed.
7. Classifying subjects into dichotomous groups (e.g., "Achievers" and "Nonachievers"), for the purpose of comparison, is fraught with problems, since categories like these are vague, variable, and transitory. Such investigations often do not yield useful findings.
8. Comparative studies in natural situations do not allow controlled selection of subjects. Locating existing groups of subjects who are similar in all respects except for their exposure to one variable is extremely difficult.

Steps:

1. Define the problem.
2. Survey the literature.
3. State the hypotheses.
4. List the assumptions upon which the hypotheses and procedures will be based.
5. Design the approach:
   a. Select appropriate subjects and source materials.
   b. Select or construct techniques for collecting the data.
   c. Establish categories for classifying data that are unambiguous, appropriate for the purpose of the study, and capable of bringing out significant likenesses or relationships.
6. Validate the data-gathering techniques.
7. Describe, analyze, and interpret the findings in clear, precise terms.

TRUE EXPERIMENTAL RESEARCH

Purpose:

To investigate possible cause-and-effect relationships by exposing one or more experimental groups to one or more treatment conditions and comparing the results to one or more control groups not receiving the treatment.

Examples:

1. To investigate the effects of two methods of teaching a twelfth grade history program as a function of class size (large and small) and levels of student intelligence (high, average, low), using random assignment of teachers and students-by-intelligence-level to method and class size.
2. To investigate the effects of a new drug abuse prevention program on the attitudes of junior high school students using experimental and control groups who are either exposed or not exposed to the program, respectively, and using a pretest-posttest design in which only half of the students randomly receive the pretest to determine how much of an attitude change can be attributed to pretesting or to the educational program.
3. To investigate the effects of two methods of pupil evaluation on the performance of children in the twenty-three elementary schools of a given suburban district. N in this study would be the number of classrooms, rather than children, and the method would be assigned by stratified random techniques such that there would be a balanced distribution of the two methods to classrooms across grade levels and socio-economic locations of schools.

Characteristics of Experimental Designs:

1. Require rigorous management of experimental variables and conditions either by direct control/manipulation or through randomization. (See page 86.)
2. Typically uses a control group as a baseline against which to compare the group(s) receiving the experimental treatment.
3. Concentrates on the control of variance:[1,2]
    a. To maximize the variance of the variable(s) associated with the research hypotheses.
    b. To minimize the variance of extraneous or "unwanted" variables that might affect the experimental outcomes, but are not themselves the object of study.
    c. To minimize the error or random variance, including so-called errors of measurement.

Best solution: Random selection of subjects, random assignment of subjects to groups, and random assignment of experimental treatments to groups.

4. Internal validity is the *sine qua non* of research design and the first objective of experimental methodology. It asks the question: Did the experimental manipulation *in this particular study* really make a difference? (See pages 67-68.)

---

[1]Based on Kerlinger, F. N. (1986). *Foundations of behavioral research* (3rd Ed.). New York: Harcourt Brace.
[2]See page 86 for a discussion of the control of variance.

5. External validity is the second objective of experimental methodology. It asks the question: How *representative* are the findings and can the results be *generalized* to similar circumstances and subjects? (See pages 69-70.)
6. In classic experimental design, all variables of concern are held constant except a single treatment variable which is deliberately manipulated or allowed to vary. Advances in methodology such as factorial designs, analysis of variance and multiple regression now allow the experimenter to permit more than one variable to be manipulated or varied concurrently across more than one experimental group. This permits the simultaneous determination of (1) the effects of the principal independent variables (treatments), (2) the variation associated with classificatory variables, and (3) the interaction of selected combinations of independent and/or classificatory variables. (See page 48.)
7. While the experimental approach is the most powerful because of the control it allows over relevant variables, it is also the most restrictive and artificial. This is a major weakness in applications involving human subjects in real world situations, since human beings often act differently if their behavior is artificially restricted, manipulated, or exposed to systematic observation and evaluation.[1]

Seven Steps in Experimental Research:[2]
1. Survey the literature relating to the problem.
2. Identify and define the problem.
3. Formulate a problem hypothesis, deducing the consequences, and defining basic terms and variables.
4. Construct an experimental plan:
   a. Identify all nonexperimental variables that might contaminate the experiment, and determine how to control them.
   b. Select a research design.
   c. Select a sample of subjects to represent a given population, assign subjects to groups, and assign experimental treatments to groups.
   d. Select or construct and validate instruments to measure the outcome of the experiment.
   e. Outline procedures for collecting the data, and possibly conduct a pilot or "trial run" test to perfect the instruments or design.
   f. State the statistical or null hypothesis.
5. Conduct the experiments.
6. Reduce the raw data in a manner that will produce the best appraisal of the effect which is presumed to exist.
7. Apply an appropriate test of significance to determine the confidence one can place on the results of the study.

---

[1]The debate between experimental precision versus its artificiality, on the one hand, and between naturalistic realism versus its imprecision, on the other, is largely a matter of appreciating what is possible and appropriate in a given set of circumstances. Both can make valuable contributions and the strengths of one often counterbalance the weaknesses of the other.
[2]Van Dalen, D. B., & Meyer, W. J. (1966). *Understanding educational research.* New York: McGraw-Hill.

QUASI-EXPERIMENTAL RESEARCH[1]

Purpose:

To approximate the conditions of the true experiment in a setting which does not allow the control and/or manipulation of all relevant variables. The researcher must clearly understand what compromises exist in the internal and external validity of the design and proceed within these limitations.

Examples:

1. To investigate the effects of spaced versus massed practice in the memorizing of vocabulary lists in four high school foreign language classes without being able to assign students to the treatment at random or to supervise closely their practice periods.
2. To assess the effectiveness of three approaches to teaching basic principles and concepts in economics to primary grade children when some of the teachers inadvertently were allowed to volunteer for one of the approaches because of its impressive-looking materials.
3. Educational research involving a pretest-posttest design in which such variables as maturation, effects of testing, statistical regression, selective attrition, and stimulus novelty or adaptation, are unavoidable or overlooked.
4. Most studies of the social problems of delinquency, rioting, smoking, or instances of heart disease, where control and manipulation are not always feasible.

Characteristics:

1. Quasi-experimental research typically involves applied settings where it is not possible to control all the relevant variables but only some of them. The researcher gets as close to the true experimental rigor as conditions allow, carefully qualifying the important exceptions and limitations. Therefore, this research is characterized by methods of partial control based on a careful identification of factors influencing both internal and external validity listed on pages 66-70.
2. The distinction between true and quasi-experimental research is tenuous, particularly where human subjects are involved as in education. A careful study of the paradigms presented on pages 70-82 will clarify the relative nature of this distinction as a matter of approximation on a continuum between "one-shot case studies" of an action research nature to experimental-control group designs with randomization and rigorous management of all foreseeable variables influencing internal and external validity.
3. While action research (see opposite page) can have quasi-experimental status, it is often so unformalized as to deserve separate recognition. Once the research plan systematically examines the validity question, moving out of the intuitive and exploratory realm, the beginnings of experimental methodology are visible.

Steps in Quasi-experimental Research: The same as with true experimental research, carefully recognizing each limitation to the internal and external validity of the design.

---

[1]The term "quasi-experimental" was first introduced into the literature in 1957 by Donald T. Campbell and reiterated in subsequent work with Julian C. Stanley.

ACTION RESEARCH

Purpose:

To develop new skills or new approaches and to solve problems with direct application to the classroom or working world setting.

Examples:

An inservice training program to help train counselors to work more effectively with minority group children; to develop an exploratory program in accident prevention in a driver's education course; to solve the problem of apathy in a required high school "orientation" class; to test a fresh approach to interesting more students in taking vocational education courses.

Characteristics:

1. Practical and directly relevant to an actual situation in the working world. The subjects are the classroom students, the staff, or others with whom you are primarily involved.
2. Provides an orderly framework for problem-solving and new developments that are superior to the impressionistic, fragmentary approach that otherwise typifies developments in education. It also is empirical in the sense that it relies on actual observations and behavioral data, and does not fall back on subjective committee "studies" or opinions of people based on their past experience.
3. Flexible and adaptive, allowing changes during the trial period and sacrificing control in favor of responsiveness and on-the-spot experimentation and innovation.
4. While attempting to be systematic, action research lacks scientific rigor because its internal and external validity are weak (see pages 66-70). Its objective is situational, its sample is restricted and unrepresentative, and it has little control over independent variables. Hence, its findings, while useful within the practical dimensions of the situation, do not directly contribute to the general body of educational knowledge.

Steps:

1. Define the problem or set the goal. What is it that needs improvement or that might be developed as a new skill or solution?
2. Review the literature to learn whether others have met similar problems or achieved related objectives.
3. Formulate testable hypotheses or strategies of approach, stating them in clear, specific, pragmatic language.
4. Arrange the research setting and spell out the procedures and conditions. What are the particular things you will do in an attempt to meet your objectives?
5. Establish evaluation criteria, measurement techniques, and other means of acquiring useful feedback.
6. Analyze the data and evaluate the outcomes.

DIFFERENCES AMONG FORMAL EDUCATIONAL RESEARCH, ACTION RESEARCH, AND THE CASUAL APPROACH TO PROBLEM SOLVING[1,2]

Area	Formal Educational Research	Action Research	Casual or "Common Sense" Approach
1. Training required	Extensive training in measurement, statistics, and research methods is needed. Much of the scientific research done in education is weak because of deficiencies of the researchers in these areas.	Only a limited training in statistics and research methods is needed because rigorous design and analysis are not usually necessary. More training in educational measurement is needed than most teachers possess. Even if teacher's research skills are low, good action research can be carried out with the aid of a consultant.	No training is needed. This is the same method used since prehistoric times to achieve faulty solutions to ill-defined problems.
2. Goals	To obtain knowledge that will be generalizable to a broad population and to develop and test educational theories.	To obtain knowledge that can be applied directly to the local classroom situation, and to give the participating teachers inservice training.	To make changes in the current procedure that appear likely to improve the situation.
3. Locating the research problem	Problems identified by a wide range of methods. Research worker must understand the problem, but is usually not directly involved in it.	Problems identified in the school situation that are causing the research worker trouble or are interfering with the efficiency of his teaching.	Problems identified in same manner as action research.
4. Hypotheses	Highly specific hypotheses are developed that employ operational definitions and are testable.	A specific statement of the problem usually serves as the research hypothesis. Ideally, action research hypotheses should approach rigor of formal research.	Specific hypotheses not established. Participants rarely progress beyond a fuzzy and ill-defined concept concerning the nature of the problem.

[1]From Borg, W. R. (1963). Educational research (pp. 319-322). New York: David McKay Company. By permission.
[2]For an alternative conceptualization involving functions of three types of research (basic, applied, & evaluation) see McMillan, J. H., Schumacher, S. (1989). Research in Education: A conceptual introduction (2nd ed.) (pp. 15-22). Glenview, IL: Scott Foresman Co.

Area	Formal Educational Research	Action Research	Casual or "Common Sense" Approach
5. Review of the literature	An extensive review of primary source material is usually carried out, giving the research worker a thorough understanding of the current state of knowledge in the research area. This enables him to build upon the knowledge accumulated by others.	A review of available secondary sources gives the teacher a general understanding of the area to be studied. Exhaustive review of primary sources is almost never done.	Usually no review of the literature is carried out, although one or two secondary sources may be checked.
6. Sampling	Research worker attempts to obtain a random or otherwise unbiased sample of the population being studied, but is usually not completely successful.	Pupils available in the class of the teacher or teachers doing the research are used as subjects.	Some casual observation of pupil behavior may be made by the teacher after the change decided upon has been in effect for a while.
7. Experimental design	Design is carefully planned in detail prior to start of the study and adhered to as closely as possible. Major attention is given to maintaining comparable conditions and reducing error and bias. Control of extraneous variables is important.	Procedures are planned in general terms prior to start of study. Changes are made during the study if they seem likely to improve the teaching situation. Little attention is paid to control of the experimental conditions or reduction of error. Because participating teachers are ego-involved in the research situation, bias is usually present.	If classroom testing of the decision is attempted, procedures are planned only in the most general terms. No attempt is made to establish common definitions or procedures among participating teachers.

[1]From Borg, W. R. (1963). *Educational research* (pp. 319-322). New York: David McKay Company. By permission.
[2]For an alternative conceptualization involving functions of three types of research (basic, applied, & evaluation) see McMillan, J. H., Schumacher, S. (1989). *Research in Education: A conceptual introduction* (2nd ed.) (pp. 15-22). Glenview, IL: Scott Foresman Co.

DIFFERENCES AMONG FORMAL EDUCATIONAL RESEARCH, ACTION RESEARCH, AND THE CASUAL APPROACH TO PROBLEM SOLVING *(cont.)* [1,2]

Area	Formal Educational Research	Action Research	Casual or "Common Sense" Approach
8. Measurement	An effort is made to obtain the most valid measures available. A thorough evaluation of available measures and a trial of these measures usually precedes their use in the research.	Less rigorous evaluation of measures than in scientific research. Participants often lack training in the use and evaluation of educational measures, but can do a satisfactory job with help of a consultant.	Usually no evaluation is made except for the casual observations of the teachers participating. The teacher's opinion as to whether the new procedure is an improvement or not depends almost entirely on whether the teacher approves the change.
9. Analysis of data	Complex analysis often called for. Inasmuch as generalizability of results is a goal, statistical significance is usually emphasized	Simple analysis procedures usually are sufficient. Practical significance rather than statistical significance is emphasized. Subjective opinion of participating teachers is often weighted heavily.	Subjective opinion of the participants is usually the only procedure used. No attempt made at objective analysis.
10. Application of results	Results are generalizable, but many useful findings are not applied in educational practice. Differences in training and experience between research workers and teachers generate a serious communication problem.	Findings are applied immediately to the classes of participating teachers and often lead to permanent improvement. Application of results beyond the participating teachers is usually slight.	Decisions reached are applied immediately in classes of participating teachers. Even if the decision leads to improvement, it is often changed later because no evidence is available to support its continuance. This approach leads to educational fads and "change for the sake of change."

[1]From Borg, W. R. (1963). *Educational research* (pp. 319-322). New York: David McKay Company. By permission.
[2]For an alternative conceptualization involving functions of three types of research (basic, applied, & evaluation) see McMillan, J. H., Schumacher, S. (1989). *Research in Education: A conceptual introduction* (2nd ed.) (pp. 15-22). Glenview IL: Scott Foresman Co.

COHORT ANALYSIS[1]

A common practice in demographic research is to compare groups of individuals within a defined age range at different points of time (e.g. five year intervals) where changes in behavior or attitude are the outcome of interest.

In such a study, the age defined group is called a cohort and the method of investigating these changes in behavior or attitude is called cohort analysis.

In general, a cohort is any group of individuals linked together in some way – usually by age, though not necessarily.

The term cohort is derived from a Roman military unit – hence, a group of soldiers. In current usage, it refers to one's companion, accomplice, peer, or associate; and collectively, a band or group of the same individuals.

Demographically, a cohort becomes those individuals within a geographical or otherwise delineated population who have experienced the same significant life event within a given time period. Most commonly, the determinant of a cohort is one's time of birth, usually within a range of one to ten years, although wider intervals are possible.

Characteristically, cohort analysis refers to any study in which there are measures of some attribute of one or more cohorts at two or more points in time: e.g., a study in which persons born between 1950 and 1954 are followed at five year intervals to determine changes in political attitudes or affiliation. As there are many variations to this format, interpretation must take into account such fluctuations as sampling error and compositional changes within aging cohorts. Three principal effects must then be considered: (1) Those produced by influences associated with aging – age effects; (2) Those produced by influences associated with cohort status – cohort effects; and (3) Those produced by influences associated with each period of time – period effects.

To complicate further the interpretation of cohort data, one must deal with sampling variability, attrition, and confounding between paired combinations of age, cohort, and period effects.

SINGLE SUBJECT EXPERIMENTS[2]

Most experimental designs depend on a sizable number of subjects in order to have reliable results. There are many instances, however, when one is working with single cases and yet would like to experiment with the effectiveness of various strategies or methods – for example, counselors working with individual clients or special education teachers working with handicapped students.

Single-subject designs offer the solution. Given such a design, a researcher can diagnose a student's problem, arrange a solution strategy, and put the matter to an experimental test based on the systematic collection of data.

---

[1]For a full discussion of this important topic see: Glenn, N. D. (1977). *Cohort analysis.* Newbury Park, CA: Sage Publications.

[2]Adapted from Borg, W. R., Gall, J. P., & Gall, M. D. (1993). *Applying Educational Research* (3rd ed.) (pp. 335-40). White Plains, NY: Longman Publishing Group.

One caveat concerning single-subject experiments is their weakened external validity– that is, their ability to generalize to other similar subjects in the same population. One way to address this problem is through replication: repeating the experiment with other subjects, perhaps using different investigators, settings, and subject attributes.

What follows is a synopsis of four examples or single-subject experimental designs, along with their respective strengths and weaknesses.

The *A-B Design*. This is the basic single-subject paradigm. Condition A is a constant environment where a certain behavior occurs at a consistent, stable rate establishing the behavior baseline. Condition B is a change in the environment instigated by the researcher and resulting in a change in behavior, other explanations are possible, such as history or maturation.

Thus, the A-B design has low internal validity. The three remaining designs each improve on internal validity by (1) Using more than one administration of the treatment (A-B-A-B); (2) Comparing two or more behaviors presumed to be influenced by the treatment (Multiple Baseline Across Behaviors); or (3) Comparing two or more individuals exposed to the same treatment (Multiple Baseline Across Individuals).

The *A-B-A-B Design*. This approach uses several baseline periods (condition A) and several treatment periods (condition B) to establish causality. If condition A is the time a student is normally observed to be on task in an independent learning situation and condition B is the intervention of praise for on task behavior, both conditions are carried out followed by a return to condition A. Results are recorded and condition B is then reinstated, accompanied by noting any behavior changes. This sequence can be repeated in a series of alternating conditions. By charting the frequency of on task behavior across the two conditions for as often as they are repeated, one can observe any trends in favor of condition B.

The differences obtained in such studies are often sufficiently clear that no test of statistical significance is needed. As generalizing results from one such single-subject experiment to other cases (external validity) is weak, replicating the experiment with other single subjects improves the basis for making such generalizations, given favorable results.

One caution in the selection of the A-B-A-B design is that not all forms of behavior can be readily reversed as is true for on task behavior. Many skill behaviors such as library reference skills and manual dexterity skills resist extinction and would mitigate against a favorable trend that depends on a reversal of behavior in the absence of a planned intervention. In such cases, the remaining two designs are better suited.

Multiple Baseline Across Behaviors Design. In this single-subject design, baseline measurements are taken on two or more behaviors exhibited by the same subject. Once the baselines are stable, a treatment condition is applied to one of the behaviors and continued until a noticeable change occurs in that behavior. Then the treatment condition is applied to the second behavior until a change is observed.

It is important in this design to work with two or more behaviors that are discrete and relatively independent of each other. Otherwise the change of the second, or subsequent, behavior could be simply a function of a change in the first rather than the treatment condition itself. For example, supposing a teacher is experimenting with three reinforcement strategies to enhance correct responses in a question-and-answer exercise: (A) Teacher smiles when student responds correctly; (B) Teacher gives such a student a token that can be exchanged for free time; and (C) Teacher praises such a student.

The Steps in carrying out this design are as follows:
1. Researcher collects baseline data on the number of times the teacher naturally exhibits any one of the three reinforcement behaviors in five half-hour lessons and records the results.
2. Researcher trains teacher to use behavior A.
3. Over the next five lessons researcher records the number of times the teacher uses all three behaviors. If the training has been effective, the teacher will exhibit an increase in behavior A, with behaviors B and C remaining at the baseline levels.
4. Researcher next trains teacher to use behavior B.
5. Again, the use of all three behaviors is recorded during five half-hour lessons. At this point, behaviors A and B should be above the baseline with behavior C remaining essentially unchanged.
6. Finally, researcher trains teacher to use behavior C.
7. Once again, all three teacher behaviors are recorded across another set of five lessons. If the training was effective, all three behaviors should occur more frequently than their baseline rates.

In reality, results are seldom so regular that differences among the treatments across time are without discrepancies. For instance, that the effects of one or more of the treatments might fade after the initial training would suggest either that its training wasn't well established or that the treatment itself was less potent. Other differences would prompt other explanations, possibly leading to other replications or variations in the procedure. What matters is that the researcher is gaining useful knowledge about the learning process.

Multiple Baseline Across Individuals Design. In this single-subject design, two or more subjects are selected for whom the behavioral goal of treatment is the same. Baseline rates of behavior are first stabilized for both subjects; then a treatment is applied with one subject. If the treated subject's behavior changes but the untreated subject's behavior remains constant, the conclusion is reached that the treatment had an effect. The treatment is then applied to the second subject and if there is a behavior change it amounts to a replication of the treatment's effect.

A word of caution in using this design: Care must be taken that the treatment of one subject doesn't influence the behavior of other subjects still in the baseline condition. Such a situation can be a problem when working with members of the same family, children from the same class, or coworkers in a work setting.

In conclusion, the A-B-A-B design is more powerful than the two multiple baseline designs just discussed because the reversal phase (the second condition A) demonstrates active control of the behavior by removing the treatment hypothesized to have caused the initial change (the initial condition B). Reinstatement of the treatment (the second condition B) offers additional evidence of the effect of the treatment.

The principal disadvantage of the A-B-A-B design lies either in dealing with behavior that is not readily reversible, noted earlier, or the ethical conflict posed by withdrawing an effective treatment to a client in a real life counseling situation. In these instances, the multiple baseline designs are practical alternatives because they can accommodate such circumstances.

OVERVIEW: INTERNAL AND EXTERNAL VALIDITY IN AN EXPERIMENTAL DESIGN[1]

Internal Validity asks the question: did, in fact, the experimental treatments make a difference *in this specific instance?* *External Validity* asks the question: to what populations settings, treatment variables, and measurement variables can this effect be *generalized*. While *internal validity* is the *sine qua non*, and while the question of *external validity* like the question of inductive inference is never completely answerable, the selection of designs strong in both types of validity is obviously the ideal. This is particularly true in education, in which generalization is to applied settings of known character.

Internal Validity–Eight classes of extraneous variables which, if not controlled in the experimental design, may produce effects becoming confounded with the effect of the experimental variable:

1. HISTORY–specific events occurring between the first and second measurement in addition to the experimental variable.
2. MATURATION–processes within the subjects operating as a function of the passage of time, per se (growing older, hungrier, fatigued, or less attentive).
3. TESTING–the effects of testing upon the scores of a subsequent testing.
4. INSTRUMENTATION–changes in obtained measurement due to changes in instrument calibration or changes in the observers or judges.
5. STATISTICAL REGRESSION–a phenomenon occurring when groups have been selected on the basis of extreme scores.
6. SELECTION–biases resulting from the differential loss of subjects from the comparison groups.
7. EXPERIMENTAL MORTALITY–the differential loss of subjects from the comparison groups.
8. SELECTION-MATURATION INTERACTION, Etc.–interaction effects between the aforementioned variables which can be mistaken for the effects of the experimental variable.

External Validity (Representativeness)–Four jeopardizing factors:
1. INTERACTION effects of SELECTION biases and the experimental variable.
2. REACTIVE or INTERACTION effect of PRETESTING–the pretesting modifies the subjects in such a way that they respond to the experimental treatment differently than will unpretested persons in the same population.
3. REACTIVE effects of experimental procedures–effects arising from the experimental setting which will not occur in nonexperimental settings.
4. MULTIPLE-TREATMENT INTERFERENCE–effects due to multiple treatments applied to the same subjects where prior treatments influence subsequent treatments in the series because their effects are not erasable.

---

[1]Campbell, D. T., & Stanley, J. C. (1966). *Experimental and quasi-experimental designs for research.* Chicago, IL: Rand McNally and Company.

INTERNAL VALIDITY[1]

When checking the internal validity of the design, an experimenter asks with reference to the just completed specific study the following question: Did the independent variable X really produce a change in the dependent variable? Many extraneous variables might have produced an effect that can be mistaken for any genuine effect of X. Internal validity is concerned with controlling as many extraneous or irrelevant variables as possible so that alternative hypotheses regarding factors other than X that could have contributed to the change in the dependent variable can be minimized or eliminated. The following factors can constitute a threat to the realization of the internal validity of an experiment:

1. *Contemporary history.*
   Sometimes the subjects experience an event–in or out of the experimental setting–besides the exposure to X, that may affect their dependent variable scores. If X is television instruction and the dependent variable is healthful practices of the students, the advent of an epidemic in the community rather than X may cause pupils to change some of their health practices. The simultaneous advent of the epidemic would be said to confound X. (An experimenter uses the term "confound" to indicate that an effect can be attributed to two or more variables, and the portion due to each cannot be determined.)

2. *Maturation process.*
   Biological and psychological processes within the subjects may change during the progress of the experiment which will affect their responses. The subjects may perform better or worse on O_2 not because of the effect of X, but because they are older, more fatigued, or less interested than when they took O_1. Their age, fatigue, or interest would confound the interpretation of the effect of X.

3. *Pretesting procedures.*
   O_1 (pretest) may serve as a learning experience that will cause the subjects to alter their responses on O_2 (posttest) whether or not X is applied.

4. *Measuring instruments.*
   Changes in the testing instruments, human raters, or interviewers can affect the obtained measurements. If O_2 is more difficult than O_1, or a different person rates subjects on the rating scales, these factors rather than X can cause the difference in the two scores. Slight fluctuations in mechanical measuring instruments can also cause the difference. If the same person judges the performance of two groups in succession or the same groups before and after the application of X, judgments may vary because the rater becomes more experienced and discriminating, or more fatigued and careless.

5. *Statistical regression.*
   In some educational research, particularly in remedial education, groups are selected on the basis of their extreme scores. When this selection procedure is employed, the effect of what is called "statistical regression" may be mistaken for the effect of X. Suppose that students who do exceptionally poor or exceptionally well on one test are

---

[1]Adapted in part from Van Dalen, D. B. (1979). *Understanding educational research* (4th ed.). New York: McGraw-Hill. (Adapted from Campbell, D. T., & Stanley, J. C. (1966). *Experimental and quasi-experimental designs for research.* Chicago, IL: Rand McNally & Co.

selected to receive an experimental treatment. The mean (average score) of either of these groups will move toward the mean of the parent population on the second test whether or not X is applied. If the mean for the top ten subjects in a class is 90, the scores of these subjects will fan out on the retest–some will be higher and some will be lower–but the mean of the group will be almost inevitably lower. Similarly, the mean for the lowest ten subjects on the second test will be almost inevitably higher.

Upon retesting, low initial means go up toward the population mean and high initial means go down toward the population mean. Why? Regression toward the mean occurs because of random imperfections in measuring instruments. The less-than-perfect capacity of O_1 and O_2 to measure knowledge will cause a variation of subjects' performances. Pupils are likely to vary within a given range because there is a less-than-perfect correlation between the two tests. The more deviant (extreme) pupils' scores are from the population mean, the more they are likely to vary. Random instability in the population may also account for regression toward the mean. Some subjects may obtain low scores on O_1 because they were upset or careless on that day. On the second test they may have better "luck," feel better, or strive harder to bring themselves up to their natural level. As a result, their higher scores will pull up the mean of their group on the second test.[1]

6. *Differential selection of subjects.*
If the experimental and control groups are exposed to X, a method of teaching spelling, and afterward are given a test, the test results may reflect a pre-X difference in the two groups rather than the effect of X. Perhaps the experimental group could spell better than the control group before X was applied.

7. *Differential experimental mortality.*
If a particular type of subject drops out of one group after the experiment is underway, this differential loss may affect the findings of the investigation. Suppose that the subjects in the experimental group who receive the lowest O_1 scores drop out after taking the test. The remainder of the experimental group may show a greater gain on O_2 than the control group, not because of its exposure to X but because the low scoring subjects are missing.

8. *Interaction of selection and maturation, selection and history, etc.*
When the experimental and control groups have the same O_1 scores, some other differences between them–such as, intelligence or motivation–rather than X may cause one of them to get higher O_2 scores. Because of this type of interaction, studies that compare volunteers (self-selected groups) with nonvolunteers must always be questioned. Suppose that an experimenter locates forty children from impoverished homes who are poor readers and twenty of them volunteer to participate in a cultural enrichment program. The volunteers may improve in reading more without X and benefit more from X than the nonvolunteers because they are different initially–they are motivated more highly toward self-improvement to begin with.

9. In summary, to the degree one achieves internal validity, it eliminates rival alternative hypotheses and supports the research hypothesis or treatment variable as the principal contributor.

---

[1]If two samples are drawn randomly from *two different populations,* so that there is no pairing or matching on a one-to-one basis, statistical regression is no longer involved.

EXTERNAL VALIDITY[1]

Discussion thus far has been confined to checking the internal validity of the design. An experimenter gives this task primary consideration but is also concerned about external validity–the generalizability or representativeness of the experimental findings. Consequently, the experimenter asks: What relevance do the findings concerning the effect of X have beyond the confines of the experiment? To what subject populations, settings, experimental variables, and measurement variables can these findings be generalized?

When checking the design of an experiment, an experimenter may ask: Can the findings be generalized to all college students? All students attending Harvard University? All Harvard freshmen who are enrolled in a particular course? Or must the findings be limited to the particular Harvard freshmen who participated in the experiment? Experimenters can strengthen the external validity of their design if they describe the population to which the results will apply *before* they conduct the experiment. If they draw a random sample from this predetermined population (say, Harvard freshmen) and expose the sample to X, they can make the following generalization: The effect that X had on the sample population (fifty Harvard freshmen) will be the same for the population that the sample represents (all Harvard freshmen).

Investigators are concerned not only about the generalizability of their findings with respect to a subject population, but also with respect to settings, independent variables, and measurement variables. Will the findings be representative of other geographical areas, sizes of schools, times of day, or time of year? Will the findings provide information about situations in which one X, no X, variations of X, or more than one X is present? Will the findings be representative of situations in which one or several types of criterion measurement are used?

The representativeness of the setting that is selected for an experiment will determine how extensively the findings can be applied. If the findings of a study are derived from data that are obtained in a deprived rural area, an experimenter cannot claim that they will hold true for wealthy metropolitan areas. If objective tests are used to measure the effect of a new teaching method, an experimenter cannot claim that the same effect would have been observed if essay tests or oral participation had been used as the measuring instruments.

When examining the external validity of a design, the experimenter checks the following threats to representativeness:

1. *Interaction effects of selection biases and X.*
   The characteristics of the subjects who are selected to participate in an experiment determine how extensively the findings can be generalized. A random sample of seventh-grade students from one school will not be representative of all seventh-grade students. The intelligence, socio-economic status, or some other characteristic of these particular students may cause X to be more effective for them than for other seventh-grade students. If X is a new textbook, it may produce excellent results in Dort School where most students have high IQs. But an experimenter cannot generalize that X will produce the same results in all seventh-grade classes, for the textbook may not be equally effective in Friar School where most students have low IQs.

[1]Adapted in part from Van Dalen, D. B. (1979). *Understanding educational research* (4th ed.). New York: McGraw-Hill. (Adapted from Campbell, D. T., & Stanley, J. C. (1966). *Experimental and quasi-experimental designs for research,*Chicago, IL: Rand McNally & Co.

2. *Reactive or interaction effect of pretesting.*
Giving a pretest may limit the generalizability of the experimental findings. A pretest may increase or decrease the experimental subjects sensitiveness to X: it may alert them to issues, problems, or events that they might not ordinarily notice. Consequently, these subjects may be no longer representative of the unpretested population from which they came. Suppose that fifty Harvard freshmen are exposed to X, a romantic film with a racial-prejudice theme. Their responses on O_2 may not reflect the effect of the film as much as the increased sensitivity to racial prejudice that taking O_1 produced. The effect of the film for the experimental subjects may not be representative of its effect for Harvard freshmen who see the romantic film without being pretested.

3. *Reactive effects of experimental procedures.*
The experimental procedures may also produce effects that limit the generalizability of the experimental findings. If the presence of observers and experimental equipment makes pupils and teachers aware of the fact that they are participating in an experiment, they may alter their normal behavior. If they alter the very behavior that is being measured, the experimenter cannot claim that the effect of X for the sample population will be the same for subjects who are exposed to X in nonexperimental situations.

4. *Multiple-treatment interference.*
When the same subjects are exposed repeatedly to two or more Xs, the effects of the previous Xs are not usually erasable; hence, the findings may be generalized only to persons who experience the same sequence of treatments repeatedly. If subjects are exposed to three types of music throughout the day, they may be more productive when marching music is played; but they might not respond in the same way if marching music were played continuously.

EXAMPLES OF EIGHT EXPERIMENTAL DESIGNS
The following sample designs are summaries of commonly used designs. It should be noted that the notation and numbering system used are based on the work done by Campbell and Stanley (1966).

A "POOR" RESEARCH DESIGN (NO CONTROL): THE "ONE-SHOT CASE STUDY[1]"

Treatment   Posttest

X	O_2

Design procedures (using example of determining whether or not a new teaching method will increase reading speed):
1. Expose subject to X, the new teaching method, for a given period of time.
2. Administer O_2, the Posttest, to measure mean reading speed *after* exposure to X.

---

[1]Adapted from Campbell, D. T., & Stanley, J. C. (1966). *Experimental and quasi-experimental designs for research.* Chicago, IL: Rand McNally & Co.

Internal validity:
1. Disadvantages:
   a. There is a complete absence of control and no internal validity. The "quick and easy" nature of this approach, often used as a basis for a change or innovation in education, is entirely misleading.
   b. No provision for comparison exists except implicitly, intuitively, and impressionistically. (*Note:* basic to science is the process of comparison and securing scientific evidence involves making at least one comparison.)
   c. This approach usually involves the "error of misplaced precision,"–a great deal of care given to the collection of data about which our conclusions can only be impressionistic and imprecise.
   d. The attempt to use standardized tests in lieu of a control group is misguided, since rival sources of difference other than X are so numerous as to render the standardization group useless as a "control" group.

2. Advantage: This method may be useful in exploring for researchable problems or developing ideas or devices, as in action research. It simply is not a basis from which we can reach defensible *conclusions* in research. The danger is that we will go this far, and no farther–that we will justify what we are doing in terms of impressionistic evidence alone.

DESIGN 2–(MINIMAL CONTROL): ONE-GROUP PRETEST-POSTTEST DESIGN[1]

Pretest	Treatment	Posttest
O_1	X	O_2

Design procedures–(using the example of determining whether or not a new teaching method will increase reading speed):
1. Administer O_1, the pretest, to measure mean reading speed of a single group *before* exposure to the new teaching method.
2. Expose subjects to X, the new teaching method, for a given period of time.
3. Administer O_2, the posttest, to measure mean reading speed *after* exposure to X. Compare O_1 and O_2 to determine what difference, if any, the exposure to X has made.
4. Apply an appropriate statistical test to determine whether the difference is significant.

Internal validity:
1. Advantages: the pretest provides a comparison between performances by the same group of subjects *before* and *after* exposure to X (the experimental treatment). It also provides a control for *selection* and *mortality* variables, if the same subjects take O_1 and O_2.

---

[1]Adapted from Campbell, D. T., & Stanley, J. C. (1966). *Experimental and quasi-experimental designs for research*. Chicago, IL: Rand McNally & Co.

2. Disadvantages:
   a. No assurance that X is the only or even the major factor in an $O_1 - O_2$ difference.
   b. Plausible rival hypotheses ("probable error"):
      (1) History–e.g., if some subjects are fitted for glasses between O_1 and O_2.
      (2) Maturation–the fact that they are growing older, or more tired, or are less enthusiastic, or less attentive.
      (3) Testing effects–the experience of O_1, by itself, may increase motivation, alter attitudes, induce learning sets, or stimulate self-pacing.
      (4) Changing effects of instrumentation–any changes in the test, its scoring, the observation or interview techniques, or calibration of an automated teaching device, that make O_1 and O_2 different events.
      (5) Statistical regression–an inevitable effect when an extreme group is being compared on pretest and posttest measures (see page 98).
      (6) Selection biases and mortality–if the same subjects did not take both O_1 and O_2, differences may be due to uncontrolled characteristics or factors related to this difference alone.

DESIGN 4–RANDOMIZED CONTROL-GROUP PRETEST-POSTTEST DESIGN[1, 2]

Group	Pretest	Treatment	Posttest
Experimental Group (R)*	O_1	X	O_2
Control Group (R)	O_1	.	O_2

*Random assignment

Design procedure
1. Select subjects from a population by random methods.
2. Assign subjects to groups and the treatment (X), or nontreatment (.), by random methods.
3. Pretest the groups on the dependent variable (O_1), finding the mean pretest score for both the experimental and control groups.
4. Keep all conditions the same for both groups, except for exposing *only* the experimental group to X, the experimental treatment (independent variable) for a specified period of time.
5. Test the groups on O_2, the dependent variable, and find the mean posttest score for both groups.
6. Find the difference between the O_1 and O_2 means for each group separately ($O_2 - O_1$).
7. Compare these differences to determine whether the application of X is associated with a change favoring the experimental group over the control group (which was not exposed to X).

---

[1]Adapted from Campbell, D. T., & Stanley, J. C. (1966) *Experimental and quasi-experimental designs for research*. Chicago, IL: Rand McNally & Co.

[2]NOTE: This numbering system is based on notation from Campbell and Stanley and therefore is not an ordinal list in this text.

8. Apply an appropriate statistical test to determine whether the difference in the scores is significant—that is, if the difference is large enough to reject the null hypothesis that the difference is simply a chance occurrence.

Design 4 can be extended to the study of two or more variations of the independent variable—for example, two methods of teaching reading:

First Experimental Group (R)	O_1	X_a (Method *a*)	O_2
Second Experimental Group (R)	O_1	X_b (Method *b*)	O_2
Control Group (R)	O_1		O_2

In this case, conclusions can be reached about the differential effects of Method *a* and Method *b*, *without* the control group. However, a more powerful conclusion can be made about both methods with a control group comparison.

Internal validity:
1. In general, internal validity gains strength in Design 4. Between-session variations (extraneous variables that occur between O_1 and O_2) are controlled since they affect both groups equally.
2. Within-session variations, however, pose problems. Such variations involve differences that the experimental and control groups may experience when they are tested and treated separately. For example, differences in room conditions, personalities of the teachers, or wording of instructions. *Solution:* Test or treat subjects individually or in small groups, randomly assigning subjects, times, and places to experimental and control conditions. The effects of any unwanted situational factors are thus randomly distributed among the subgroups, allowing them to be ignored.
3. To control for within-session instrument differences, it is necessary also to assign mechanical instruments, teachers, observers, and raters to sessions—or preferably to a single session. Ideally, if observers or judges are involved, they should remain unaware of which groups are being used for control or experimental purposes, since they may have subtle biases that could influence their observations.
4. Differential selection is controlled by random selection methods, *maturation* and *pretesting* effects occur equally for all groups, *differential mortality* can be assessed for nonrandom patterns, and *statistical regression* is controlled when extreme scorers from the same population are randomly assigned to groups (statistical regression will occur but it will occur equally with all groups).

External validity: Do the results allow valid generalizations to other persons and situations for which the subjects and settings of this study are presumably representative? More specifically, can extraneous variables interact with the experimental treatment and make the subjects unrepresentative of the population from which they were selected? Can the claim be made that the effect which X had on the subjects will be the same for other members of the population who did not participate in the experiment?

1. *Interaction of pretesting* and X—Design 4 does not control for this possibility. If the pretesting somehow sensitizes or alters the subject so that the response to X is different than if no pretesting had taken place, then the external validity will have been compromised. (See Design 5 for solution.)

2. *Interaction of selection* and *X*–If the subjects in the experiment are different in any particular way from persons to whom one wishes to generalize, biased influences can arise. If subjects are from a university community, or if they come from only a few schools that were willing to cooperate out of many schools approached, subtle factors can enter the picture which compromise the generalization.

3. *Interaction of history* and *X*–If an experiment coincides with a dramatic event or an atypical condition (e.g., war, depression, scandal, and local strife), subjects may respond to *X* differently than during normal circumstances.

4. The *reactive effects* of *experimental procedures* may hamper generalization. If subjects know they are in an experiment they may react differently (put forth unusual effort or cooperate to an unnatural degree). *Solution:* Either avoid letting the subjects know they are in an experiment or treat both the experimental and control groups with equal attention so that they are unable to distinguish which is which. Many times O_1 and O_2 measures can be part of routine school testing or evaluation with *X* presented as part of the normal instructional or counseling program. The question of ethical practices must, of course, be carefully examined and proper authorization secured in advance.

DESIGN 5–RANDOMIZED SOLOMON FOUR-GROUP DESIGN[1]

Group	Pretest	Treatment	Posttest	Difference*
1–Pretested (R)**	O_1	X	O_2	$1D = O_1, X, M, H$
2–Pretested (R)	O_3	.	O_4	$2D = O_3, M, H$
3–Unpretested (R)		X	O_5	$3D = X, M, H$
4–Unpretested (R)		.	O_6	$4D = M, H$

*D–The difference between O_1 and O_2 mean scores represents the effects of various combinations of variables, such as: pretesting O_1, independent variable *X*, history *H*, maturation *M*. To find *the effect of X alone*, subtract $4D$ from $3D$. To find *the effect of pretesting alone*, subtract $4D$ from $2D$. To find *the effect of the interaction of pretesting and X*, add $2D$ and $3D$ and subtract the sum for $1D$.

**(R): Random assignment

Design 5 overcomes the external validity weakness in Design 4. When pretesting may affect the subjects in an experiment such that they become sensitized to *X* in a way that they respond differently than unpretested subjects, external validity is compromised and one cannot generalize the experimental findings from the sample to the population. Design 5 solves this problem by adding two "Unpretested" groups (3 and 4) to the study.

---

[1]Adapted from Campbell, D. T., & Stanley, J. C. (1966). *Experimental and quasi-experimental designs for research*. Chicago, IL: Rand McNally & Co.

Design 5 requires that the subjects be assigned at random to the four groups. The random assignment of subjects makes it possible to assume that the pretest scores for groups 3 and 4 would have been similar to the pretest scores attained by groups 1 and 2. But since groups 3 and 4 are not pretested, no interaction between X and the effects of O_1 can be reflected in their O_1 scores.

Design validity–Design 5 permits the control and measurement of both (1) the *main effects of pretesting* and (2) the *interaction effects of pretesting* and X. Furthermore, the combined effects of *maturation* and *history* can be measured if the O_2 mean for group 4 is compared with the O_2 means. This design actually amounts to doing the experiment twice (once with pretests and once without). Consequently, if the results of the "two experiments" are consistent, greater confidence can be placed in the findings than would otherwise be possible.

Supplementary matching procedures may be used with Designs 5 and 6. If matching is employed, the subjects are matched on some factor other than the dependent variable. If O_1 and O_2 are reading achievement tests, for example, the matching may be done on IQ scores, but not the reading scores. In general, matching without random assignment is not recommended.

DESIGN 6–RANDOMIZED CONTROL-GROUP POSTTEST ONLY DESIGN[1]

	Pretest	Treatment	Posttest
Experimental Group (R)*		X	O_2
Control Group (R)		.	O_2

*Random assignment

Design procedures–Design 6 consists of the last two groups in the Solomon design: the two unpretested groups.

As in all rigorously controlled designs, prior to the application of X the subjects are assigned at random to the experimental and control groups. Why can the experimenter omit the pretest? Because randomization techniques permit the experimenter to declare that at the time of assignment the groups were equal. The probability theory defines to what extent the randomly assigned subjects in the two groups might have been expected to differ by chance on O_1, and the test of significance takes account of such chance differences.

---

[1]Adapted from Campbell, D. T., & Stanley, J. C. (1966). *Experimental and quasi-experimental designs for research*. Chicago, IL: Rand McNally & Co.

After the subjects are assigned at random to groups, the experimental group is exposed to X, such as a film with a racial-prejudice theme, and the control group is not. During or after the exposure to X, the two groups are tested for the first time. Their scores are compared to ascertain the effect of X, and an appropriate test of significance is applied to determine whether this difference is greater than might have occurred by chance.

Design validity–Design 6 is superior to Design 4 because no interaction effect of pretesting and X can occur. Groups are assumed to be equivalent on the basis of random selection. It controls for, but does not measure the effects of, history, maturation and pretesting. It is particularly useful when pretests are unavailable, inconvenient, or too costly; when subjects' anonymity must be kept; and when a pretest may interact with X. (Note: Design 4 is superior to Design 6 when the sample size is small and a check on equivalence is appropriate. Also, if O_1 information is routinely available, Design 4 is probably preferable.)

DESIGN 10–NONRANDOMIZED CONTROL-GROUP PRETEST-POSTTEST DESIGN[1]

	Pretest	Treatment	Posttest
Experimental Group	O_1	X	O_2
Control Group	O_1	.	O_2

Design procedures–Same as Design 4, except subjects are not assigned to groups at random. Preassembled groups that are as similar as availability permits are selected and are given pretests. Pretest means and standard deviations are then compared for similarity.

Internal validity:

1. Fairly satisfactory if groups have similar means and standard deviations on pretest.

2. Control group insures against mistaking effects of history, pretesting, maturation, and instrumentation, for the main-effects of X.

3. Differences in within-session history and instrumentation can be sources of contamination, if not carefully checked, however.

4. Mortality effects are controlled by checking pretest and posttest records.

---

[1]Adapted from Campbell, D. T., & Stanley, J. C. (1966) *Experimental and quasi-experimental designs for research.* Chicago, IL: Rand McNally & Co.

5. Main threats to internal validity arise from interaction between such variables as selection and maturation, selection and history, or selection and testing. In the absence of randomization, the possibility always exists that some critical difference, not reflected in the pretest, is operating to contaminate the posttest data. For example, if the experimental group consists of volunteers, they may be more highly motivated; or if they happen to have a different experience background which affects how they interact with the experimental treatment–such factors rather than X by itself, may account for the differences.

6. Statistical regression can be avoided but should be checked. For example, if two different schools have substantially different means on a criterion test, one might match students from both schools to insure a sample of "equal" ability so that the lower school is not "penalized." However, on the posttest, both groups will regress toward the mean of their respective schools, creating an artificial difference.

External validity: The same general questions apply here as with Design 4. Design 10 has some practical advantages, since it deals with intact classes and does not disrupt the school's program. By involving a wide variety of classes from several settings it is possible to achieve an even higher degree of external validity. This is especially true for *interaction* of *selection* and X. The *reactive effects of experimental procedures* may hamper generalizations, but to a lesser extent than in Design 4. Conducting an authorized experiment without the subjects being aware of it is easier with intact classes than when subjects are assigned at random to treatment groups.

DESIGN 11–COUNTERBALANCED DESIGN[1]

Application: When random assignment of subjects is not possible and intact groups must be used. Advantages over Design 10: When a limited number of subjects is available, no pretest is given, and more than one variation of X is tested.

Treatment Variations

Replication	X_a	X_b	X_c	X_d
1	A	B	C	D
2	B	D	A	C
3	C	A	D	B
4	D	C	B	A

Column Mean Scores:

Design procedures:
1. Each group of subjects (*A, B, C,* or *D*) is exposed to each variation of X (or absence of X, if a control group is used) at different times during the experiment. In the

---

[1]Adapted from Campbell, D. T., & Stanley, J. C. (1966). *Experimental and quasi-experimental designs for research*. Chicago, IL: Rand McNally & Co.

above example, there are four variations of X applied to four different groups in such a way that: (a) a different X is presented to each group each time, and (b) each X precedes and follows each other X an equal number of times.

2. After all the experimental sessions are completed, the column mean for each variation of X is computed. A column mean represents the average score for all groups when exposed to the particular X in the column heading. A comparison of these column mean scores reveals what effect the different Xs have upon group performance.

Design validity:
1. Design 11 controls for weakness inherent in Design 10–namely, the possibility that the nonrandomized groups might not be equivalent in all important respects, introducing differences that are mistaken for the effects of X. The Counterbalanced Design rotates out these subjects' differences by exposing all variations of X to all groups, at the same time controlling for order-of-presentation effects. If one group happens to be more intelligent than the others, each X will profit from this superiority.
2. Interaction effects can contaminate the findings if, for example, one group fatigues dramatically on one trial (*selection-maturation interaction*), or if the interaction for some reason affects a different group each time over several replications.
3. Primary weakness of Design 11 for education: Does not control for the effect of an exposure to one X if it carries over and combines with measurements of the next X. When the possibility of carry-over effects exist, sufficient time should elapse between replications to permit these effects to dissipate. If the assumption that there are no residual or carry-over effects, operating cannot be satisfied, and Design 10 will not be appropriate. (Example of carry-over effects: In a drug experiment, the effect of a given drug may remain in the body and combine with the effect of a subsequent drug. The measurement of the effect of the second drug is now contaminated by the first. Another illustration highly relevant to education is the transfer of training effect where cognitive processes are involved.)

DESIGN 7–ONE-GROUP TIME-SERIES DESIGN[1]

This design is the same as Design 2, except that several measurements are taken before and after the introduction of X.

Pretest	Treatment	Posttest
O_1 O_2 O_3 O_4	X	O_5 O_6 O_7 O_8

Internal validity:
1. The several tests given over a period of time provide more control over possible sources of internal invalidity than Design 2. If, for example, there is no appreciable difference in the first four O scores, the difference between the O_4 and O_5 scores cannot reasonably be due to *maturation, testing,* or *regression.* Changes in *instrumentation,* or effects of *selection* or *mortality* can be largely controlled, or accounted for, also.
2. The chief potential source of internal invalidity is *contemporary history*–for instance, the coincidence (with X) of some influential event such as the simultaneous appearance of a televised program related to the experimental instruction, an environmental change (such as weather, public scandal) or cyclic variation (e.g.,

---

[1]Adapted from Campbell, D. T., & Stanley, J. C. (1966). *Experimental and quasi-experimental designs for research.* Chicago, IL: Rand McNally & Co.

weekend, end-of-semester examinations). The role of such factors must be carefully observed and assessed.

External validity:
1. Generalization of findings of Design 7 depends upon the experimental conditions. An *interaction* between *pretesting* and *X* can occur if the pretesting introduces factors which somehow modify the subjects so that they are no longer representative of the population from which they were drawn. Atypical tests, for example, might induce an attitude or set in the subjects which will never be experienced by the general population of subjects. Standardized achievement tests, on the other hand, are common experiences to nearly all subjects.
2. A *selection-X interaction* can occur if not carefully avoided. For example, if the subjects are volunteers, or come from groups with special characteristics, or if the repetition of the unique *O*s cause selective absenteeism, they may not represent the general population of possible subjects.

DESIGN 14–CONTROL-GROUP TIME-SERIES DESIGN[1]

Design 14 follows from Design 7 by simply adding a control group, thus controlling for the effects of *contemporary history,* the main weakness within Design 7. If the control group fails to show a gain from O_4 to O_5 and the experimental group yields a gain, the plausibility of some contemporary event accounting for the gain is greatly reduced, since both groups have experienced this particular event.

	Pretest	Treatment	Posttest
Experimental Group:	O_1 O_2 O_3 O_4	X	O_5 O_6 O_7 O_8
Control Group:	O_1 O_2 O_3 O_4	.	O_5 O_6 O_7 O_8

This design is also superior to Design 10 by controlling for *selection-maturation interaction.* If one group shows a greater rate of gain than the other, this accelerated gain would also appear in the pre-*X* testing.

The multiple posttests employed in Designs 7 and 14 can be the source of vital information that a single posttest design will not reveal. For instance, if *X* is a short-term influence which tends to disappear with time, these designs will pick up this trend. Or, one variation of *X* may have strong but *short-term* effects while another variation of *X* may have mild but *long-term* effects.

An alternative design strategy to control for the effects of maturation, pretesting, regression, and contemporary history (cf. Design 14) begins with several groups which are pretested at the same time but which are posttested at different intervals of time:

Group A:	O_1	X	O_2			
Group B:	O_1	X		O_2		
Group C:	O_1	X			O_2	
Group D:	O_1	X				O_2
Group E:	O_1	X				O_2

---

[1]Adapted from Campbell, D. T., & Stanley, J. C. (1966). *Experimental and quasi-experimental designs for research.* Chicago, IL: Rand McNally & Co.

By adding a control group with the same pretest and posttest pattern, but without the treatment, the effects of the treatment can be assessed. This strategy is particularly appropriate where maturational factors are involved and where the effects of serial testing within groups should be minimized.

FACTORS JEOPARDIZING THE VALIDITY OF EXPERIMENTAL DESIGNS[1]

Sources of Invalidity	EXPERIMENTAL DESIGNS*							
	Little Control	Rigorous Control			Partial Control			
	2	4	5	6	10	11	7	14
Internal validity								
Contemporary history	−	+	+	+	+	+	−	+
Maturation processes	−	+	+	+	+	+	+	+
Pretesting procedures	−	+	+	+	+	+	+	+
Measuring instruments	−	+	+	+	+	+	?	+
Statistical regression	?	+	+	+	?	+	+	+
Differential selection of subjects	+	+	+	+	+	+	+	+
Experimental mortality	+	+	+	+	+	+	+	+
Interaction of selection and maturation, etc.	−	+	+	+	−	?	+	+
External validity								
Interaction of selection and X	−	?	?	?	?	?	?	−
Interaction of pretesting and X	−	−	+	+	−	?	−	−
Reactive experimental procedures	?	?	?	?	?	?	?	?
Multiple-treatment interference								−

*Names of Designs 2 to 14 are:

2. One-Group Pretest-Posttest
4. Randomized Control-Group Pretest-Posttest
5. Randomized Solomon Four-Group
6. Randomized Control-Group Posttest only

10. Nonrandomized Control-Group
11. Counterbalanced
7. One-Group Time-series
14. Control-Group Time-series

Note: A plus symbol indicates control of a factor, a minus indicates lack of control, a question mark suggests there is some source for concern, and a blank indicates that the factor is not relevant.

AN EXTENSION OF THE WORK OF CAMPBELL AND STANLEY

In 1979 Cook and Campbell expanded upon the work of Campbell and Stanley (1966) in terms of formulating four broad types of threats to the validity of experimental and quasi-experimental designs. The four broad threats were categorized as those pertaining to (1) statistical conclusion validity, (2) internal validity, (3) construct validity of cause and effects, and (4) external validity. Briefly considered, statistical conclusion validity refers essentially to whether the statistical procedures were properly applied to the data analysis and whether the assumptions underlying these procedures were adequately met. Internal validity was conceptualized almost in the same way as that

---

[1]Material on this page and on the preceding page is adapted in large measure from Van Dalen, D. B. (1979). *Understanding educational research* (4th ed.) (pp. 279-280). New York: McGraw-Hill.

which has just been presented with a few additional considerations. Construct validity of cause and effects was examined in terms of (a) whether the independent or treatment variable was actually applied in the manner intended, and (b) whether the measures of the dependent variable actually reflected in an accurate way the underlying constructs that the experimenter desired to have represented by the one or more dependent variables. External validity was conceptualized very much in the same manner as that which has already been presented. The accompanying table adapted by Michael and Benson (1994) from material presented in Cook and Campbell (1979) serves to summarize quite succinctly the four major categories of threats to the validity of designs as well as the corresponding features associated with these threats as set forth by these two authors.

THREATS TO THE VALIDITY OF DESIGNS

Threats	Features
(1) Statistical conclusion validity	Was the study sensitive enough to detect whether the variables covary?
(a) Low statistical power	Type II error increases when alpha is set low and sample is small; also refers to some statistical tests.
(b) Violated statistical assumptions	All assumptions must be known and tested when necessary.
(c) Error rate	Increases, unless adjustments are made with the number of mean differences possible to test on multiple dependent variables.
(d) Reliability of measures	Low reliability indicates high standard errors which can be a problem with various inferential statistics.
(e) Reliability of treatment implementation	Treatments need to be implemented in the same way from person to person, site to site, and across time.
(f) Random irrelevancies in setting	Environmental effects which may cause or interact with treatment effects.
(g) Random heterogeneity of respondents	Certain characteristics in subjects may be correlated with dependent variables.
(2) Internal validity	Was the study sensitive enough to detect a causal relationship?
(a) History	Event external to treatment which may affect dependent variable.
(b) Maturation	Biological and psychological changes in subjects which will affect their responses.
(c) Testing	Effects of pretest may alter responses on posttest regardless of treatment.
(d) Instrumentation	Changes in instrumentation, raters, or observers (calibration difficulties).
(e) Statistical regression	Extreme scores tend to move to middle on posttesting regardless of treatment.
(f) Selection	Differences in subjects prior to treatment.
(g) Mortality	Differential loss of subjects during study.
(h) Interaction of selection with maturation, history and testing	Some other characteristic of subjects is mistaken for treatment effect on posttesting; differential effects in selection factors.
(i) Ambiguity about direction of causality	In studies conducted at one point in time, problem of inferring the direction of causality.
(j) Diffusion/imitation of treatments	Treatment group members share the conditions of their treatment with each other or attempt to copy treatment.

Continued on next page.

THREATS TO THE VALIDITY OF DESIGNS[1]

Threats	Features
(k) Compensatory equalization of treatments	It is decided that everyone in experimental or comparison group receive the treatment that provides desirable goods and services.
(l) Demoralization of respondents	Members of group not receiving treatment perceive they are inferior and give up.
(3) Construct validity of cause and effects	Which theoretical or latent variables are actually being studied?
(a) Inadequate explication of constructs	Poor definition of constructs.
(b) Mono-operation bias	Measurement of single dependent variable.
(c) Mono-method bias	Measurement of dependent variable in only one way.
(d) Hypothesis-guessing	Subjects try to guess researcher's hypothesis and act in a way that they think the researcher wants them to act.
(e) Evaluation apprehension	Faking well to make results look good.
(f) Experimenter expectancies	Experimenters may bias study by their expectations entering into and during study.
(g) Confounding constructs and levels of constructs	All levels of a construct are not fully implemented along a continuum, they may appear to be weak or non-existent.
(h) Interaction of different treatments	Subjects are a part of other treatments rather than of an intended one.
(i) Interaction of testing and treatment	Testing may facilitate or inhibit treatment influences.
(j) Restricted generalizability	The extent to which a construct can be generalized from one study to another.
(4) External validity	Can the cause and effect noted in the study be generalized across individuals, settings, and occasions?
(a) Interaction of selection and treatment	Ability to generalize the treatment to persons beyond the one studied.
(b) Interaction of setting and treatment	Ability to generalize the treatment to settings beyond the one studied.
(c) Interaction of history and treatment	Ability to generalize the treatment to other times (past and future) beyond the one studied.

[1]Reprinted from Husen, T. & Postlethwaite, T. H. (1994). *The international encyclopedia of education* (2nd ed.) from vol. 4 *Evolution of Evaluation Design* by Michael, W. B., & Benson, J. (pp. 2079-2089) with kind permission from Elsevier Science, Ltd. the Boulevard, Langford Lane, Kidlington OX5 IGB UK.

FACTORIAL DESIGNS

Classical experimental design allows the variation of a single X at a time, holding all other conditions constant. Complex behavior, however, usually will not be fitted into such an artificial situation. Furthermore, factors influencing behavior frequently *interact* to produce differences that do not occur when only one factor is free to vary at a time. For example, there might be an interaction between intelligence and method of teaching such that authoritarian methods work better with low intelligence subjects and democratic methods work better with high intelligence subjects. A study of the two teaching methods which holds intelligence constant will lead to misleading conclusions, just as would a study allowing intelligence to vary but holding the teaching method constant. To permit research studies where more than one factor is free to vary at a time, *factorial designs* have become increasingly prominent. They have several advantages over the classical experimental design:

1. They permit the testing of several hypotheses simultaneously, rather than having to conduct a series of single X experiments to study the effects of different Xs on, for example, learning.
2. They permit the conduct of only one experiment to answer several complex questions at once, such as: What effect does X_1-type teacher have on learning achievement when using X_2-type methods in X_3-length classes with X_4-type students?
3. Where *interaction* between two or more variables simultaneously makes a difference, it reveals this difference.
4. Where the classical experimental control of all variables but one is impractical or impossible.

Note: The basic statistical technique used to test the null hypothesis in factorial designs is analysis of variance (see pages 189-191).

THE 2 x 2 FACTORIAL DESIGN[1]

	Length of Period (X_2)			
	50'	30'	Mean	Difference
Teaching Method (X_1) — Lecture	A — 59.0	B — 58.0	58.5	−1.0
Teaching Method (X_1) — Discussion	C — 82.0	D — 84.0	83.0	+2.0
Mean:	70.5	71.0		
Difference	+23.0	+26.0		

This is the simplest factorial design, permitting the study of the effects of two Xs (treatments), each of which is varied in two ways (levels or values).

Example:
1. Let X_1 represent two teaching methods and X_2 represent two lengths of time for a class period.
2. Assign subjects at random to each of the four possible combinations of experimental treatment. Group A is exposed to 50-minute lecture periods, Group B to 30-minute lecture periods, Group C to 50-minute discussion, and Group D to 30-minute discussion periods.

---

[1]Adapted from Van Dalen, D. B. (1979). *Understanding educational research* (4th ed., pp. 256-262). New York: McGraw-Hill. (Adapted from Campbell, D. T., & Stanley, J. C. (1966). *Experimental and quasi-experimental designs for research*. Chicago, IL: Rand McNally & Co.

3. After a predetermined period of time, the achievement of each subject is measured and the mean scores of each of the groups are recorded in their appropriate cells (e.g., Group A = 59.0, Group B = 58.0, etc.).
4. Mean scores are also computed for the pairs of groups exposed to the lecture method (A and B = 58.5) and the discussion method (C and D = 83.0); the 50-minute period (A and C = 70.5) or the 30-minute period (B and D = 71.0). These combined means are placed in their respective row or column margins.

Design information:
1. What is the main effect of teaching method (X_1) on achievement scores? Answer: A comparison of the mean score of the two lecture groups (58.5) with that of the two discussion groups (83.0) appears to favor the latter as more effective.
2. What is the main effect of length of class (X_2) on achievement scores? Answer: A comparison of the mean score of the two groups with 50-minute periods (70.5) and the two groups with 30-minute periods (71.0) suggests no particular difference.
3. What is the interaction effect, if any, of teaching method and length of class period on the achievement scores? Answer: If there is an interaction, the effect that a teaching method has on the achievement scores will differ for 30- and 50-minute classes. If the discussion method, for example, is more effective with one length of class than it is with the other, there is an interaction. If there is no interaction, the effect of a teaching method on achievement scores will be the same for both lengths of class periods. The data in the above example, therefore, reveal no appreciable interaction effect.

EXTENDED FACTORIAL DESIGNS

Factorial designs more complex than the 2 x 2 model are often employed. For example:

2 x 3 Design–two independent variables: One varied in two ways; the other varied in three ways. Example:
First variable: Sex (*male* or *female*).
Second variable: Method of teaching reading *(reading experience approach, phonics approach,* and *word recognition approach).*
3 x 3 Design–three independent variables: Each varied three ways. Example:
First variable: Intelligence *(Above* 110 *IQ, Between* 90-110 *IQ,* and *Below* 90 *IQ).*
Second variable: Problem-solving approach *(individual, small group,* and *large group).*
Third variable: Time allotment *(2 hours without interruption, 2 1-hour sessions with a 1 hour break, 2 1-hour sessions with a 24-hour break).*
2 x 2 x 2 Design: Three independent variables: Each varied two ways. Example:
First variable: Age *(12 year olds* and *15 year olds).*
Second variable: Sex *(boys* and *girls).*
Third variable: Counseling atmosphere *(directive* or *nondirective).*
Note: This design requires eight treatment groups (2 x 2 x 2 = 8) and can answer the following seven questions: What is the main effect on (for example) achievement scores of (1) X_1, (2) X_2, and (3) X_3? What is the interaction effect on the achievement scores of (4) X_1 and X_2, (5) X_1 and X_3, (6) X_2 and X_3, and (7) X_1, X_2, and X_3?

Designs of greater complexity than the above illustrations are possible, though they tend to be unwieldy and highly sophisticated.

An important characteristic of factorial designs is that several hypotheses can be tested simultaneously, releasing researchers from the rigidity of classical designs. Whereas classical designs allowed only the study of a single variable at a time, factorial designs permit several variables to be investigated in one experiment. An example of this multi-factor approach would be an experiment investigating simultaneously the following question: What effect does teacher personality (X_1) have on student achievement when using a particular teaching method (X_2) in a particular classroom situation (X_3) with students of a particular ability level (X_4)?

ADDITIONAL CONCERNS, STRATEGIES, AND PITFALLS IN THE DESIGN OF RESEARCH

The payoff in research studies comes in reaching significant and useful conclusions after the data have been collected and analyzed within the *framework of the design*. Good planning and careful design anticipate which questions will be open to investigation and establish the conditions under which conclusions can be defensibly drawn.

The major difficulty, discussed earlier in this section, arises from the role of *plausible rival hypotheses* which the design must minimize if the results are to be meaningful. In other words, can the findings be explained for reasons other than those advanced by the research hypotheses? Subtle biases, contaminating factors, inadequate controls and numerous oversights and oversimplifications conspire to waylay the obvious interpretation which seems to follow so directly from the research framework.[1]

In essence, then, the goal of good design is to maximize internal and external validity and minimize error. To bolster the probability of this outcome, the remaining pages of this section summarize further concerns, strategies, and pitfalls often neglected in unsophisticated or carelessly designed research. They are organized under the following topical headings:

1. Control–a key concept in experimental design
2. Confounding and cancellation of effects; two pitfalls of interaction
3. Generalizability of research findings
4. Interaction between variables
5. Some common sources of error
6. Making meaningful comparisons
7. Reactive versus nonreactive measures
8. Measurement; single versus multiple outcomes–*triangulation*
9. Statistical regression effects
10. Short-term and long-term studies

---

[1]Varying degrees of "confirmation" are conferred upon a theory by examining the number of *plausible rival hypotheses* available to account for the data. As the number of such rival hypotheses decreases, confirmation increases. Equally important, the more numerous and independent the ways in which the experimental effect is demonstrated, the less numerous and less plausible any single rival hypothesis becomes. The appeal is to parsimony. If several sets of differences can all be explained by a single hypothesis claiming that X has an effect, while several distinct uncontrolled-variable effects otherwise must be hypothesized, a different one for each observed difference, then the effect of X becomes the most tenable. In other words, a general finding among several studies, which is contested on different grounds from one study to another, is strengthened by that fact alone. (From Campbell, D. T., & Stanley, J. C. (1966). *Experimental and quasi-experimental designs for research.* Chicago: Rand McNally & Co.

11. Five points about research design
12. Large samples versus small samples
13. Individual differences
14. Matching as a control technique; some disadvantages

CONTROL–A KEY CONCEPT IN EXPERIMENTAL DESIGN[1]

Research design has two basic purposes: First and most obvious, to provide answers to research questions and, second, to *control variance* (variability).[2] There are three kinds of variance that must be controlled according to the following set of "minimax" principles if answers to research questions are to be valid:

1. *Maximize the experimental variance*–the systematic effects of the variable(s) associated with the research hypotheses. This is done by designing, planning, and conducting research so that the experimental conditions are as different as possible, emphasizing their importance.

2. *Control the extraneous variance*–the effects of other systematic but "unwanted" variables that might influence the experimental outcomes but are not themselves the object of study. There are five ways to do this:
    a. Simply prevent the variation of an extraneous variable such as IQ by holding it *constant*. For example, choose subjects that are homogeneous on this variable by holding IQs within a range between 90-110.
    b. The most powerful technique is *randomization* which controls for all possible extraneous variables simultaneously. Ideally, this means randomly selected subjects who are randomly assigned to groups which, in turn, are randomly assigned the treatment or control conditions.
    c. Build the extraneous variables right into the design as if they were independent variables. This achieves control and yields additional information about their effect on the dependent variable and their possible interactions with other independent or classificatory variables.
    d. Perhaps the most commonly used method for controlling extraneous variables is *matching* the subjects on one or more variables. Matching has many disadvantages and is now generally discouraged (see page 103), but it occasionally remains useful if a substantial correlation ($\geq$.50) between the matching variable(s) and the dependent variable exists.
    e. The final method of control is *statistical* and is inherent in all research design since it is inseparable from other control techniques. The method of analysis of covariance is particularly useful in place of matching, but still requires randomization.

3. *Minimize the error variance*–the effects of random fluctuations including so-called errors of measurement. This is achieved largely by careful control of the measurement conditions and by increasing the reliability of the measures themselves. While error variance is unpredictable and self-cancelling around a mean of zero, if it is sizable it can swallow up the systematic variance of the experimental variables just as a signal is lost in a high-noise background. Sampling error is minimized by increasing the sample size.

---

[1]Adapted from Kerlinger, F. N. (1986). *Foundations of behavioral research* (3rd ed.) (Chapter 17). New York: Harcourt Brace.

[2]"Variance" is a statistical way of looking at the variability of scores or means. "Control of variance" is taking into account all factors which systematically contribute to the generation of individual differences in scores or measures on the outcome or dependent variable.

CONFOUNDING AND CANCELLATION OF EFFECTS: TWO PITFALLS OF INTERACTION

The interaction between variables, intentional or incidental, poses at least two difficulties for research design, if unforeseen.

Confounding. Confounding exists when the variance of one or more independent variables, usually outside the focus of the research, mixes with the variance arising from the independent variable(s) built into the research problem. Consequently, it is unclear whether the relationship found is between the independent/classificatory and dependent variables in the research design, or between the extraneous independent/classificatory variables and the dependent variable, or both. Succinctly, whenever the effects of the independent variables cannot be evaluated unambiguously, confounding probably is present.[1]

EXAMPLE: Two groups of students, A, the control group, and B, the treatment group, obtain the following mean performance scores:

Group A	Group B
$M = 60$	$M = 69$

If the mean scores between the two groups are taken at their face value, assuming their difference is statistically significant, we would conclude that the treatment was effective. Suppose, however, we learn afterward that Group A had a mean IQ of 109 and Group B, a mean IQ of 115. Because the treatment and intelligence were unwittingly *confounded*, it is no longer clear which made the difference.

Cancellation of effects. Sometimes, instead of finding a difference whose source is confounded, a difference will be hidden from view because the design failed to identify and/or distinguish between variables whose effects counteract each other or, within a single variable, failed to compare contrasting levels or amounts resulting in the same cancellation of effect.

EXAMPLE: Consider an investigation of the differential effects of either small or large steps in programmed instruction, in terms of mean terminal achievement test scores, yielding these results:

	Group I small steps	Group II large steps	
High IQ	70	90	$\overline{M}_{Ach.score} = 80$
Low IQ	50	30	$\overline{M}_{Ach.score} = 40$
	$\overline{M}_{Ach.score} = 60$	$\overline{M}_{Ach.score} = 60$	

If the original analysis dealt only with randomly selected subjects, with no distinction between levels of IQ, no differences between Group I and Group II would have been observed, since means of 60 were reported for both groups. A differential analysis of the data, on the other hand, reveals an interaction between IQ and step size such that High IQs do better with large steps and Low IQs with small steps. Obviously, if the IQ levels are indiscriminately combined, their differential effects are cancelled and remain hidden.

Kerlinger, F. N. (1986). *Foundations of behavioral research* (3rd ed.) (Chapter 17). New York: Harcourt Brace.

GENERALIZABILITY OF RESEARCH FINDINGS[1]

Generalizability is the problem of external validity. Having done research with satisfactory internal validity, to what other situations do the results apply? In educational research, generalizability of the results is often the crucial practical question--what is learned in a single research setting ought to apply generally to many actual classroom settings. Here are three useful considerations to increase the generalizability of results:

1. *Generalizability of Results and Selection of Subjects:*
   Oftentimes, a researcher casts about for a school in which to conduct a study until one is found that is willing to cooperate. If several schools have turned the researcher down, it is reasonable to suspect that the cooperating school may not be representative of schools in general. Sampling biases often occur because of the inertia of researchers to assure representativeness in their selection procedures which, in turn, assures generalizability of the findings to the largest number of schools.
   Solution No. 1: Select subjects at random from a variety of classes and/or schools, rather than taking entire classes from a single school or school district. This minimizes the impact on any given school and maximizes the representativeness of the educational sample. This strategy is also apt to be more economical, less conspicuous, less disruptive to the classroom, and reduces overtesting (if testing only involves the sample).
   Solution No. 2: Use classrooms as the unit and randomly select these from a representative population of school districts to which generalizations of the findings would be appropriate.

2. *Generalizability of Results and Variation of the Input or Stimulus Source:*
   Contrary to a prevalent notion about the importance of *exact* replications of the stimulus source in experimental design (e.g., providing exactly the same recorded stimulus to all groups), varying the stimulus source may actually increase the generalizability of the results. This is particularly true when the task is to communicate effectively the main point of a message or treatment to new users. With the taped interview, for example, repeated each time are the same irrelevant features which may account for the effect rather than the message, per se. By varying the stimulus source, but keeping the intended communication intact, the conclusion that the source of effects lies in the message is strengthened.
   Another example of this principle is to have every teacher using every treatment within the research design, thus distributing all specific irrelevancies across all treatments and preventing the confounding of any particular irrelevancy with any particular treatment. While this design feature enhances the generalizability of the results, it frequently is impractical because of the obvious burden it places on the participating teachers.

3. *Generalizability Among Observations:*
   Just as any given treatment carries with it irrelevant characteristics which may turn out to cause the effect, so any given observation or measuring instrument is imbedded among characteristics irrelevant to the intended assessment but which may be mistaken for it.
   Solution: Use multiple measures of outcomes; e.g., essay examinations, objective tests, and indices of classroom participation. (See page 97.)

---

[1]Adapted from Campbell, D. T., & Stanley, J. C. (1966). *Experimental and quasi-experimental designs fo research.* Chicago, IL: Rand McNally & Co.

INTERACTION BETWEEN VARIABLES

Patterns of Interaction
The current emphasis in behavioral research is upon interactions between variables. The old questions, "What method works best?" or "What factor is most important?" have given way to questions specifying, "What variables?" "In what combinations and amounts?" "Under what conditions?" "With what subjects?" and "To meet what objectives?"

Interaction-proneness
Some factors are more interaction-prone than others. It is important to look for the interaction between variables, combining them to optimize outcomes.

Main Effects Versus Interactions[1]
In cases of ignorance, however, a main effect of one variable is to be judged more likely than the interaction of two other variables. More generally, main effects are more likely than interactions. If every highest order interaction is significant, if every effect is specific to certain values on all other potential treatment dimensions, then a science is not possible. If generalizations are ever possible, it is because the great bulk of potential determining factors can be discarded.

Use of Inappropriate Independent Variables[2]
It is useful to select independent variables such that they are relevant and arranged in realistic combinations with each other to take into account the interaction relationships. If researchers question whether they have defined their variables properly, they are likely to discover new things. Often the researcher selects what appear to be obvious and important variables as if they were independent of the others. If an interaction relationship exists between two or more of these independent variables, however, highly important and useful information is likely to be overlooked.

Examples: Class size is an important independent variable only in relationship with different teaching methods; to consider it separately is to miss its relevance to teaching. Another example of interaction between independent variables comes from Gage's research on the *Minnesota Teacher Attitude Inventory* (MTAI). This is a well-developed test based on the conception that teachers who are warm, gentle, democratic, and child-centered, have a superior relationship with the class and it has validity ratings near .40. However, when Gage developed another test of cognitive versus emotional orientation and compared "interpersonal relations-valuing" classes with "cognitive learning-oriented" classes—classes where the teacher and pupil are collaborating in a learning enterprise—MTAI predictive validities remained around .40 for the former but fell to zero in the latter case. Thus, an oversimple conception of the independent variable led apparently to a false interpretation of previous results.

---

[1]Adapted from Campbell, D. T., & Stanley, J. C. (1966). *Experimental and quasi-experimental designs for research.* Chicago, IL: Rand McNally & Co.
[2]Based on notes by Stephen Isaac of suggestions made by Lee J. Cronbach at a California Educational Research Association meeting, c. 1960.

The Fixed Treatment Assumption[1]

In the validation of tests involving personality categories, evidence is typically sought to match these personality categories with success in particular treatment outcomes. For example, Strong's Vocational Interest Test is used to fit the client's answers to similar patterns in various occupations. The end effect of this orientation is to select persons of a single type for any given occupation, leading to social stereotyping. Other research suggests that atypical patterns predict success for some of the less common pathways within a particular vocational field.

Solution: Allow for the relationship between personality characteristics and validation criteria in a flexible, rather than a fixed, fashion. Instead of predicting whether type A does better than type B in a given treatment, look for ways to change the treatment to fit individuals of different kinds. It is important to ask: What teaching methods work best for what kinds of students under what conditions?

SOME COMMON SOURCES OF ERROR

THE HALO EFFECT

This is the tendency for an irrelevant feature of a unit of study to influence the relevant feature in a favorable or unfavorable direction. Typically, a strong initial positive or negative impression of a person, group, or event tends to influence ratings on all subsequent observations. Impressions formed early in a series of observations often affect later observations; or impressions based on high or low status attributes of the unit of study affect observations on unrelated attributes—quoting a celebrity's opinion on an educational issue or associating emotionally-loaded labels with candidates in a hotly contested school board election. The more vague and impressionistic the variable to be rated, the more powerful is the effect; the more specific and clearly defined the variable, the less evident is the effect.

RATING ERRORS

In addition to the halo effect, three other tendencies plague the validity of ratings:
1. The over-rater error—rating subjects in general on the side of leniency or favorableness.
2. The under-rater error—rating subjects in general on the side of severity or unfavorableness.
3. The central tendency error—rating subjects toward the middle of the scale. This often occurs when the observer is unfamiliar with or uncertain about what is being rated.

---

[1]Based on notes by Stephen Isaac of suggestions made by Lee J. Cronbach at a California Educational Research Association meeting, c. 1960.

THE HAWTHORNE EFFECT

In an industrial efficiency study performed at the Hawthorne Plant of Western Electric in Chicago during the 1920's it was observed that to single out a group of workers for a special research project makes them feel and act differently compared to regular workers. The effect of this was to bring about a *consistent increase in productivity* in spite of changes in the working conditions intended both to increase and decrease efficiency. Explanations for this effect point to the factors of: (1) novelty; (2) awareness that one is a participant in an experiment; (3) a modified environment involving observers, special procedures, and new patterns of social interaction; and (4) knowledge of results in the form of daily productivity figures and other feedback, ordinarily not systematically available.

THE EXPERIMENTER BIAS EFFECT OR "SELF-FULFILLING PROPHECY" IN RESEARCH

Well documented in articles by Dr. Robert Rosenthal of Harvard, this is the bias a researcher is inclined to project into methodology and treatment that subtly shapes the data in the direction of foregone conclusions. What the researchers "expect to see," where they direct their attention, ignore or forget, remember or record, and even the way they interact with subjects to alter their own expectations and motivational states, all can influence the results to fit preconceptions.

THE "JOHN HENRY" EFFECT

The phenomenon in a research study involving human subjects assigned to experimental and control groups, when those who are identified as "controls" discover their status and, by that fact, are determined "to show the experimental group a thing or two," actually outperforming them.

THE PLACEBO EFFECT

A placebo is an inert or neutral stimulus given to subjects as if it were the active treatment variable itself. In medical research the placebo often is an injection of sterile water or a chemically inert pill administered so that the subject cannot distinguish between the neutral and the active ingredient. This allows the observer to separate treatment effects from psychological reactions induced by the treatment situation involving, in particular, the patient's expectations and suggestibility. For this reason, background elements in an educational research setting often turn out to be the agents of change in addition to the active treatment variable. For example, in a research study to examine the effects of videotape playback on increasing participation in class discussions using treatment and control groups, it might turn out that the presence of videotape recording equipment and any operators or observers were of equal or greater importance in contrast to the actual videotape playback. Unless the same equipment and personnel are present in at least some of the control classes as a placebo condition, the actual effectiveness of the playback may be misconstrued.

THE POST HOC ERROR

"After this, therefore because of this." Many events follow one another without having a cause-and-effect relationship. The reasons for this vary all the way from simple coincidence to complex relationships with other factors. For example, an increase in the ocean's temperature is directly related to the number of drownings along the California coast. We do not conclude that the warmer surf, per se, is more dangerous but that it attracts larger numbers of swimmers, exposing more people to the probability of drowning.

ERROR OF MISPLACED PRECISION

To collect data with great care and precision but within the framework of a faulty design invalidates the findings and the painstaking work that produced them. When properly evaluated, this is also demoralizing to the staff associated with the project.

BEWARE OF "TYPICAL" CASE STUDIES

Studies based on "typical" cases are usually biased and nonrepresentative. Such cases too often are more ideal than typical, or better fit the reporter's biases than others which might have been cited. A defendable alternative would be to select and review several cases *at random*, a procedure rarely followed.

THE LAW OF THE INSTRUMENT

This refers to the human inclination to become attached to a certain instrument or procedure and apply it as an across-the-board solution to every problem. As one pair of authors put it, "If you give a small boy a hammer, he will find that everything he encounters needs pounding!"[1] Most of the popular devices, innovations, and panaceas in education are vulnerable to this overreaction. In such instances, the focus is on the instrument or procedure and not the problem, placing the cart before the horse. This error is avoided by examining the problem first and then seeking appropriate instruments and procedures that best fit the properties of the problem.

MAKING MEANINGFUL COMPARISONS

BASELINE DATA[2]

To observe changes in behavior, it is first necessary to establish baseline data against which to make meaningful comparisons. Such data establish what the subjects were like before the treatments and/or observations began. To be valid, baseline data must allow appropriate adaptation periods to any unusual modifications of the research setting such as television cameras, observers in the room, new equipment, and other noticeable changes in the environment. Common procedures for gathering baseline data are the *pretest* and the *control group*. The latter is important where there is an expected treatment effect and the absence of treatment is the baseline. Control groups are also necessary where the baseline is a subjective judgment in a rater's head which is likely to change with experience.

---

[1] Resta, P. E., & Baker, R. L. (1967). *Formulating the research problem*. Inglewood, CA: Southwest Regional Laboratory for Educational Research and Development.
[2] Based on notes taken at a Field Studies Workshop given by staff members of the Far West Regional Laboratory, Berkeley, CA, 1968.

PITFALL OF "DO NOTHING" CONTROL GROUPS[1]

Control groups ordinarily should experience *all things* in common with the treatment group *except* the critical factor, per se. Control groups that "do nothing" are apt to differ from the treatment groups in more ways than just the isolated treatment variable. For example, if technicians or observers are present in the classrooms of treatment groups, they should also be present for the control groups since their presence may account for the effect rather than the treatment itself. The same is true for special equipment, visitors, interruptions, and other events that tend to single out treatment groups but ignore control groups.

EXPERIMENTAL DESIGN AND RANDOM ASSIGNMENT[2]

The most rigorous means of making meaningful comparisons is the controlled experiment with random assignment of subjects, occasions, and treatment conditions. While many research problems do not lend themselves to this technique, many more opportunities exist than are used.

USE OF INDEX NUMBERS[3]

Irrelevant sources of variance in raw data can be controlled by transforming these data into weighted, compensated, or counter-balanced aggregates. Intelligence quotients, the "labor force," and "real wages" are examples where such adjustments make meaningful comparisons possible. Such transformations are particularly critical in historical or longitudinal comparisons.

For example, the problem of measuring "mental ability" or "intelligence" across age ranges so that younger children of a given ability level could be equated to older children of the same comparative ability level, was solved by inventing the concept of *mental age*. Categories of test items, each serially ordered in difficulty, were given to children representing various chronological age intervals. The average score for each of these intervals became the "mental age" level for that corresponding chronological age level. By dividing the child's obtained mental age by his chronological age, and multiplying the resulting ratio by 100 to clear decimals, an index was devised called the intelligence quotient, or IQ, allowing direct comparisons, independent of chronological age differences. (For a restriction on this procedure, see page 100, "Two Statistical Points, item 1.")

ELIMINATION OF PLAUSIBLE RIVAL HYPOTHESES[4]

These ask the question: What other plausible interpretations are allowed by the research setting and the measurement processes? The fewer of these, and the more implausible each is, the more validly interpretable is the comparison.

---

[1]Based on notes taken at a Field Studies Workshop given by staff members of the Far West Regional Laboratory, Berkeley, CA, 1968.
[2,3]Adapted from Webb E. J., Campbell, D. T,. Schwartz, R. D., & Sechrest L. (1966). *Unobtrusive measures*. Chicago, IL: Rand McNally & Co.
[4]Adapted from Campbell, D. T., & Stanley, J. C. (1966). *Experimental and quasi-experimental designs for research*. Chicago, IL: Rand McNally & Co.

INITIAL DIFFERENCES BETWEEN CONTROL AND EXPERIMENTAL GROUPS[1]

It is often misleading to determine *critical ratio* or *t* tests on a before-and-after basis without first comparing initial differences between control and experimental groups There are two solutions:

1. *Gain scores:*[2] For each group, compute pretest-posttest gain scores and then calculate *t* between gain scores for the experimental and control groups.
2. *Covariance:* A better solution than simple gain score comparisons is to carry out randomized "blocking" or "leveling" on pretest scores or perform an analysis of covariance with the pretest scores as the covariate. Random assignment is essential.

Caution: The use of matched pairs to avoid initial differences seldom is a satisfactory alternative. See page 103.

THE RETROSPECTIVE PRETEST[3]

Sometimes a researcher would like to have pretest information on groups of subjects after it is too late to collect it. A possible solution is the "retrospective pretest": subjects simply are asked to *reflect* on their attitudes or behavior prior to some given event on which they are being compared.

This procedure was validated in a military setting when Caucasian soldiers in all-Caucasian or mixed-race units evidenced no differences in their pre-military attitudes toward African Americans, whereas Caucasians in the mixed-race units revealed more favorable attitudes toward African Americans after their experiences with military integration. Surprisingly, though experience with African Americans led to these more favorable attitudes on the part of Caucasians, this same experience apparently did not exercise a "halo effect" upon their recollections of how they felt before the integration experience.

PITFALL IN "METHOD" STUDIES

In method-of-teaching studies, it is dangerous to assume that two teachers are actually teaching with the same method. Observers often report critical differences that suggest two versions of a given method. Such an interaction is crucial in making meaningful interpretations.

---

[1]Based on notes by Stephen Isaac of suggestions made by Lee J. Cronbach at a California Educational Research Association meeting c. 1960.
[2]Gain scores often are highly unreliable and hazardous to use. For an authoritative discussion of this problem see: Lord, F. M. (1956). The measurement of growth, *Educational And Psychological Measurement, 16*, 421-427. Also see Cronbach, L. J., & Furby, L. (1970). How we should measure 'change'--or should we? *Psychological Bulletin, 74*, 68-80.
[3]Adapted from Campbell, D. T., & Stanley, J. C. (1966). *Experimental and quasi-experimental designs for research.* Chicago, IL: Rand McNally & Co.

REACTIVE VERSUS NONREACTIVE MEASURES

REACTIVE MEASURES[1]

A measurement is reactive whenever the subject is directly involved in a study and is reacting to the measurement process itself. The risk of introducing changes peculiar to the measurement process takes several forms:

1. *The guinea pig effect*: To the extent that one feels like a "guinea pig" and must do their best or that the method of data collection starts trains of thought not previously characteristic of the subject or makes them defensive, antagonistic or unusually cooperative, the measuring process itself changes the respondent and biases the research results.

2. *Role selection:* When approached as a respondent in a research study, an individual tends to assume a role of "the kind of person they think they should be" in this situation. To the extent that this assumed role differs from their natural behavior in situations similar to, but outside, the research setting, validity decreases.

3. *Measurement as change agent:* The *preamble effect* described by Cantril[2] indicates that the instructions to a test or questionnaire induce certain attitudes or sets in the respondent which even persist beyond the research situation. Initial "don't know" answers on opinion surveys frequently set into motion opinion-forming processes which otherwise would not have happened. *Practice effects* are also observed where exercise on the pretest accounts for gains on the posttest. "Testwise" subjects who develop skills in test-taking exhibit this same change tracing back to the measurement act.

4. *Response sets:* This is the tendency of subjects to respond to questions in certain predictable ways. The *acquiescence response set* describes the phenomenon that respondents will more frequently endorse a positive statement than disagree with its opposite. Respondents more often than not will prefer strong statements to moderate or inconclusive ones. Sequences of questions presented in a similar format lead to response patterns affecting items in the last half of a test differently than in the first half, possibly because the respondent becomes aware of his adaptation pattern by the middle of the instrument and shifts to a variation to avoid monotony or conformity. The *social desirability response set* refers to items where one alternative is more acceptable socially than another.[3]

5. *Interviewer effects:* The sex, age, race, manner of dress, and speech patterns or accents of the interviewer all interact with the attitudes or expectations of the respondent toward these characteristics.

6. *Change in the research instrument:* Differences often appear *within* the same interviewer or panel of judges over time; increasing skill, sensitivity, sophistication, fatigue, boredom, or a shifting adaptation level modifies the interviewer's effect as a "stimulus" upon the subject. If the instrument is a record-keeping system which changes over the years with new ways of collecting and classifying information, then impressions of changing behavior may be nothing more than artifacts of an altered measurement process. For example: an apparent increase in the suicide rate resulting from improved reporting procedures.

---

[1]Adapted from Webb, E. J., Campbell, D. T., Schwartz, R. D., & Sechrest, L. (1966). *Unobtrusive measures.* Chicago, IL: Rand McNally & Co.

[2]Cantril, H. (1944). *Gauging public opinion.* Princeton, Princeton Univ. Press.

[3]Edwards, A. L. (1957). *The social desirability variable in personality assessment and research.* New York: Dryden Press.

NONREACTIVE MEASURES[1]

A measurement is nonreactive when it does not change that which is being measured It is a passive or unobtrusive measure of behavior and does not introduce stimulus factors to which the subject might otherwise react. Nonreactive measures have been categorized into the following types:

1. *Physical traces:*
   a. Erosion—For example, examination of library books for physical "wear and tear" as an index to their actual use.
   b. Accretion—For example, measuring the amount of campus litter before and after an administration-sponsored "cleanup campaign" as an index of student attitude toward administrative authority.
2. *Archives and records:* Actuarial, governmental, mass media, industrial, personnel, and miscellaneous running records, public and private. For example, changes in library withdrawal patterns as an index of the effectiveness of a reading appreciation program in a high school.
3. *Unobtrusive observation:* Expressive behavior, physical activity, language behavior, conversion sampling, time duration, and time sampling of behavior. An example is counting the number of times students raise their hands, smile, or participate in class discussions as indices of their interest in a particular instructional program.

Nonreactive measures are vulnerable to sampling biases and other non-representative distortions that influence kinds and rates of physical change, record-keeping procedures, and observable human behavior patterns. In ridding a measurement of its reactive characteristics, the risk of even more serious consequences is not eliminated. A reasonable measurement strategy is *triangulation:* incorporate more than one measure of the phenomena in question. For example, to measure the effectiveness of a particular reading program, obtain: (1) scores on a standardized reading achievement test; (2) school attendance record patterns; and (3) their preference for books in their free time compared with nonreading activities. This would combine one reactive with two nonreactive measures of the program's effect. (See page 97.)

MAKING CLASSROOM RESEARCH NONREACTIVE[2]

To reduce the Hawthorne or guinea pig effect which causes subjects to respond differently from that under normal classroom conditions, the following inconspicuous strategies are suggested:

1. Build the research measures into the regular classroom examinations or through tests presented as regular examinations and similar in content.
2. Involve alternative teaching procedures presented without announcement or apology in the regular teaching process.
3. Use the regular staff to conduct experimentation within schools, especially where findings are to be generalized to other classroom situations.

---

[1]Based on discussion from, Webb, E. J., Campbell, D. T., Schwartz, R. D., & Sechrest, L. (1966). *Unobtrusive measures.* Chicago, IL: Rand McNally & Co.
[2]Based on discussion from, Campbell, D. T., & Stanley, J. C. (1966). *Experimental and quasi-experimental designs for research.* Chicago, IL: Rand McNally & Co.

MEASUREMENT: SINGLE VERSUS MULTIPLE OUTCOMES - *TRIANGULATION*

The operational definition of a concept, leading to its measurement in behavioral terms, has led to the self-defeating practice of arbitrarily selecting a single measurement criterion or class of observations. For example, the questionnaire or interview technique together account for about 90 percent of research in the social sciences. Operationalism is better served by *multiple measures* of a given concept or attribute, each sharing a portion of the theoretically relevant components but each having different loadings of irrelevant factors or "noise." Once a proposition has been confirmed by two or more independent measurement processes, the uncertainty of its interpretation is greatly reduced. The *triangulation of measurement* process is far more powerful evidence supporting the proposition than any single criterion approach.[1] Two problems are raised:

1. Multiple measures of a given concept are often disappointing and inconsistent, pointing to the gravity of the measurement problem in the social sciences and the risks of false confidence where single criterion methods are employed. Such results are also awkward to report coherently.
2. Since all components of a multi-method approach may not deserve equal weighting, they ideally should be weighted according to the amount of extraneous variation each is known to have and then taken in combination according to its independence from similar sources of bias.

For example:[2] In a study of the effect of praise or blame on the outcome of reading instruction, no significant differences were found among the various groups on the criterion of *gain in reading*. If a second criterion had been used, such as *attitudes toward reading*, a highly significant treatment difference might have been found. Most research of this kind looks at an achievement or skill outcome rather than the development of attitudes. The failure of people to choose to read following their formal education, or to choose mathematics in their higher education, given the skill development to do both, strongly suggests that a counter-current of *negative attitudes* to avoid these experiences, lies hidden underneath.

Using more than one outcome measure or criterion simply means the selection of more than one *dependent variable,* such as achievement *plus* attitudes *plus* transfer to a new process. If no differences are obtained on one criterion, differences on another may prove equally valuable and relevant. Cronbach reports a study by Brownell of four methods of teaching subtraction; he found only small differences both on a skill criterion and on a retention criterion but clearly superior results favoring one method over all the others when he measured transfer to a new process. There are serious risks in making recommendations based on a single criterion which fails to consider the whole outcome of an educational process.[2]

---

[1]Adapted from Webb, E. J., Campbell, D. T., Schwartz, R. D., & Sechrest, L. (1966). *Unobtrusive measures.* Chicago, IL: Rand McNally & Co.
[2]Notes by Stephen Isaac based on a talk by L. J. Cronbach, Invited Address, California Educational Research Association, c. 1960.

STATISTICAL REGRESSION EFFECTS

Subjects selected because they are particularly high or low on some variable, on an equivalent form of the variable will tend to regress toward the mean because of imperfect correlation between the two measures of the variable. Since children are selected into special programs on the basis of extreme scores ("gifted," "retarded," "slow readers," etc.), there is a danger that the role of statistical regression will be overlooked in the outcomes. Thus, a Booster Reading Program for the "bottom 25 percent" of third graders on a standardized reading achievement test will be assured of increased scores on a posttest, by that fact alone. The same youngsters probably will not place so low a second time because the same set of penalizing chance factors will not operate to make all of them so "unlucky" again.

Statistical regression involves several considerations:[1]

1. Extreme groups, on a second testing or posttest, behave as if the bright subjects are becoming less bright and the dull subjects are becoming less dull.
2. The greater the deviation of the extreme scores, the greater the regression to the mean.
3. The lower the correlation, the greater the regression toward the mean.
4. Groups selected for independent reasons, but which just happen to have extreme scores on a given variable, will tend not to regress so much on the retest as they would on a measure highly correlated with the selection variable. (The random or extraneous sources of variance have been allowed to affect the initial scores in *both* directions.)
5. Groups selected on the basis of extreme scores on one variable but evaluated on an unrelated dependent variable should be reasonably free of the regression effect on that second variable.
6. An indirect pseudo-gain can occur when subjects are selected on some criterion other than the pretest (e.g., "failing scores on a class examination"). Because the class examination and the pretest are closer to each other in time, they tend to correlate higher than does the class examination and the posttest administered much later. If the treatment is a "How to Study" program, and with more regression to the mean on the posttest because of the somewhat lower correlation with the class examination, a pseudo-gain may be mistaken for an actual gain. The lower the correlation, the greater will be the regression.
7. When subjects are matched according to a pretest criterion, there is risk of regression effects if the matching involves two different populations. Suppose, for example, pairs are made up from two schools representing middle and lower socio-economic levels, respectively, but "equating" the subjects by matching them on the basis of IQ scores. Since the two schools probably have different mean population IQs, students from each school will tend to regress toward their respective population means on a second intelligence test, yielding a difference which may be only a statistical artifact.[2]

---

[1]Based on discussion from Campbell, D. T., & Stanley, J.C. (1966). *Experimental and quasi-experimental designs for research.* Chicago, IL: Rand McNally & Co.

[2]For a most enlightening discussion of regression artifacts see the contribution by Campbell, D. T., & Erlebacher, A. How regression artifacts in quasi-experimental evaluations can mistakenly make compensatory education look harmful, in J. Hellmuth (Ed.) *Compensatory Education: A National Debate,* Vol. III of The Disadvantaged Child. New York: Brunner/Mazel.

SHORT-TERM AND LONG-TERM STUDIES

1. *Short-term and long-term effects:*[1]
   Short-term and long-term effects tend to differ both quantitatively and qualitatively. For example, research by Hovland has shown that long-range effects are greater than immediate effects for general attitudes, although weaker for specific attitudes. To check for such differences extended over time, serial posttests such as one month later, six months later, and one year later, might be designed into the study. In the short-duration studies, the possibility of getting significant results depends upon the power of the treatment variable. Strong stimuli (e.g., operant conditioning techniques) yield results very early in the treatment. Weak stimuli tend to get lost in the error variance of the environmental surroundings.

2. *Three points are necessary to define a function:*
   Two-point before-and-after designs have a serious fault when investigating behavior related to underlying growth or change functions. Such functions require a minimum of three measurement points in order to determine whether they resemble a simple linear function or a curvilinear one. To get at still more complex functions involving periodic fluctuations, cycles, accelerations and decelerations, temporary effects, step-like patterns or delayed reactions, more than three points are required. A longitudinal design may be necessitated.

   For example, in many Headstart programs initial gains achieved during a special summer program disappear after a few months unless they are systematically maintained by an ongoing treatment program. Also, studies of intelligence have shown that the IQ undergoes a complex series of accelerations and decelerations during childhood and adolescence. Learning curves often are complex functions with step-like characteristics combining ascending and descending slopes with plateaus.

3. *Possible experimental design:*
   A design strategy to get at changing functions and to control for the effects of maturation, pretesting, regression, and contemporary history (see page 79) begins with several groups which are pretested at the same time but which are posttested at different time intervals, respectively:

Group A:	O_1	X	O_2		
Group B:	O_1	X		O_2	
Group C:	O_1	X			O_2
Group D:	O_1	X				O_2
Group E:	O_1	X					O_2

   By adding a control group with the same pretest and posttest pattern, but without the treatment, the effects of the treatment can be assessed. This strategy is particularly appropriate where maturational factors are involved and where the effects of serial testing within groups should be minimized.

---

[1]Adapted from Campbell, D. T., & Stanley, J. C. (1966). *Experimental and quasi-experimental designs for research.* Chicago, IL: Rand McNally & Co.

FIVE POINTS ABOUT RESEARCH DESIGN[1]

1. Measurement of multiple outcomes is preferable to a single outcome. In other words use more than one *dependent variable:* for example, achievement, attitudes, and transfe: to a new process. Result: if no differences are obtained on one, differences on anothe: may prove equally valuable and relevant.

2. Begin with *dependent variables* each having sufficient criterion reliability to minimize the probability that measurement error, per se, will mask a significant difference actuall present in the outcomes.

3. Select appropriate *independent variables* such that they are relevant and are arranged in realistic combination with each other to take advantage of interaction relationships. Fo example, it makes little sense to study class size as a variable unless one also brings in its relationship to teaching method, pupil characteristics, and other factors.

4. Allow for the relationship between personality characteristics and validation criteria in a flexible, rather than a fixed, fashion. For instance, rather than using the Strong Inventory to select medical school candidates across the board, look for the additiona subpatterns which fall outside the "typical" medical interest profile but would predic success in some of the less prominent specialty fields as medical research, and medica school instruction. Otherwise, there is a risk of selecting out potentially successfu candidates and creating professional stereotypes that are absolute rather than relative.

5. Emphasize the interaction between individual differences and particular learning principles or methods. Too much reliance has been placed on randomization, equatec groups and formal statistical controls; too little reliance on controls by individua differences. In other words, instead of seeking general principles of education applying to everyone, seek empirically established principles about how to deal with people of particular types.

TWO STATISTICAL POINTS[1]

1. When matching is appropriate, avoid matching groups on the basis of IQ. Equating should be done on the basis of mental age, achievement, or some other nonrelative measure. Pupils of a given IQ are not at all alike if their ages are different.[2]

2. Analysis of covariance is greatly neglected as a means of controlling for individual differences. When the assumptions underlying covariance cannot be met, there is a simple nonparametric analogue available. It permits adjustment for initial differences between groups that arise by chance. (Valid application of analysis of covariance adjusts for usually relatively small differences in pretest or covariate means that have arisen as a function of random sampling error.)

---

[1]Based on notes by Stephen Isaac of an address by Lee J. Cronbach to the California Educationa Research Association, c. 1960.

[2]For a discussion of the disadvantages of matching see page 103.

LARGE SAMPLES VERSUS SMALL SAMPLES[1]

The advantages of using *large samples* in educational research have been enhanced with computer technology. Large-sample statistics involve smaller sampling errors, greater reliability, and increase the power of a statistical test applied to the data. Other things being equal, large samples are preferable to small samples. Despite the advantages of using large representative samples, there are, however, several arguments favoring research with small samples under certain conditions:

1. *Small sample economy:*
   When it is not economically feasible to collect or analyze large sample data, small samples will be appropriate. Small-sample statistics assure the researcher of acceptable reliability in estimating sampling error before making decisions about data.

2. *Computer monitoring:*[2]
   Even when large samples are being used and the data are being analyzed by computer programs, there are problems:
   a. *Errors*—Preparing and processing data in a computer environment risks many sources of error: incorrectly keyed-in data; program errors, often obscure and complex; errors in the special instructions controlling the programs; and mishandled magnetic tapes.
   b. *The "black box" problem*—The complexities of a constantly changing computer technology usually force the researcher to accept the printout of final results on faith. A helpful safeguard is to draw a small sample of data and run a parallel analysis by hand. This illuminates the mechanics of the statistical analysis and serves as an independent check against errors.

3. *Exploratory research and pilot studies:*[3]
   To find promising leads or alternatives in research, it is essential to stay close to data. Samples with *N*'s between 10 *and* 30 have many practical advantages:
   a. A quick, convenient sample size with which to work.
   b. Provides easy multipliers and divisors, facilitating calculations.
   c. Samples of this size are large enough to test the null hypothesis, yet small enough to overlook weak treatment effects. Remembering that statistically-significant findings for any relevant variable appear simply by increasing the sample size toward the universe, such findings are not apt to be *educationally significant* since the variable in question is too diluted to make a practical difference.

4. *N in large studies:*[4]
   In large educational studies, *N* actually equals the number of classrooms, not the number of individuals. This distinction increases in importance as the number of classrooms approaches 20 to 30, and is a critical consideration in analyzing and interpreting the data, since it involves the distinction between large and small sample statistics.

---

[1]See page 74 for instances when large samples are necessary.
[2]See page 44.
[3]Suggested by Dr. Harry Munsinger, University of California at San Diego.
[4]Based on notes taken at a Field Studies Workshop given by staff members of the Far West Regional Laboratory, Berkeley, CA, 1968.

INDIVIDUAL DIFFERENCES

INDIVIDUAL DIFFERENCES AND LAWS OF BEHAVIOR[1, 2]

Most research in education concerns groups with conclusions based on group averages. The risk in this approach is the loss of important information about *laws of behavior* and individual differences. Consider the following learning plots where each dotted line represents a different individual and the solid line the group mean:

From the group data alone, it might be erroneously concluded that, since the three learners began and ended at the same levels, the learning was equivalent. The individual learning plots, based on serial measures, tell a strikingly different story of three quite distinct events. Learner A made the most initial progress but peaked early and actually lost ground at the end. Learner B made consistent progress with many minor plateaus. Learner C was a slow starter but came through with an impressive spurt at the last minute. Clearly, three different learning events were taking place and no meaningful "law of learning" ever would be discovered using the group data.

Each of the differences between individuals points to a difference in how a behavioral law or laws might be operating at that moment, and that is the crucial question. It is conceivable, for instance, that the above individual differences are all functions of a single reinforcement principle operating in similar ways but at different times and in varying amounts. If so, the discovery of this function depends upon the discrete observations of individuals. Also, to discover *functions* more than two observations are needed, a condition not met by the typical before-and-after paradigm and one that increases in importance if the function is cyclical. Individual serial observations, as often as practical, are essential in research designed to reveal the shape of learning functions. If the three individual learning plots are not variations of a single reinforcement factor, but represent complex differences between the three learners and what causes them to learn, this again is the only method that will isolate the kinds of determinants, their characteristics, and the manner of their interaction.

---

[1]Based on notes taken at a Field Studies Workshop given by staff members of the Far West Regional Laboratory, Berkeley, CA, 1968.
[2]See item 2, page 99.

PATTERNS AMONG INDIVIDUALS AND THE
USEFULNESS OF SUBGROUPS

Between the overall group average and the infinity of individual differences, it is reasonable to expect meaningful and useful intermediate patterns. Consider this commonplace example: In a before-and-after evaluation design involving a class of 33 children, the teacher notes that the posttest mean is 7 points higher than the pretest mean and concludes that "the class improved and the teaching methods are working." Suppose, however, that closer examination of the data reveals a disconcerting fact: while 22 of the children had higher posttest scores, 11 actually had lower scores. Because the children who gained outnumbered the children who lost, there was a deceptive net gain overall. Besides overlooking the losses, the mean gain of 7 points is misleadingly low for those who did improve. More realistic analysis would have reported a mean gain of 17.5 points for the 22 who improved and a mean loss of 14 points for those who regressed. Underneath these several observations lies the problem of test unreliability and the regression effect between the two testings. A conscientious teacher armed with these considerations might ask such questions as: What caused two-thirds of my students to do better on the posttest and one-third to do worse? What do children in each category have in common? Do I interact differently with these two groups? Or, are my tests reliable enough to give me the answers I seek?

Types of people, styles of learning, and background factors such as socioeconomic and cultural differences invite research questions about patterns and interactions. For instance, the researcher might want to know what kinds of teachers interact more effectively with what kinds of students, or what kinds of learning environments interact favorably with these patterns.

MATCHING AS A CONTROL TECHNIQUE:
SOME DISADVANTAGES[1,2]

1. *In general*, the technique of matching subjects to form pairs for later comparison tends to create more control problems than it solves. Therefore, the matching technique is coming under increasing criticism and should generally be set aside in favor of control by random selection and assignment methods. Random assignment is also required when the technique of *analysis of covariance* is applied. This statistical tool allows the adjustment of posttest scores to compensate for a lack of equivalence between control and experimental groups observed on a pretest or initial measure correlated with a posttest. See footnote 2, however, for another option. Also, see page 86, item 2d.

---

[1]Adapted in part from Van Dalen, D. B. (1979). *Understanding educational research* (4th ed.). New York: McGraw-Hill. (Adapted from Campbell, D. T., & Stanley, J. C. (1966). *Experimental and quasi-experimental designs for research*. Chicago, IL: Rand McNally & Co.

[2]A solution for avoiding the problems of matched pairs is *matched groups*, grouping subjects into blocks on the basis of their expected homogeneous response on some dependent variable, in the absence of treatment effects, compared to an expected heterogeneous response of subjects selected completely at random. The advantage of matched groups over randomized groups is an expected smaller error mean square in the analysis of variance, for the same number of observations. See Edwards, A. L. (1968). *Experimental design in psychological research* (3rd ed.) (Chapter 9: Randomized Block Designs). New York: Holt, Rinehart, & Winston, Inc.

2. *Matching with identical twins using random assignment:* Nature provides an excellent control situation in the case of identical twins, though their relatively rare occurrence poses serious practical limitations on their use. The rule of *random assignment* to treatments or groups must still be observed.

3. *Matching with ordinary subjects on a O_1 variable using random assignment:* While there is some validity in using ordinary subjects matched on some pretest (O_1) criterion (e.g., IQ, achievement, age, or socio-economic status) and where random assignment to treatments or groups is still observed, certain problems are created. For example:
    a. The problem of deciding on *which* variables to base the matching.
    b. The problem of obtaining satisfactory measures of variables which influence the dependent variable, so that they can be reliably and validly used. Many such variables reported in the literature are too vague, ill-defined, or over-determined to identify or measure objectively.
    c. The problem of statistical regression when matching subjects or groups which turn out to represent different populations with respect to the matching variable(s). Suppose, for example, pairs are made up to represent two different schools, matching subjects on the basis of IQ scores. If the two schools have different mean population IQs, students from each school will tend to regress toward their respective school means on a second intelligence test, creating a difference which may be only a statistical artifact.
    d. The problem of discarding subjects who do not fit the matching criteria, especially if extreme scores are involved or if matching is based on two or more variables. Depending on the number and restrictiveness of the matching variables, the ratio of matching pairs to discards quickly becomes a costly one—twenty acceptable matchings perhaps running into hundreds or even thousands of subjects.

REFERENCES

Borg, W. R., & Gall M. D. (1989). *Educational research: An introduction* (5th ed.). White Plains, NY: Longman.

Keppel, G. (1991). *Design and analysis: A research handbook* (3rd ed.). Englewood Cliffs, NJ: Prentice Hall.

Kerlinger, F. N. (1986). *Foundations of behavioral research* (3rd ed.). New York: Holt, Rinehart, and Winston.

Pedhazur, E. J., & Schmelken, L. P. (1991). *Measurement, design, and analysis: An integrated approach.* Hillsdale, NJ: Erlbaum.

If a thing exists, it exists in some amount. If it exists in some amount, it can be measured.

E. L. Thorndike

CHAPTER FIVE

INSTRUMENTATION AND MEASUREMENT

In reaching conclusions in research and evaluation studies it is necessary, first, to establish the *criteria* upon which such conclusions will be based and, second, to provide *measurements* of these criteria.

Instrumentation is the process of selecting or developing measuring devices and methods appropriate to a given evaluation problem. While a variety of approaches to the problem of measurement have been developed, two principal questions confront them all:

1. Is it *reliable*? Is it an accurate, consistent, and stable measuring instrument?
2. Is it *valid*? Is it really measuring what it claims to measure? and, Is it relevant?

Note to the reader: This chapter, more than the others, tends to be a series of relatively autonomous exhibits and may seem disjointed. No attempt is made to create an impression of continuity but the various topics covered were selected on the basis of their utility and representativeness.

A FORM FOR EVALUATING TESTS[1]

1. Title

2. Author

3. Publisher

4. Forms and groups to which applicable

5. Practical features

6. General type

7. Date of publication

8. Cost, booklet; answer sheet

9. Time required

10. Purpose for which evaluated

11. Description of test, items, scoring

12. Author's purpose and basis for selecting items

13. Adequacy of directions; training required to administer

14. Mental functions or traits represented in each score

15. Comments regarding design of test

16. Predictive validation (criterion, number and type of cases, result)

17. Concurrent validation (criterion, number, and type of cases, result)

18. Other empirical evidence indicating what the test measures

19. Comments regarding validity for particular purposes

20. Equivalence of forms or internal consistency (procedure, cases, result)

21. Stability over time (procedure, time interval, cases, result)

22. Norms (type of norms, cases)

23. Comments regarding adequacy of reliability and norms for particular purpose

24. Comments of reviewers

25. General evaluation

26. References

---

[1]Cronbach, L. J. (1990). *Essentials of psychological testing*. (5th ed.) (p. 148). New York: Harper & Collins College Publishers.

CHART COMPARING VARIOUS TEST SCORES
AND THEIR CORRESPONDENCE TO EACH OTHER[1]

[1]Test Service Bulletin Number 48, The Psychological Corporation, 304 East 45th Street, New York, NY: 10017.

INTERPRETING TEST SCORES

To interpret a test score, two things must be known:
1. The nature of the score itself—what kind of scoring or scaling system was used in its calculation?
2. The basis for comparison underlying the score—what reference population or norm group does it represent, if any?

TYPES OF TEST SCORES

1. *Raw Scores*—Simply the total number of points an individual earns on a test before it is converted to any formal or standardized scoring system. A raw score, by itself, is uninterpretable, as there is no way of knowing how it compares with anything else.

EXAMPLE: A high school student obtains the following raw scores: English— first test, 35; second test, 70; and Algebra—96. By these facts alone we have no idea how the student is doing. Which of these scores are above average? below average? Which score is actually the highest? the lowest? Compared to the first test in English, did the student do twice as well on the second test? With the limited information provided in the absence of any frame of reference, none of these questions is answerable.

2. *Percentile (Centile) Ranks* and *Percentiles (Centiles)*—Raw scores begin to have meaning when they are rank ordered from high to low. Because this procedure ignores the sample size, a convenient solution is to convert the scores into percentage values. There are two statistics used for this purpose: (1) the *percentile (centile) rank* of any given score, which is a number between 0 and 100 indicating the percent of cases in a norm group falling at or below that score; and, conversely, (2) the *percentile (centile)*, which is a point on a scale of scores at or below which a given percent of the cases falls. For example, an individual obtaining a score on a test with a percentile rank of 68, or whose score lies at the 68th percentile, can be said to be doing *as well as, or better than*, 68 percent of the persons being compared. Percentiles of 25, 50, and 75 divide a distribution of scores into four quarters and are called the first, second, and third *quartiles,* respectively. The 50th percentile, or second quartile, is also the *median* or the point on the scale of scores, above and below which lies the top 50 percent and bottom 50 percent of cases, respectively. It is important to remember, however, that each quartile is a *point* on a scale and is not a quarter of the distribution. A score cannot lie *within* any quartile; rather, it lies between two quartiles, below the first quartile, or above the third quartile. Occasionally, a score will fall exactly *at* a particular quartile. If the term *quarter* is used, then it is correct to say a score falls within, for example, the bottom quarter of the distribution.

Percentile ranks and percentiles have three important advantages: (1) they are easily understood by lay audiences; (2) they allow exact interpretation; and (3) they are more appropriate for markedly skewed data than scores based on the normal probability curve. There are also some disadvantages. Because a percentile scale consists of 100 points, it is misleading to report results in percentage terms when the sample size is under 100, a distortion which increases as the sample size approaches zero. Furthermore, percentile ranks and percentiles only permit statements about rank (greater than, equal to, or less than) and the intervals between units are not equal (the interval between the 60th and 70th percentiles is not equal to the interval between the 80th and 90th percentiles). Because the intervals are unequal, their values are misleading near the center of a distribution where they exaggerate small differences (the raw score difference between the percentiles of 50 and 55 may be infinitesimal) and especially misleading at the extremes of a distribution (the raw score difference between the percentiles of 98 and 99 may be quite large). The distortion is apt to be greatest when dealing with several percentiles reported as 99 where raw score differences can vary tremendously (a "brilliant" student may answer twice as many questions as a "bright" student, but both might be reported as having percentiles of 99, if the two performances fall in the top one percent of the reference group). The same is true at the opposite end of the scale. As a general rule of thumb, percentiles between 10 and 90 reflect minimal distortion; beyond these limits in either direction they should be interpreted with the distortion factor in mind.

3.   *Stanine Scores*—Stanine ("standard nine") scores combine the understandability of percentages with the properties of the normal curve of probability. A scale is created with nine intervals, each interval representing half of a standard deviation. The middle interval (5th stanine) straddles the midpoint of the distribution, encompassing the middle 20 percent of cases. The 4th, 3rd, 2nd, and 1st stanines, moving from the center to the extreme lower end of the distribution in increments of one-half of a standard deviation, encompass respectively, 17, 12, 7, and 4 percent of the cases. Correspondingly, the 6th, 7th, 8th, and 9th stanines, moving from the center to the extreme upper end of the distribution in like increments, also encompass respectively, 17, 12, 7, and 4 percent of the cases. Examination of the chart on page 107 graphically illustrates these characteristics and allows direct comparisons to other scales. Note that a stanine is not a point on a scale like a percentile but a relatively broad interval. It is, therefore, insensitive to sizeable differences within a stanine interval and misleadingly sensitive to small differences on either side of the point separating adjacent stanine intervals. Nevertheless, stanine scores are coming into increasing use because of their simplicity and utility.

4.   *Standard Scores*—The most powerful scores, statistically, are standard scores derived from the properties of the normal probability curve and preserving the absolute differences between scores, a feature percentile or stanine scores do not possess. Furthermore, they can be used in calculating averages and correlations yielding the same results as the original raw scores. Standard scores from a variety of tests also have the advantage of being directly comparable if the reference groups are equivalent. Their major disadvantages are two: If data are markedly skewed, they are inappropriate, and, because of their dependence on the standard deviation, they are difficult to explain to lay audiences.

   a.   *z-scores*—If a mean and standard deviation are computed for a given set of raw scores, each raw score can be expressed in terms of its distance from the mean in standard deviation units or z-scores:

$$z\text{-score} = \frac{\text{Raw Score} - \text{Mean}}{\text{Standard Deviation}} = \frac{X - M}{\sigma}$$

From the formula it is clear that z-scores at the mean have a value of zero, increasing in numerical size the farther they lie from the mean. Since 99.74 percent of all scores in a normal distribution fall between a range of three standard deviations above the mean and three standard deviations below the mean, z-scores greater than 3.00 are seldom reported though, theoretically, they have no limit. The z-score above the mean carries a plus sign; below the mean, a minus sign. The utility of z-scores comes from their relationship to properties of the normal curve of probability (see chart, page 107). Using a table for the area underneath a normal curve (see Table A, page 248), statements can be made about the proportion of cases above or below any z-score value or between any two z-score values.

b. *T-scores*—Because z-scores have a mean of zero and involve decimals as well as plus and minus signs, they are awkward to interpret. T-scores get around this problem by arbitrarily setting a new mean equal to 50 and the standard deviation equal to 10. By understanding the properties of z-scores and the normal curve of probability, and making the simple conversion to T-scores, the advantages of both systems are combined (see chart, page 107).

c. *Other Standard Scores*—Many other scoring systems are based on properties of the normal probability curve. The *College Entrance Examination Board* (CEEB) simply multiplies the T-score system by 10, creating a mean of 500 and a standard deviation of 100. Tests of intelligence set the mean IQ at 100 and their standard deviations at 15, 16, or 20, depending on the test. Note that these differences in standard deviations further complicate comparisons of IQs between tests which differ in this respect.

5. *Normal Curve Equivalent Scores* (NCEs)[1]—Percentiles are scores widely used in reporting test results. Their principal limitation lies in the fact that units along the percentile scale are rank order or ordinal only and therefore have unequal intervals. Hence, the distance between the percentiles of 1 and 2 is not the same as the distance between the percentiles of 21 and 22 or 51 and 52. This feature further limits the mathematical operations that can be applied to percentiles such as addition, subtraction, multiplication, and division – all functions that are desirable in assessing program effects where test scores are the dependent variable.

A useful alternative is normal curve equivalent scores (NCEs) which are based on an equal interval scale. The distance between any two adjacent units of the NCE scale is the same, regardless of its location on the scale. This allows all the arithmetic calculations mentioned above, including advantages involved in associated statistical applications. In this connection the mean of the NCE distribution is set at 50 with a standard deviation of 21.06.

One caution to be aware of is the possible confusion inherent in the superficial resemblance of the numbers used to represent percentiles and NCEs. As the following conversion chart demonstrates, the two sets of scores are roughly comparable toward the middle of the distribution with increasing discrepancies as the extremes are approached. It is worth noting that the two scales exactly coincide at 1, 50, and 99.

---

[1]Horst, D. P., Tallmadge, G. K., & Wood, T. C. (1975). *A practical guide to measuring project impact on student achievement.* (Monographs on Evaluation in Education No. 1), RMC Research Corporation. Mountain View, CA: Government Printing Office, Stock No. 017-080-01460.

Percentile to Normal Curve Equivalent Conversion

%	NCE	%	NCE	%	NCE	%	NCE	%	NCE
1	1.0	21	33.0	41	45.2	61	55.9	81	68.5
2	6.7	22	33.7	42	45.8	62	56.4	82	69.3
3	10.4	23	34.4	43	46.3	63	57.0	83	70.1
4	13.1	24	35.1	44	46.8	64	57.5	84	70.9
5	15.4	25	35.8	45	47.4	65	58.1	85	71.8
6	17.3	26	36.5	46	47.9	66	58.7	86	72.8
7	18.9	27	37.1	47	48.4	67	59.3	87	73.7
8	20.4	28	37.7	48	48.9	68	59.9	88	74.7
9	21.8	29	38.3	49	49.5	69	60.4	89	75.8
10	23.0	30	39.0	50	50.0	70	61.0	90	77.0
11	24.2	31	39.6	51	50.5	71	61.7	91	78.2
12	25.3	32	40.1	52	51.1	72	62.3	92	79.6
13	26.3	33	40.7	53	51.6	73	62.9	93	81.1
14	27.2	34	41.3	54	52.1	74	63.5	94	82.7
15	28.2	35	41.9	55	52.6	75	64.2	95	84.6
16	29.1	36	42.5	56	53.2	76	64.9	96	86.9
17	29.9	37	43.0	57	53.7	77	65.6	97	89.6
18	30.7	38	43.6	58	54.2	78	66.3	98	93.3
19	31.5	39	44.1	59	54.8	79	67.0	99	99.0
20	32.3	40	44.7	60	55.3	80	67.7		

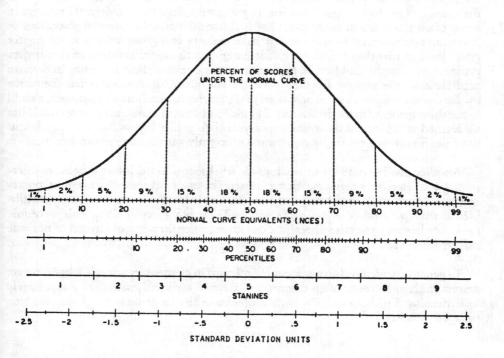

6. *Grade Level Scores*[1]—Grade level scores are based on the relationship between scores on a test and the *average* performance of children at each of a series of grade levels. The average score for fourth graders in the norm group at the beginning of the fourth grade, for example, is assigned a grade level value of 4.0, for fifth graders, 5.0, and so forth. Each grade level is broken down further into ten substeps roughly equivalent to a ten-month school year, beginning, for example, in September for the fourth grade with 4.0 and ending in June with 4.9. Grade level scores are popular with educators and parents because they fit the framework of a pupil's progress from one level to the next in the school system. They have several serious shortcomings, however. They suggest an interval scale such that the growth of one grade level is an equivalent unit of growth throughout the system. This conclusion is seldom true, since progress at different grade levels depends heavily on the nature of the instructional program. It is a relationship supportable only when the instruction is continuous throughout the grades as in the case of mathematics and starts breaking down in an area such as reading after the primary grades when instruction, per se, ceases. From the eighth grade through high school, grade level scores are virtually meaningless since they are extrapolations from lower grade performance levels or represent subject matter taught in only one or two grades. Developmental characteristics peculiar to certain age levels that appear to be more often a function of maturational age rather than instruction further complicate the notion that a grade level is an equivalent unit of growth throughout the grades.

The fact that gains slow down in the upper grades greatly compromises the interpretation of the performance of children with superior ability, as they often exceed the average of the highest grade covered by the norms. Superior children at lower grade levels often score two or more grade levels above their actual classroom placement; it is inaccurate, however, to assume they have mastery of a given subject at the higher grade level or that they could work efficiently with the older children in that higher grade. Many bright children obtain high scores because they are faster and more accurate than the average for their own age and grade. To conclude that they have mastery of the subject at some advanced grade level is misleading. For instance, a child in the third grade, who might have a 6.5 grade level score in Arithmetic, most likely has *not* learned arithmetic as the average mid-year sixth grader knows it—to a large extent the child is simply performing rapidly and efficiently with third grade arithmetic.

Another disadvantage arises when grade level scores in the lower ranges are interpreted too literally, suggesting that children "below grade level" are either poorly motivated (underachievers) or poorly taught. Grade level scores are normally distributed as are IQs, standard scores, and stanines. These other scores, along with percentile ranks, are less likely to raise unrealistic questions, since they do not remind us of grade placement, *per se.*

In general, grade level scores are most relevant in elementary schools where subject matter tends to be more often continuous. Beyond the sixth grade they progressively lose meaning. Furthermore, the same problems besetting grade level scores hold true for *age level scores.*

---

[1]The authors are indebted for many of these observations to Thorndike, R. L., & Hagen, E. (1977). *Measurement and evaluation in psychology and education* (4th ed.). New York: Wiley.

REFERENCE POPULATIONS—NORM GROUPS

Once a raw score is converted to some scale of measurement, usually in terms of a rank or deviation from the mean, the next question is, *To whom is the student being compared?* Just to the other students in the classroom, as in the case of most teacher-made tests? To all other students at that age or grade level in the school or school district? To all other students at that age or grade level in the state or nation? Standardized tests report scores based on a norm group representing a defined population and until this comparison group is clearly known, a satisfactory interpretation of the score is not possible.

For many evaluation purposes, the selection of a norm group is crucial. The same raw score on the *College Board Examination* may represent, for example, the 90th percentile for typical four-year liberal arts colleges but only the 20th percentile for the highly selective Ivy League institutions. The appropriate norm group is even more critical where second languages and different socio-economic and subculture patterns are concerned. Another caution where age, grade, or class level norm groups are involved, is to be sure the points in time when the measurements were made are comparable. For example, were the local fourth graders tested at the same point during the year as the fourth grade norm group? Are the "freshmen" norms for entering freshmen, mid-year freshmen, or end-of-the-year freshmen?

Still another pitfall appears after all other considerations have been checked out, should the norm group have had different kinds or amounts of instruction in a given subject matter area. Some reading tests, for instance, are normed on populations whose average daily exposure to reading instruction is twice that of the local pupils; they may also differ as to the instructional emphasis or approach, one group receiving instruction more closely related to the test content than the other.

COMPARING NORM-REFERENCED WITH CRITERION-REFERENCED TESTS

Over the years, a controversy has arisen concerning the merits of norm-referenced tests in relation to those of criterion-referenced tests. As is often the case in such controversial matters, both types of tests have their advantages and limitations. Instead of addressing the concern of which form of measurement is better, a balanced viewpoint would ask this question: When is it appropriate to use one or the other type of measure? The answer is seldom straightforward or simple. It depends on (a) an adequate familiarity with the attributes of selected versions of both types of tests and (b) the requirements of the particular situation being assessed.

Typically, widely used norm-referenced and criterion-referenced tests are standardized. A standardized test is one that has been carefully constructed and field-tested as well as one that has carefully prepared and uniform directions for administration and scoring. Generally speaking, standardized tests are commercially produced.

A norm-referenced standardized test affords a comparison of the performance of each student to that of the norm group across a certain content coverage. Customarily, this content coverage tends to be general and broad, and the norm group is representative of students of a given age or grade level within a large geographical unit such as a county, state, or the nation. Norm-referenced tests vary in the degree to which they measure how much a student has learned. Nevertheless, they do emphasize reporting results in terms of where each student stands on the test in relation to the placement of students in the norm group. In standardized achievement tests of either a norm-referenced or criterion-referenced orientation, content validity is of supreme importance. Even in a norm-referenced test reflecting curricular objectives, content validity usually takes some precedence over the capability of the test to differentiate between high-performing and low-performing students. To provide a basis for the distribution of these two groups of differentially scoring students, the items of norm-referenced tests are selected, in part, such that students who pass any single item also tend to earn high scores on the total test, whereas students who fail on any single item are likely to earn low scores on the total test.

As a result of this practice, a score continuum ranging from high to low is created along which students can be spread and identified as showing different degrees of competence or capability. To afford a means of comparing the standings of students along the score continuum, percentile ranks (numbers indicating the percentages of students in the norm group who fall below given scores) are often employed, particularly to facilitate communication of the results of a testing experience. Sometimes, grade equivalents (numbers revealing the estimated grade level standing corresponding to given raw scores) are used. Researchers often prefer standard scores, which furnish a unit-free index revealing how many standard deviations above or below the mean a given raw score falls.

A criterion-referenced standardized test yields a comparison of each student's level of mastery to that of the total body of knowledge that the test has been designed to cover. Typically, this level of mastery is indicated by the percentage of items answered correctly among all possible items. The test is based on a criterion (or standard) of achievement that focuses solely on the mastering of content rather than on a determination of the rank ordering of students for evaluative purposes. For residents of California, a familiar example of a criterion-referenced test is the State of California Motor Vehicle Department's written examination for the driver's license. Test items are selected primarily to ensure content coverage irrespective of whether they prove to be easy or difficult. Many items that nearly everyone has answered correctly are retained, as this response behavior reflects a high level of mastery that is the ideal for the competence or proficiency standard desired as a consequence of a public school or private school training course. (It should be noted that such items are usually eliminated from norm-referenced tests, as they contribute nothing to the ranking of students.) The essential task in constructing sound criterion-referenced tests is the clear and specific definition of the content or subject matter to be covered by a particular instructional program in terms of comprehensive and measurable objectives. Scores on criterion-referenced tests are usually reported as "pass" or "fail" depending upon whether or not the criterion level has been attained.

It is possible for a standardized test to be both norm-referenced and criterion-referenced, although this circumstance is not common in most educational practice, as criterion-referenced tests are so specific that they have limited application. Moreover, it frequently occurs that the score distributions of criterion-referenced tests as well as the difficulty levels of a large proportion of the items provide a sufficiently wide range in resulting numerical values that traditional approaches of psychometric evaluation can still be employed.

In summary, a norm-referenced test indicates one's standing in the score distribution compared to that of students comprising a norm group (although it often provides additional information concerning which items in content areas have been answered correctly), and a criterion-referenced test reveals one's mastery level of a given body of knowledge anchored to specific curricular objectives. Both types of tests require a careful definition of the curricular or content objectives to be covered, comparable skills in writing items, and seasoned judgment in interpretation and use of scores for evaluation purposes.

The table below is an attempt to summarize some typical generalizable similarities and differences in the types of attributes or characteristics associated with norm-referenced and criterion-referenced tests. However, as norm-referenced tests often have criterion-referenced characteristics–a circumstance showing an increasingly evident trend–and as criterion–referenced tests for some groups can become norm-referenced for the same or other groups, each attribute needs to be examined carefully in light of possible unique or joint relevancies.[1]

SIMILARITIES AND DIFFERENCES IN NORM-REFERENCED AND CRITERION-REFERENCED TESTS

Attribute	Norm-Referenced Test (NRT)	Criterion-Referenced Test (CRT)
State of the Art	Highly developed; technically sound	Mixed & variable; technology developing
Developmental Cost	Major	Moderate to major
Consumer Cost	Relatively inexpensive	Relatively expensive
Utility	General purpose; long-lived	Situation-specific; short-lived
Content Validity & Coverage	Based on a specified content domain, appropriately sampled, and tending to have fewer items per objective. Tends to be general and broad.	Based on a specified content domain, appropriately sampled, and tending to have more items per objective. Tends to be specific and narrow.
Score Interpretation	In terms of a specified norm group (e.g., percentile ranks, grade equivalents)	In terms of a specified criterion of proficiency (e.g.. percent mastery)
Item Development	Two main considerations: content validity and item discrimination	One main consideration: content validity
Standardized	Yes	Usually
Sensitivity to Instruction	Tends to be low to moderate, because of its general purpose nature	Tends to be high, when closely matched to a particular instructional situation
Reliability	High	Can be high, but sometimes hard to establish
Application	To assess the effectiveness of given instructional treatments in achieving general instructional objectives	To assess the effectiveness of given instructional treatments in achieving specific instructional objectives

---

The authors are indebted for much of this material to W. A. Mehrens and R. L. Ebel who expressed their ideas about criterion-referenced and norm-referenced tests in their article, "Some comments on criterion-referenced and norm-referenced achievement tests" Mehrens, W. A., & Ebel, R. L. (Winter, 1979). *NCME Measurement in Education, 10.*

REFERENCES

Ebel, R. L., & Frisbee. (1990). *Essentials of educational measurement* (5th ed.). Englewood Cliffs, NJ: Prentice Hall.

Linn, R. L., & Gronlund, N. E. (1995). *Measurement and assessments in teaching* (7th ed.). Englewood Cliffs, NJ: Simon & Schuster.

Mehrens, W. A., & Ebel, R. L. (Winter, 1979). Some comments on criterion-referenced and norm-referenced achievement tests. *NCME Measurement in Education, 10,* 1-8.

Mehrens, W. A., & Lehmann, I. J. (1991). *Measurement and evaluation in education and psychology* (4th ed.). New York: Holt, Rinehart, & Winston.

Millman, J. (1974). Criterion-referenced measurement. In W. J. Popham (Ed.), *Evaluation in education: Current applications.* (Chapter 6). Berkeley, CA: McCutchan Publishing Company.

Popham, W. J. (1978). *Criterion-referenced measurement.* Englewood Cliffs, NJ: Prentice Hall.

Popham, W. J., & Lindheim, E. (Spring, 1980). The practical side of criterion-referenced test-development. *NCME Measurement in Education, 10,* 1-8.

Sax, G. (1989). *Principles of educational and psychological measurement and evaluation* (3rd ed.). Belmont, CA: Wadsworth.

Thorndike, R. L., Cunningham, Thorndike, E. L., & Hagen, E. (1991). *Measurement and evaluation in psychology and education* (5th ed.). Englewood Cliffs, NJ: Prentice Hall.

THE RELATIONSHIP BETWEEN TYPE OF TEST AND CLASSROOM INSTRUCTION

The figure on page 117 was designed (Baker & Hanson, 1978) to clarify the relationship between the type of test and its sensitivity to classroom instruction. The instruments available for assessment procedures are arrayed along a continuum of instructional influence, from most influenced to least influenced by classroom instruction. Further, the dotted lines around the three sets of boxes illustrate the "is happening–should be happening–planning to happen" concept as it is dealt with internally at the local district level. The types of tests represented within each set of dotted lines provide the most appropriate information for that particular level of educational responsibility. It is clear that the two most useful types of measurement instruments for making instruction-related decisions are the program-specific and domain-referenced measures.

INFLUENCE OF CLASSROOM INSTRUCTION
ON TEST PERFORMANCE[1]

MOST INFLUENCED
BY CLASSROOM INSTRUCTION

LEAST INFLUENCED
BY CLASSROOM INSTRUCTION

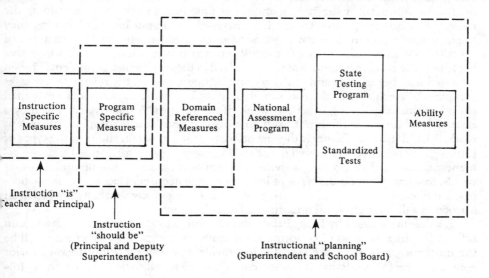

Instruction "is"
(Teacher and Principal)

Instruction
"should be"
(Principal and Deputy
Superintendent)

Instructional "planning"
(Superintendent and School Board)

PERFORMANCE-BASED (AUTHENTIC) ASSESSMENT

With the increasing emphasis that has been placed on the accountability of administrative and teaching personnel in both public and private education, especially in the context of the realization of student competencies in academic subjects, it is crucial to obtain valid assessments of student performance. Many educators and community members have criticized the appropriateness of the use of traditional standardized objective achievement tests comprising largely multiple choice and matching items as not being valid measures of student achievement. Although it is quite possible to construct objective test items to represent competencies reflecting higher level cognitive processes, many teachers and curriculum specialists have thought that such measures have not constituted meaningful indicators of complex performances in realistic and authentic life situations.

Assessment policies and practices have been transformed at local, state, and national levels to the increasing use of what are considered realistic or authentic forms of assessment. These approaches to assessment include use of (a) portfolios of student work such as samples of writing and art work, (b) hands-on laboratory and field experiences in the sciences, (c) open-ended exercises and problems in mathematics and the sciences requiring a step-by-step demonstration of the problem-solving process,

Baker, R. L., & Hanson, R. A. (1978). *Information requirements for assessing the effects of formal schooling.* Los Alamitos, CA: SWRL Educational Research & Development. (Reproduced with permission.)

(d) computer simulations duplicating problems of the real world, and (e) group discussions by class members and teachers of problems of vital social interest. Such activities have been thought by many to represent a more valid indication of student competencies than that furnished by scores on a standardized objective test.

Several difficulties underlie the use of performance-based assessment measures. First, it is difficult to obtain reliable evaluations (consistency of judgments across raters of student products). A substantial amount of time needs to be spent in training the raters to conform to a given set of scoring criteria which, despite intensive training, they might still interpret in different ways. Second, an adequate sample of given types of so-called authentic indicators of student performance is often difficult to achieve because of the excessive amount of time involved in the completion by students of even a limited number of tasks and in the scoring by raters of even the relatively few tasks completed. To achieve an adequate sampling of student work may require an extended period of time amounting to several weeks if not months. A one-day test given by a state or local agency is often not likely to represent an adequate sampling of student work. A third major difficulty is the one on transfer and generalizability of the types of learning experiences encountered in the tasks comprising a performance-based assessment measure to other learning activities of equal or even greater importance. In other words, to what extent do the types of learning experiences reflected in a performance-based task carry over to other learning experiences or portray what already has been learned in a different but still important educational context?

In a definitive paper by Linn, Baker, and Dunbar[1] (1991), eight criteria have been offered for the validation of performance-based assessments. This paper may well be the most comprehensive one available to provide an overview of the areas of major concern in performance-based assessment. These eight validation criteria are as follows: (a) *consequences*—a consideration of the positive and negative effects of test score interpretation in relation to the instructional process, (b) *fairness*—the realization of equity in the interpretation of test scores for individuals of different cultural, ethnic, and experiential backgrounds, a factor largely dependent upon what uses and interpretations are made of the assessment results, (c) *transfer and generalizability*—the lack of which could lead to the risk of a nonrepresentative and limited sampling of items (tasks) that prevent a basis for meaningful generalization of the degree to which successful performance in the knowledge domain of interest has been adequately measured so that inferences can be made concerning how well an examinee can transfer the body of knowledge and skills demonstrated to other tasks in the same domain, (d) *cognitive complexity*—the need to establish that the authentic assessment items such as those in an open-ended mathematics or science test really reflect higher–order skills rather than rote memorization of the steps involved in almost identically presented previous problems, an occurrence that might take place when instructors teach to the test, (e) *content quality*—the need to ensure that the content of the items is not only consistent with the best current understanding of the subject matter area but also indicative of the prolonged significance of the content, a goal highly dependent upon the input of educators with subject matter expertise, (f) *content coverage*—the need to establish an adequate sampling of the content of a given subject matter area, the absence of which could lead teachers to under-emphasize those significant portions of the content domain that had been excluded from the assessment process, (g) *meaningfulness*—a motivationally-related criterion thought to reflect one of the great advantages of

[1]Linn, R. L., Baker, E. L., & Dunbar, S. B. (1991). Complex, performance-based assessment: Expectations and validation criteria. *Educational Researcher, 20, 15-21.*

uthentic assessment, but one which might be overlooked by those item writers who have self-serving or idiosyncratic interests, and (h) *cost and efficiency*—the need to maintain costs of large-scale assessments at acceptable levels, a challenge hard to meet n the time-consuming tasks of preparing and especially scoring tests items.

It is the view of the authors of this book that not only traditional forms of assessment uch as those provided by standardized objective tests but also the performance-based ypes of authentic assessment are needed to evaluate the effectiveness of the educational rocess. Traditional modes of testing afford a greater sampling of activities, a higher egree of reliability, and probably a more cost-effective approach than that provided by uthentic assessment. It is possible to construct objective test items that do indeed tap igher level cognitive processes and meaningful tasks. It is probably somewhat easier lso to have a more nearly comparable basis for arriving at a generalization of how well ducational outcomes anchored to universally agreed upon objectives have been chieved across the nation from administration of carefully normed standardized chievement tests than from use of performance-based measures that tend to be dministered to meet the expectations of educators at a local or state level. On the other and, authentic assessment might be expected to have a greater impact upon the motivation of both students and teachers in the instructional and learning process. nformation from one approach can be expected to supplement that gained from the ther in a positive and constructive manner.

The recent definitive paper on performance-based assessment presented by Baker nd Dunbar has appeared which also includes a comprehensive set of references:

Baker, E. L., O'Neil, H. F., & Linn, R. L. (1993). Policy and validity prospects for performance-based assessment. *American Psychologist, 48*, 1210-1218.

Burger, S. E., & Burger, D. L. (1994). Determining the validity of performance-based assessment. *Educational Measurement: Issues and Practice, 13*, 9-15.

Linn, R. L., & Burton (1994). Performance-based assessment: Implication of task specificity. *Educational Measurement: Issues and Practice, 13*, 3-8, 15.

THE RASCH SCALING MODEL

The Rasch Model is a method of constructing tests. It provides a theory for (1) item analysis and selection, and (2) a measurement scale for reporting scores.

Essential Characteristics

The Rasch Model states that the probability of a person answering correctly a test item s a function of two attributes or parameters:

1. The *person* attribute – theoretically, any trait of interest in the measurement situation, but most often "ability," "achievement," and "aptitude." More specifically, it is the amount of such a trait the person possesses to answer correctly a certain number of items like the ones on a given test.
2. The *item* attribute – in effect, the difficulty level, defined as that point on the ability scale where the person has a fifty percent chance of answering the item correctly.

As a result, the Rasch Model puts people and test items on the same scale. The stimation of these two attributes – person ability and item difficulty – is termed *calibration*. Item calibration involves the evaluation of the fit of the difficulty parameter Test calibration requires the evaluation of the fit of the persons to the Rasch Model and the estimation of the ability parameter corresponding to each test score.

Underlying Assumptions

The fit of the items and persons to the Rasch Model depends on whether or not the following assumptions are met:

1. *Unidimensionality:* assumes that items can be arranged in order of difficulty along a single continuum such that the performance of a person on these items can be represented by a single score that is on the same continuum as the items. Implication difficult items should be more often answered correctly by persons with high ability rather than by those with low ability.

2. *Equal Item Discrimination:* assumes that items represent equal units when summed to yield a total score.

3. *No Guessing:* assumes that no one correctly guesses an answer. Implication: when low ability persons guess correctly on difficult items, the unidimensionality assumption is violated.

4. *Independence of Items:* assumes, for a person of a given ability, a response to one item is independent of a response to any other item; that is, a correct response to one item cannot depend on a correct response to any other item.

It is noteworthy that, although a great deal of research has focused on the effects of violating these assumptions, classical test theory makes these assumptions too – for example, when the test score equals the sum of all correct answers. Moreover, if the assumptions of the Rasch Model are met – specifically, the items and the persons fit the model – the estimates of ability and item difficulty are taken to be "specifically objective" or invariant. Implications: (1) for *items*, the estimates of item difficulty are independent of both particular persons and all other items in the calibration situation; (2) for *persons* the estimates of their abilities are independent of both the particular items used in this determination and all other persons being measured. The invariance of item calibrations and person measurement has led to the concepts of "item-free," or "test-free," measurement and "person-free," or "sample-free," item calibration – concepts particularly appealing to test developers.

Implications for Test Development

Given the three basic components of test development – (1) content specification and item writing, (2) item analysis, and (3) test form assembly – the principal difference between the Rasch Model and traditional methods centers on item analysis. Traditional item analysis is based on two statistics: *item difficulty* (p) – the proportion of examinees correctly answering an item; and *item discrimination* (r) – the extent to which an item differentiates between high- and low-scoring students. The problem inherent in this procedure is that both item statistics vary from one group of examinees to another with the result that these statistics are sample-bound.

Rasch item statistics have the following attributes (at least theoretically) to overcome this limitation:

1. They are invariant from group to group – hence, sample free.
2. An estimate of the examinee's ability level can be made independent from the set of items on a particular test – hence, item-free person measurement.

3. Item difficulty and examinee's ability levels are referenced on the same scale.
4. The ability scale is equal-interval.

The Rasch Model remains both a promising and perplexing method. The validity of its assumptions have been called into question and yet it continues to gain in use each year. Perhaps its two greatest drawbacks are the complex mathematical foundation which makes it extremely difficult to understand or to explain to non-technical audiences, and some emerging problems regarding the underlying assumptions and their empirical validations.

REFERENCES

Demaline, R. (March, 1979). *The Rasch Model and Title I Evaluation*. Portland, OR: Northwest Regional Educational Laboratory.
Journal of Educational Measurement, 14 (Summer, 1977). (Entire issue devoted to latent trait models.)
Lenke, J. M. (April, 1978). The Rasch Model – An overview. Paper presented at the meeting of the Tenth Annual Large School Systems Invitational Conference on Measurement in Education (The Psychological Corporation), Houston, TX.
Rentz, R. R., & Rentz, C. C. (Spring, 1979). Does the Rasch Model really work? *NCME Measurement in Education, 10*.

STANDARD SCORE AND PERCENTILE RANK EQUIVALENTS FOR NORMAL DISTRIBUTIONS OF SCORES

Standard Score		Approx. Percentile	Standard Score		Approx. Percentile	Standard Score		Approx. Percentile
z	T	Rank	z	T	Rank	z	T	Rank
-3.0	20	0.1	-0.9	41	18.4	1.2	62	88.5
-2.9	21	0.2	-0.8	42	21.2	1.3	63	90.3
-2.8	22	0.3	-0.7	43	24.2	1.4	64	91.9
-2.7	23	0.4	-0.6	44	27.4	1.5	65	93.3
-2.6	24	0.5	-0.5	45	30.8	1.6	66	94.5
-2.5	25	0.6	-0.4	46	34.5	1.7	67	95.5
-2.4	26	0.8	-0.3	47	38.2	1.8	68	96.4
-2.3	27	1.1	-0.2	48	42.1	1.9	69	97.1
-2.2	28	1.4	-0.1	49	46.0	2.0	70	97.7
-2.1	29	1.8	0.0	50	50.0	2.1	71	98.2
-2.0	30	2.3	0.1	51	54.0	2.2	72	98.6
-1.9	31	2.9	0.2	52	57.9	2.3	73	98.9
-1.8	32	3.6	0.3	53	61.8	2.4	74	99.2
-1.7	33	4.5	0.4	54	65.5	2.5	75	99.4
-1.6	34	5.5	0.5	55	69.2	2.6	76	99.5
-1.5	35	6.7	0.6	56	72.6	2.7	77	99.6
-1.4	36	8.0	0.7	57	75.8	2.8	78	99.7
-1.3	37	9.7	0.8	58	78.8	2.9	79	99.8
-1.2	38	11.5	0.9	59	81.6	3.0	80	99.9-
-1.1	39	13.6	1.0	60	84.1	3.1	81	99.9
-1.0	40	15.9	1.1	61	86.4	3.2	82	99.9+

Note: If one wishes to normalize a distribution of scores that may depart from normality, one first finds the percentile rank for a given raw score and then finds the approximate *z* or *T* score that corresponds to the percentile rank that was determined. This procedure is very common among test publishers who in having found a somewhat skewed distribution of scores wish to express the given raw scores in the form of standard score equivalents that can be conventionally interpreted for either research or dissemination purposes.

THE DELPHI TECHNIQUE
Reaching Group Consensus Individually

When group consensus is desired, the traditional approach is a round table discussion of those concerned or their representatives. Disadvantages of this process are numerous: (1) the bandwagon effect of a majority opinion; (2) the power of a persuasive or prestigious individual to shape group opinion; (3) the vulnerability of group dynamics to manipulation; and (4) the unwillingness of individuals to abandon publicly stated positions.

The Delphi Technique (Helmer, 1967) was designed to generate group consensus while minimizing the foregoing disadvantages. In essence, it identifies the group members who will generate the consensus position but interacts with them individually to provide collective feedback of the emerging consensus to each member privately. Individuals then reconsider their initial positions in light of the group trends and make any adjustments felt to be appropriate. The final result is an informed consensus insulated from the forces of face-to-face group interaction.

Typical Sequence of Events

1. Identify the group members whose consensus opinions are sought. If the study goes beyond an intact group such that representatives must be selected, care must be taken to insure that all the various publics or positions are proportionally sampled.
2. *Questionnaire One.* Have each member generate a list of goals, concerns, or issues toward which consensus opinions are desired. Edit the results to a manageable summary of items presented in random order. Prepare the second questionnaire in an appropriate format for rating or ranking. (Note: if an established or acceptable listing of such items already exists, this first step can be bypassed.)
3. *Questionnaire Two.* Have each member rate or rank the resulting items.
4. *Questionnaire Three.* Present the results of Questionnaire Two in the form of Questionnaire Three, showing the preliminary level of group consensus to each item and repeating each member's earlier response. The respondent rates or ranks each item a second time, now aware of the preliminary group trend. For each item where the individual differs substantially from the group, and chooses to remain so on Questionnaire Three, the respondent should provide a brief reason or explanation.
5. *Questionnaire Four.* The results of Questionnaire Three are presented in the form of Questionnaire Four, showing the new level of group consensus for each item and repeating that member's latest rating or ranking, along with a listing by item of the major reasons members had for dissent from the prevailing group position. Each member rates or ranks each item for the third and final time, in light of the emerging pattern of group consensus and the reasons for dissent.
6. The results of Questionnaire Four are tabulated and presented as the final statement of group consensus.

REFERENCES

Cyphert, F. R., & Grant, W. L. (1971). The Delphi Technique, *Phi Delta Kappan, 42*, 272-273.

Helmer, O. (1967). *Analysis of the future: The Delphi Technique.* Santa Monica, CA: Rand Corporation.

Rasp, A., Jr. (July, 1973). Delphi: A decision-maker's dream. *Nation's Schools, 92*, 29-32.

ITEM ANALYSIS[1]

Item analysis is a procedure to increase the reliability and validity of a test by separately evaluating each test item to determine whether or not that item *discriminates* in the same way the overall test is intended to discriminate. For example, given a test of academic aptitude or achievement, will students in the top half of the test score distribution also tend to get a particular item correct and students in the bottom half of this distribution tend to miss this same item? If so, such an item has favorable discriminating power and contributes to the overall reliability and validity of the test.

EXAMPLE A—*Steps in the Item Analysis of a True-False or Multiple Choice Aptitude or Achievement Test:*
1. Rank order the distribution of test scores from high to low.
2. Divide these ranked scores into two contrasting groups. The division point is arbitrary but common practice is to split the data in half, forming the Top and Bottom Halves; or, to increase the contrast, compare Upper and Lower Quarters. For ease of computation, use two groups of equal size.
3. Construct a four-fold table based on two pairs of categories. The first pair is simply the category *Wrong-Right* (for a specific test item); the second pair is the category *High-Scorers-Low Scorers* (depending on how the ranks were divided):

	Wrong	Right
High		
Low		

4. Calculate the chi square (χ^2) value of the resulting proportions using Computing Guide 12, page 185.
5. If χ^2 is significant, it can be concluded that a dependable difference exists in the proportion of high and low scoring subjects who gave correct answers. Items that meet this criterion should be retained; items that fail to meet it should be discarded.

EXAMPLE B—*Steps in the Item Analysis of a Three-Choice Interest Inventory:*

Interest or personality inventories often attempt to discriminate between the preferences of two subgroups on a given series of items. For instance, if the following item is given to a group of art majors and physical education majors in four-year colleges, will it discriminate between them?

I would enjoy browsing through old curio
shops on weekends or vacations. *A* ? *D**
*A, Agree; ?, Undecided; D, Disagree.

---

[1] See page 178 for a correlational approach to item analysis.

2. Construct a 2 x 3 contingency table:

	Disagree	?	Agree
Art Majors			
P.E. Majors			

3. Calculate χ^2 using Computing Guide 14, page 187.
4. If χ^2 is significant, it can be concluded that a dependable difference exists in the proportion of Art and P.E. majors who answered appropriately—presumably art majors tending to agree and P.E. majors tending to disagree.

REFERENCES

Standard Tests and Measures:
1. Kramer, J. J., & Conoley, J. C. (Eds.). (1992). *The Eleventh Mental Measurements Yearbook* (Vols. 1, 2). Lincoln, NB: Buros Institute of Mental Measurements.
2. Murphy, L. L., Conoley, J. C., & Impala, J. C. (Eds.). (1994). *Tests in print IV.* Lincoln, NB: Buros Institute of Mental Measurements.
3. Sweetland, R. C., & Keyser, D. J. (1983). *Tests.* Kansas City, MO: Test Corporation of America.
4. Keyser, D. J., & Sweetland, R. C. (1988). *Test Critiques* (Vols. I-VII). Kansas City, MO: Test Corporation of America.
5. *Journal of Educational Measurement.* Quarterly Journal.
6. *Educational and Psychological Measurement.* Bi-monthly Journal.
7. *Review of Educational Research.* Every three years: *1968,* 1965, 1962, etc. Beginning in 1970, however, an unscheduled publication pattern replaced the cyclical one.
8. Miscellaneous test publishers' catalogs–most *current* source of information. See Buros and Sweetland & Keyser for listing of publishers.
9. *Psychological Abstracts.*
10. *Educational Index.*
11. *ERIC* (Educational Resources Information Center): Nineteen clearing-houses, depending on the nature of the need. For general information regarding information retrieval resources, procedures, and publications, contact: USOE, 400 Maryland Avenue SW, Washington, DC 20202.
12. Thorndike, R. L., Cunningham, Thorndike, E. L., & Hagen, E. (1991). *Measurement and evaluation in psychology and education* (5th ed.). Englewood Cliffs, NJ: Prentice Hall.

Nonstandard Tests and Measures:
1. *Psychological Abstracts.*
2. *Educational Index.*
3. Webb, E. J., Campbell, D. T., Schwartz, R. D., & Sechrest, L. (1966). *Unobtrusive measures: Nonreactive research in the social sciences.* Chicago, IL: Rand McNally.
4. Educational Testing Service, Microfiche File, Princeton, NJ. This is a comprehensive file of measures and instruments reported by researchers in the literature. It is important to state your measurement needs in clear and specific terms in order for ETS to match your request to an appropriate measure, if one exists.
5. Shaw, M. E., & Wright, J. M. (1967). *Scales for the measurement of attitudes.* New York: McGraw-Hill Book Co. A review of the literature, with comprehensive exhibits and applications.
6. Oppenheim, A. N. (1966). *Questionnaire design and attitude measurement.* New York: Basic Books, Inc.
7. *ERIC.* (See item 12, above.)

THREE TYPES OF VALIDITY

	QUESTION	METHOD	COMMON USE	EXAMPLE
Content Validity	How well does the content of the test sample the kinds of things about which conclusions are to be drawn?	Logically conclude whether or not the test content comprises an adequate *definition* of what it claims to measure.	Achievement tests.	A test of school readiness is examined to see whether the content relates to knowledge and skills expected of first grade children following the kindergarten program.
Criterion-related Validity[2]	Does the test compare well with external variables considered to be direct measures of the characteristic or behavior in question?	Give the test and compare it with the criterion variable. The latter may be obtained concurrently or predicted, and then obtained in the future, depending on the recommended use of the original test.	Tests used in place of a more complicated procedure; or to select and classify persons.	Diagnosis of mental instability based on a card-sorting test compared with a more elaborate psychiatric examination; intelligence test scores used to predict future performance.
Construct Validity	To what extent do certain explanatory concepts or qualities account for performance on the test?	Based on the theory underlying the test, set up hypotheses regarding the behavior of persons with high or low scores. Test the hypothesis.	Tests used for description, or in scientific research.	A test of personality types is studied to see how well theoretical implications of the typologies account for actual results obtained.

Note: The term *"face validity"* often is used to indicate whether the instrument, on the face of it, appears to measure what it claims to measure. Will persons making use of this instrument accept it as a valid measure in the everyday sense of the word? While face validity is not a rigorous concept, its importance never can be ignored on that basis. Its presence, in conjunction with the above categories of validity, reinforces overall acceptance. It also is true that face validity, in the absence of these other standards, can be dangerously misleading, just as its absence, when these other validities are, in fact, present, can lead to disbelieving and frustrating resistance among potential users.

1. Based on format originally developed by Lee J. Cronbach.
2. Formerly, Concurrent Validity and Predictive Validity.

TEST ITEM BIAS

Considerable concern in recent years has been raised about test item bias – in particular, items on tests which favor one group over others, independent of the ability of those making up the groups. As the implicit goal of any test instrument is its fairness, methods have been devised to ensure such an outcome.[1]

An unbiased test item is one for which the probability of success is the same for equally able test takers of the same population regardless of their subgroup membership.

To illustrate an instance of a biased item, consider the following example comparing results of five test items given to two groups where p represents the proportion of students answering the item correctly.

Item	Rank Order for Group I (p value)	Rank Order for Group II (p value)
1	3rd (p = .62)	2nd (p = .64)
2	1st (p = .93)	1st (p = .81)
3	4th (p = .55)	3rd (p = .51)
4	2nd (p = .71)	5th (p = .19)
5	5th (p = .28)	4th (p = .38)

Note that the similarity of p values for the two groups on four of the five items indicates no obvious case of bias. Item 4, however, with quite different p values, reveals a test item that clearly favors Group I over Group II. At issue in this situation is the construct validity of the test which, if satisfactory, should allow examinees of comparable ability to have the same chance of answering the item correctly.

Although this example illustrates the problem of test bias, more sophisticated techniques have been developed to determine its presence. In his review of these methods, Osterlind offers five approaches, each with its own merits.

Analysis of Variance (ANOVA). This is a strategy where two or more groups sampled from the same population are given a common test. The resulting variations in individual item scores are then examined using analysis of variance, where the focus is upon the interaction of groups x items rather than main effects. The interaction contrast for every item within each group forms the criterion on which judgments about item bias are made.

Transformed Item Difficulties (TID). This approach assumes bias to be characteristic of all test items and the focus is on the degree that bias is present. It is conceptually similar to the ANOVA strategy: relative item difficulties for the performances of two or more groups on a set of test questions covering a single skill or mental construct and revealed by the interaction of groups with items. It goes beyond interaction, however, and identifies particular biased test items by their degree of aberration.

Chi Square (χ^2). This technique examines the probability of correctly responding to an item for test takers from different groups with the same ability levels. It follows a goodness-of-fit logic by testing the null hypothesis of no significant difference between an expected number of examinee responses in a particular ability level category and the actual number observed to respond in that category. Thus the χ^2 approach to test item bias is sensitive to within groups' item discrimination in addition to the differences between groups in item difficulty levels.

---

[1] Adapted from Osterlind, S. J. (1983). *Test item bias.* Thousand Oaks, CA: Sage.

Item Characteristic Curve (ICC). Although this approach is the most elegant of all models to get at test item bias, it is also the most complex both conceptually and procedurally as it necessitates computer processing and the grasp of advanced statistical methodology. In essence, it compares probabilities of responding correctly to an item for each of two groups. The overall notion is that the item characteristic curves that it produces for each group should be alike for an item to be considered unbiased.

Distractor Response Analysis (Distractor). As the name states, this strategy addresses the incorrect alternative to a test item – the distractors or question foils – by examining differences in response patterns among the various subgroups of a population. It determines the significance of differences among two or more groups' response frequencies in the discrete categories of question distractors. If two or more groups according to a distinguishing criterion are in fact differentially attracted to the distractors of one or more test items, the null hypothesis of no differences may be rejected and a bias inferred to be present.

Of the foregoing five strategies, the decision among them depends on answers to such questions as: What hypotheses are to be tested? Are the sample sizes adequate for the statistics employed? Are computers and software available if required? What is most appropriate for any given audience?

Both ANOVA and TID strategies examine the interaction of groups x items as an adequate indicator of bias. TID takes matters one step farther identifying individual items with pronounced interaction values. Both focus solely on item difficulty. This fact poses several problems, most notably that groups x items interaction can occur regardless of bias.

Chi-square avoids this difficulty by examining differences in proportions across total score categories. It is relatively easy to compute but has the disadvantage of an arbitrary selection of ability levels.

Item characteristic curve is the most sophisticated technique indicating item difficulty, item discrimination, and some guessing levels. Its drawback is its technical complexity both to apply and to comprehend, along with its requirement of a very large sample.

Lastly, the distractor response analysis, like chi-square, examines a difference in proportions. Its focus, however, is on the incorrect answer choices to a test item, seeking to reveal whether or not there is a differential pull toward distractors between groups.

In summary, the intent of this section is simply to open the door of inquiry where test bias is concerned. It turns out to be a many-faceted topic necessitating in-depth knowledge both to use and to comprehend. The reader should consult references giving full treatment to this subject, beginning with Steven Osterlind's monograph noted previously.

REFERENCE

Crocker, L., & Algina, J. (1986). *Introduction to classical and modern test theory.* New York: Holt, Rinehart and Winston. (See Chapter 16).

VALIDITY[1, 2]

Validity information indicates the degree to which the test is capable of achieving certain aims. Tests are used for several types of judgment, and for each type of judgment, a different type of investigation is required to establish validity. For purposes of describing the uses for three kinds of validity coefficients, we may distinguish three of the rather numerous aims of testing:

1. *The test user wishes to determine how an individual performs at present in a universe of situations that the test situation is claimed to represent.* For example, most achievement tests used in schools measure the student's performance on a sample of questions intended to represent a certain phase of educational achievement or certain education objectives.

2. *The test user wishes to forecast an individual's future standing or to estimate an individual's present standing on some variable of particular significance that is different from the test.* For example, an academic aptitude test may forecast grades, or a brief adjustment inventory may estimate what the outcome would be of a careful psychological examination.

3. *The test user wishes to infer the degree to which the individual possesses some hypothetical trait or quality (construct) presumed to be reflected in the test performance.* For example, the level of standing of an individual on some proposed abstract trait such as "intelligence" or "creativity" that cannot be observed directly may want to be determined. This may be done to learn something about the individual, or it may be done to study the test itself, to study its relationship to other tests, or to develop psychological theory.

Different types of tests are often used for each of the different aims, but this is not always the case. There is much overlap in types of tests and in the purposes for which they are used. Thus, a vocabulary test might be used as: (a) simply a measure of present vocabulary, the universe being all the words in the language; (b) a screening device to discriminate present or potential schizophrenics from organics; or (c) a means of making inferences about "intellectual capacity."

To determine how suitable a test is for each of these uses, it is necessary to gather the appropriate sort of validity information. The kind of information to be gathered depends on the aim or aims of testing rather than on the type of test. The three aspects of validity corresponding to the three aims of testing may be named content validity, criterion-related validity, and construct validity.

---

[1]This material was taken from the *Standards for Educational and Psychological Tests and Manuals,* American Psychological Association (Co-chairmen of joint committee, APA, AERA, NCME: John W. French and William B. Michael). Revised, 1966. Supplementary information with slightly different emphases about validity may now be found in a report by a new joint committee entitled *Standards for Educational and Psychological Tests,* published by the American Psychological Association in 1974 under the chairmanship of the late Frederick B. Davis.

[2]While reliability coefficients are customarily greater than validity coefficients, validity is always the important question. Maximum possible validity $= \sqrt{\dfrac{\text{Reliability}}{\text{of}} \times \dfrac{\text{Reliability}}{\text{of}}}$

$$\text{Maximum possible validity} = \sqrt{\begin{array}{c}\text{Reliability}\\\text{of}\\\text{Test}\end{array} \times \begin{array}{c}\text{Reliability}\\\text{of}\\\text{Criterion}\end{array}}$$

Content validity is demonstrated by showing how well the content of the test samples the class situations or subject matter about which conclusions are to be drawn. Content validity is especially important for achievement and proficiency measures and for measures of adjustment or social behavior based on observation in selected situations. The manual should justify the claim that the test content represents the assumed universe of tasks, conditions, or processes. A useful way of looking at this universe of tasks or items is to consider it to comprise a *definition* of the achievement to be measured by the test. In the case of an educational achievement test, the content of the test may be regarded as a definition of (or a sampling from a population of) one or more educational objectives. The aptitudes, skills, and knowledges required of the student for successful test performance must be precisely the types of aptitudes, skills, and knowledges that the school wishes to develop in the students and to evaluate in terms of test scores. Thus, evaluating the content validity of a test for a particular purpose is the same as subjectively recognizing the adequacy of a definition. This process is actually quite similar to the subjective evaluation of the criterion itself. Unless, however, the aim of an achievement test is specifically to forecast or substitute for some criterion, its correlation with a criterion is *not* a useful evaluation of the test.

Criterion-related validity is demonstrated by comparing the test scores with one or more external variables considered to provide a direct measure of the characteristic or behavior in question. This comparison may take the form of an expectancy table or, most commonly, a correlation relating the test score to a criterion measure. Predictive uses of tests include long-range forecasts of one or more measures of academic achievement, prediction of vocational success, and prediction of reaction to therapy. On some occasions the criterion data are collected concurrently with the test; for example, when one wishes to know whether a testing procedure can take the place of more elaborate procedures for diagnosing personality disorders. A test that is related to one or more concurrent criteria will not necessarily predict status on the same criterion at some later date. Whether the criterion data should be collected concurrently with the testing or at a later time depends on whether the test is recommended for prediction or for assessment of present status.

Construct validity is evaluated by investigating what qualities a test measures, that is, by determining the degree to which certain explanatory concepts or constructs account for performance on the test. To examine construct validity requires a combination of logical and empirical attack. Essentially, studies of construct validity check on the theory underlying the test. The procedure involves three steps. First, the investigator inquires: From this theory, what hypotheses may we make regarding the behavior of persons with high or low scores? Second, data are gathered to test these hypotheses. Third, in light of the evidence, an inference is made as to whether the theory is adequate to explain the data collected. If the theory fails to account for the data, the test interpretation should be revised, the theory reformulated or the theory rejected altogether. Fresh evidence would be required to demonstrate construct validity for the revised interpretation.

A simple procedure for investigating what a test measures is to correlate it with other tests. We would expect a valid test of numerical reasoning, for example, to correlate more highly with other numerical tests than with clerical perception tests. Another procedure is experimental. If it is hypothesized, for example, that form perception on a certain projective test indicates probable ability to function well under emotional stress, this inference may be checked by placing individuals in an experimental situation producing emotional stress and observing whether their behavior corresponds to the hypothesis.

Construct validity is ordinarily studied when the tester wishes to increase under standing of the psychological qualities being measured by the test. A validity coefficien relating test to criterion, unless it is established in the context of some theory, yields n information about *why* the correlation is high or low, or about how one might improv the measurement. Construct validity is relevant when the tester accepts no existin measure as a definite criterion of the quality being measured (e.g., in measuring postulated drive such as need for achievement), or when a test will be used in so man diverse decisions that no single criterion applies (e. g., in identifying the ability of Peac Corps trainees to adapt to new cultures). Here the traits or qualities underlying tes performance are of central importance. It must be remembered, however, that, withou a study of criterion-related validity, a test developed for diagnosis or prediction can b regarded only as experimental.

These three aspects of validity are only conceptually independent, and only rarel is just one of them important in a particular situation. A complete study of a test woul normally involve information about all types of validity. A first step in the preparatio of a predictive (*criterion-related*) instrument may be to consider what *constructs* are likel to provide a basis for selecting or devising an effective test. Sampling from a *conten universe may also be an early step in producing a test whose use for *prediction* is th ultimate concern. Even after satisfactory *prediction* has been established, informatio regarding *construct* validity may make the test more useful; it may, for example, provide a basis for identifying situations other than the validating situation where the test i appropriate as a predictor. To analyze *construct* validity, all the knowledge regardin validity would be brought to bear.

The three concepts of validity are pertinent to all kinds of tests. It is the intended use of the test rather than its nature that determines what kind of evidence is required.

Intelligence or scholastic aptitude tests most often use criterion-related validity to show how well they are able to predict academic success in school or college, but the nature of the aptitudes measured is often judged from the content of the items, and the place of the aptitude within the array of human abilities is deduced from correlations with other tests.

For achievement tests, content validity is usually of first importance. For example, a testing agency has a group of subject-matter specialists devise and select test items that they judge to cover the topics and mental process relevant to the field represented by the test. Similarly, teachers judge whether the final test in their course covers the kinds of situations, certain principles or understandings about which they have been trying to teach their students. Teachers also judge content when using a published test, but can appropriately investigate criterion-related validity by correlating this test with tests they have prepared or with other direct measures of their chief instructional objectives. When the same published achievement test is used for admissions testing, it may reasonably be checked against a later criterion of performance. In any theoretical discussion of what is being measured by the achievement test, a consideration of construct validity is required. Whether the score on a science achievement test, for example, reflects reading ability to a significant degree, and whether it measures understanding of scientific method rather than mere recall of facts are both questions about construct validity.

Development of a personality inventory will usually start with the assembly of items covering content the developer considers meaningful. Such inventories are then likely to be interpreted with the aid of theory; any such interpretation calls for evidence of construct validity. In addition, a personality inventory must have criterion-related validity, if, for example, it is to be used in screening military recruits who may be maladjusted.

Interest measures are usually intended to predict vocational or educational criteria, but many of them are also characterized by logical content and constructs. This makes it more likely that they can provide at least a rough prediction for the very many occupations and activities that exist and for which specific evidence of criterion-related validity has not been obtained.

For projective techniques, construct validity is the most important, although criterion-related validity using criteria collected either concurrently with the testing or afterwards may be pertinent if the instruments are to be used in making diagnostic classifications.

REFERENCES

Crocker, L., & Algina, J. (In press, 1996). *Introduction to classical and modern test theory.* New York: Holt, Rinehart, & Winston.

Cronbach, L. J. (1971). Test validation. In R. L. Thorndike (Ed.), *Educational measurement* (2nd ed.) (pp. 443-507). Washington, DC: American Council on Education.

Guilford, J. P., & Fruchter, B. (1978). *Fundamental statistics in psychology and education* (6th ed.). New York: McGraw-Hill. (See Chapter 18 on validity.)

Guion, R. M. (1976). Recruiting, selection, and job placement. In M. D. Dunnette (Ed.), *Handbook of industrial and organizational psychology.* Chicago, IL: Rand McNally. (Section IV, Chapter 18.)

Linn, R. L. (Ed.). (1989). *Educational measurement* (3rd ed.). New York: Macmillan.

Nunnally, J. C., & Bernstein, I. H. (1994). *Psychometric theory* (3rd ed.). New York: McGraw-Hill. (See Chapter 3 on validity.)

Suen, H. K. (1990). *Principles of test theories.* Hillsdale, NJ: Lawrence Erlbaum.

RELIABILITY COEFFICIENTS

1. *Reliability* means the consistency of scores between measurements in a series.
2. The *reliability coefficient* tells what proportion of the test score variance is nonerror variance.
3. The *reliability coefficient* increases with the length of the test, a relationship which is much less pronounced for validity. (See Spearman-Brown formula, page 179.)
4. The *reliability coefficient* increases with the spread or variance of scores.
5. A test may measure reliably at one level of performance and unreliably at another level. Items too difficult for some cause them to guess, yielding "reliable" but chance results; items too easy for others also provide "reliable" but nondiscriminatory information. The difficulty level of a test must be adjusted to the purposes of the testing.
6. Relationship between reliability and validity:
   a. For a test to predict a particular criterion, *predictive (criterion related) validity* is more important than reliability. When predictive validity is satisfactory, low reliability is not a serious problem (e.g., tests of creativity).
   b. Given two tests measuring the same thing, the test with the higher reliability will also have the higher *validity coefficient.*
   c. Rule for the limit reliability places on validity: The correlation between the test and independent criterion can never be higher than the square root of the product of the reliability of the test and the reliability of the criterion variable.

7. Types of reliability coefficients:
   a. *Coefficient of Stability ("test-retest")*: Correlation between two successive measurements with the same test. Critical problem: Optimizing the delay between the two administrations to offset a spuriously high effect due to recall, if too short; or spuriously low effect due to the change in the make-up of the subject, if too long.
   b. *Coefficient of Equivalence ("alternate forms")*: The successive administration of two parallel forms of the same test. (In terms of test theory, this is the most desirable index of test reliability, since it involves two different representative samples of items.)
   c. *Internal-Consistency Reliability:* Whenever only one form of a test is available, an indication of its internal consistency (i.e., the extent to which there is cohesiveness or interrelatedness among the items) is often desired. In the instance of true-false or multiple-choice items in a scale, the content of which is quite homogeneous in the characteristic being measured, it is common practice to score the alternative response keyed as correct or appropriate with the numerical value of one and to score all remaining alternatives (i.e., the distorters or foils representing incorrect responses) with a value of zero. In such a situation, it is customary to obtain an internal-consistency estimate of reliability from application of the well-known procedure called Kuder-Richardson formula 20 provided that the items are not administered under highly-speeded conditions.

      The difficulty of any test item i is represented by the proportion of individuals who respond to it in a correct or appropriate manner and is designated by the symbol p_i. The proportion of individuals not responding correctly to the item is designated by q, which is equal to $1 - p_i$. The variance of a single item can be shown to be equal to p_iq_i, and its standard deviation to be $\sqrt{p_iq_i}$. The mean and standard deviation of the scores of all individuals in the total sample (N) taking the test are defined as M_t and σ_t, respectively. The total number of items is defined as k. The formula for the estimation of the internal-consistency reliability of a measure is given as follows:

      $$\text{KR-20} \qquad r_{tt} = \frac{k}{k-1} \cdot \frac{\sigma_t^2 - \Sigma p_iq_i}{\sigma_t^2}$$

      In Computing Guide 8 on page 179 a hypothetical item score matrix of ten examinees (A, B, . . ., J) in a four-item total test is presented in which the computational steps are shown for calculating the estimate of the internal-consistency reliability from Kuder-Richardson formula 20.
   d. *Coefficient Alpha; Internal Consistency Reliability Generalized:* Approximately 14 years after the Kuder-Richardson formula 20 appeared, Cronbach (1951) generalized the procedure to the case in which differential weights or scores might be assigned to the alternatives of several test items or to parts of a measuring instrument. A typical example in which the use of coefficient alpha would be appropriate is that of estimating the internal-consistency reliability of an attitude scale in a Likert-like format. Thus, if the respondent was to indicate to each of several items within a homogeneous scale one of five responses of *strongly agree, agree, undecided, disagree,* or *strongly disagree* carrying respective weights of 5, 4, 3, 2, or 1, coefficient alpha would be appropriate. The formula associated with coefficient alpha is very similar to that of Kuder-Richardson 20. For each item, its variance (σ_t^2) across persons over the possible range of scores, say from 1 to 5, is calculated. Then a sum of the variances across items is obtained just as the sum of p_iq_i was determined for dichotomously scored items (+1 or zero) associated with the Kuder-Richardson formula 20.

The formula for coefficient alpha is given as follows:

$$\alpha = \frac{k}{k-1} \cdot \frac{\sigma_t^2 - \Sigma\sigma_i^2}{\sigma_t^2}$$

An illustrative example is presented in Computing Guide 9, on page 180. In this guide a hypothetical item score matrix comprising a five-item scale administered to eight persons is presented along with the variance for each item and the variance of the total scores.[1]

RELIABILITY: POSSIBLE SOURCES OF VARIANCE IN A TEST SCORE[2]

I. Lasting and general characteristics of the individual
   1. General skills (e.g., reading)
   2. General ability to comprehend instructions, testwiseness, techniques of taking tests
   3. Ability to solve problems of the general type presented in this test
   4. Attitudes, emotional reactions or habits generally operating in situations like the test situation (e.g., self-confidence)

II. Lasting and specific characteristics of the individual
   1. Knowledge and skills required by particular problems in the test
   2. Attitudes, emotional reactions, or habits related to particular test stimuli (e.g., fear of high places brought to mind by an inquiry about such fears on a personality test)

III. Temporary and general characteristics of the individual (systematically affecting performance on various tests at a particular time)
   1. Health, fatigue, and emotional strain
   2. Motivation, rapport with examiner
   3. E.g., effects of heat, light, and ventilation
   4. Level of practice on skills required by tests of this type
   5. Present attitudes, emotional reactions, or strength of habits (insofar as these are departures from the person's average or lasting characteristics—e.g., political attitudes during an election campaign)

IV. Temporary and specific characteristics of the individual
   1. Changes in fatigue or motivation developed by this particular test (e.g., discouragement resulting from failure on a particular item)
   2. Fluctuations in attention, coordination, or standards of judgment
   3. Fluctuations in memory for particular facts
   4. Level of practice on skills or knowledge required by this particular test (e.g., effects of special coaching)
   5. E.g., temporary emotional states and strength of habits, related to particular test stimuli (e.g., a question calls to mind a recent bad dream)
   6. Luck in the selection of answers by "guessing"

---

[1]For additional information on internal-consistency reliability, see Cronbach, L. J. (1990). *Essentials of psychological testing* (5th ed.). New York: Harper Collins College Publishers. Also consult Guilford, J. P., & Fruchter, B. (1978). *Fundamental statistics in psychology and education* (6th ed.). New York: McGraw-Hill.

[2]Source: After Thorndike, R. L (1949). *Personnel selection* (p. 73). New York: Wiley. Adapted for Cronbach, L. J. (1970). *Essentials of psychological testing* (3rd ed.) (p. 175). New York: Harper & Brothers.

RELIABILITY[1]

Reliability refers to the accuracy (consistency and stability) of measurement by a test. Any direct measurement of such consistency obviously calls for a comparison between at least two measurements. (Whereas "accuracy" is a general expression, the terms "consistency" and "stability" are needed to describe, respectively, form-associated and time-associated reliability.) The two measurements may be obtained by *retesting* an individual with the identical test. Aside from practical limitations, retesting is not a theoretically desirable method of determining a reliability coefficient if, as usual, the items that constitute the test are only one of many sets (actual or hypothetical) that might equally well have been used to measure the particular ability or trait. Thus, there is ordinarily no reason to suppose that *one* set of (say) 50 vocabulary items is especially superior (or inferior) to another comparable (equivalent) set of 50. In this case it appears desirable to determine not only the degree of response variation by the subject from one occasion to the next (as is accomplished by the retest method), but also the extent of sampling fluctuation involved in selecting a given set of 50 items. These two objectives are accomplished most commonly by correlating scores on the original set of 50 items with scores by the same subjects on an independent but similar set of 50 items—an "alternate form" of the original 50. If the effect of content-sampling *alone* is sought (without the effects of response variability by the subject), or if it is not practical to undertake testing on two different occasions, a test of 100 items may be administered. Then the test may be divided into two sets of 50 odd-numbered items and 50 even-numbered items; the correlation between scores on the odd and the even sets is a "split-half" or "odd-even" correlation, from which a reliability (consistency) coefficient for the entire test of 100 items may be estimated by the Spearman-Brown formula (involving certain generally reasonable assumptions). Essentially the same type of estimated reliability coefficient may be obtained from item-analysis data through use of the Kuder-Richardson formulas (which involve various assumptions, some more reasonable and exact than others). It should be noted that despite the possible heterogeneity of content, the odd-even correlation between the sets of items may be quite high if the items are easy and if the test is administered with a short time limit. Such odd-even correlations are in a sense spurious, since they merely reflect the expected correlation between two sets of scores each of which is a measure of rate of work.

From the preceding discussion, it is clear that *different methods of determining the reliability coefficient take account of different sources of error.* Thus, from one testing to the other, the retest method is affected not only by response variability of the subjects but also by differences in administration (most likely if different persons administer the test on the two occasions). Reliability coefficients based on the single administration of a test ignore response variability and the particular administrative conditions: their effects on scores simply do not appear as errors of measurement. Hence, "reliability coefficient" is a generic term referring to various types of evidence; each type of evidence suggests a different meaning. It is essential that *the method used to derive any reliability coefficient should be clearly described.*

---

[1]This material was taken from the *Standards for Educational and Psychological Tests and Manuals,* American Psychological Association (Co-chairmen of joint committee, APA, AERA, NCME: John W. French and William B. Michael). Revised, 1966. Supplementary information with slightly different emphases about validity may now be found in a report by a new joint committee entitled *Standards for Educational and Psychological Tests,* published by the American Psychological Association in 1985 under the chairmanship of Melvin R. Novick, chairman of the APA, AERA and NCME joint committee.

As a generic term, reliability refers to many types of evidence, each of which describes the agreement or consistency to be expected among similar observations. Each type of evidence takes into account certain kinds of errors or inconsistencies and not others. The operation of measurement may be viewed as a sample of behavior; in a typical aptitude or achievement test students are observed on a particular date as they respond to a particular set of questions or stimuli, and their responses are recorded and scored by a particular tester or system. The occasion is a sample from the period of time within which the same general inquiry would be pertinent; some sampling error is involved in selecting any one date of observation. The items that constitute the test are only one of many sets (actual or hypothetical) that might have been used to measure the same ability or trait. The choices of a particular test apparatus, test administrator, observer, or scorer, are also sampling operations. Each such act of sampling has some influence on the test score. It is valuable for the test user to know how much a particular score would be likely to change if any one of these conditions of measurement was altered.

There are various components that may contribute to inconsistency among observations: (a) response variation by the subject (due to changes in physiological efficiency, or in such psychological factors as motivation, effort, or mood): These may be especially important in inventories of personality; (b) variations in test content or the test situation (in "situational tests" which include interacting persons as part of the situation, this source of variation can be relatively large); (c) variations in administration (either through variations in physical factors, such as temperature, noise, or apparatus functioning, or in psychological factors, such as variation in the technique or skill of different test administrators or raters); and (d) variations in the process of observation. In addition to these errors of observation, scoring-error variance in test scores reflects variation in the process of scoring responses as well as mistakes in recording, transferring, or reading of scores.

The estimation of clearly labeled components of error variance is the most informative outcome of a reliability study, both for the test developers wishing to improve the reliability of those users and for those users desiring to interpret test scores with maximum understanding. The analysis of error variance calls for the use of an appropriate *experimental* design. There are many different multivariate designs that can be used in reliability studies; the choice of design for studying the particular test is to be determined by its intended interpretation and by the practical limitations upon experimentation. In general, where more information can be obtained at little increase in cost, the test developer should obtain and report that information.

Although estimation of clearly labeled components of error variance is the most informative outcome of a reliability study, this approach is not yet prominent in reports on tests. In the more familiar reliability study the investigator obtains two measures and correlates them, or derives a correlation coefficient by applying one of several formulas to part or item scores within a test. Such a correlation is often interpreted as a ratio of "true variance plus error variance." Many different coefficients, each involving its own definition of "true and "error" variance, may be derived from a multivariate reliability experiment with the presence of controls for such factors as those of content, time, and mode of administration. Hence, any single correlation is subject to considerable misinterpretation unless the investigator makes clear just what sampling errors are considered to be error in the particular coefficient they report. The correlation between two test forms presented on different days has a different significance from an internal-consistency coefficient, for example, because the latter allocates day-to-day fluctuations in a person's efficiency to the true rather than to the error portion of the score variance.

In the present set of *Standards*, the terminology by which the 1954 *Technical Recommendations* classified coefficients into several types (e.g., coefficient of equivalence) has been discarded. Such a terminological system breaks down as more adequate statistical analyses are applied and methods are more adequately described. Hence, it is recommended that test authors work out suitable phrases to convey the meaning of whatever coefficients they report; as an example, the expression, "the stability of measurements by different test forms as determined over a seven-day interval," although lengthy, will be reasonably free from ambiguity.

REFERENCES

Guilford, J. P., & Fruchter, B. (1978). *Fundamental statistics in psychology and education* (6th ed.). New York: McGraw-Hill. (See Chapter 17 on reliability.)

Linn, R. L. (1989). *Educational measurement* (3rd ed.). New York: Macmillan.

Nunnally, J. C., & Bernstein, I. H. (1994). *Psychometric theory* (3rd ed.). New York: McGraw-Hill. (See Chapter 7 on reliability.)

Stanley, J. C. (1971). Reliability. In R. L. Thorndike (Ed.). *Educational measurement* (2nd ed.) (pp. 356-442). Washington, DC: American Council on Education.

SURVEY DESIGN AND TECHNIQUES FOR SCHOOL-RELATED USE

Purpose

Surveys are the most widely-used technique in education and the behavioral sciences for the collection of data. They are a means of gathering information that describes the nature and extent of a specified set of data ranging from physical counts and frequencies to attitudes and opinions. This information, in turn, can be used to answer questions that have been raised, to solve problems that have been posed or observed, to assess needs and set goals, to determine whether or not specific objectives have been met, to establish baselines against which future comparisons can be made, to analyze trends across time, and generally, to describe what exists, in what amount, and in what context.

Characteristics

The guiding principles underlying surveys are that they should be:
1. Systematic – carefully planned and executed to insure appropriate content coverage and sound, efficient data collection.
2. Representative – closely reflecting the population of all possible cases or occurrences, either by including everyone or everything, or by using scientific sampling procedures.

3. Objective – insuring that the data are as observable and explicit as possible.
4. Quantifiable – yielding data that can be expressed in numerical terms.

Limitations

With the exception of surveys based on a search of records, surveys are dependent on direct communication with persons having characteristics, behaviors, attitudes, and other relevant information appropriate for a specific investigation. This makes them *reactive* in nature; that is, they directly involve the respondent in the assessment process by eliciting a reaction. Although direct interactions are often the most cost-effective, efficient, and credible means of collecting data, because the respondents are usually in the best position to speak for themselves and "tell it like it is," reactive methods run many risks of generating misleading information. Among these risks are the following:

1. Surveys only tap respondents who are accessible and cooperative.
2. Surveys often make the respondent feel special or unnatural and, thus, produce responses that are artificial or slanted.
3. Surveys arouse "response sets" such as acquiescence or a proneness to agree with positive statements or questions.
4. Surveys are vulnerable to over-rater or under-rater bias—the tendency for some respondents to give consistently high or low ratings.
5. In the case of interviews, biased reactions can be elicited because of characteristics of the interviewer or respondent, or the combination, that elicit an unduly favorable or unfavorable pattern of responses.

General Guidelines for Designing Surveys

1. Define the purpose and scope of the surveys in explicit terms–avoid "fishing expeditions" and rambling, redundant, ill-conceived approaches.
2. Avoid using an existing survey, if it was designed for a different purpose, population, or circumstance. Although they may serve as a point of departure, surveys usually have aims or situational factors that are specific to each application.
3. In designing questionnaires or interviews, one often finds it helpful to sit down with a group of potential respondents and explore what is meaningful or important to them, and how best to phrase questions to reflect their attitudes or opinions.
4. Field test instruments to spot ambiguous or redundant items and to arrive at a format leading to ease of data tabulation and analysis.
5. Examine the merits of using machine-scored answer sheets to facilitate tabulation and analysis.
6. As often as possible, use structured questions as opposed to unstructured and open-ended ones for uniformity of results and ease of analysis.
7. Do not ask questions out of idle curiosity–this approach will overtax the respondents. Avoid questions that are redundant or have obvious answers.
8. Avoid loaded or biased questions (usually by involving others in the wording process and by field testing) and be watchful of biased sampling.
9. Keep the final product as brief, simple, clear, and straightforward as possible. Complex instruments, while justified under special circumstances, generally will be resisted or rejected by most respondents, and cloud the analysis of the data.
10. Brainstorm the analysis needs to insure the clarity and comprehensiveness of the instrument.
11. Consider the necessary and sufficient characteristics of the respondent that must be collected at the time the survey is administered and on which the data analysis will be based: e.g., name, sex, address, age, race, occupation, education, and related background, life-history, and demographic factors. Be realistic and keep such

characteristics to an absolute minimum, as they add to the length of the survey, the
complexity of the analysis, and often invade the privacy of the respondent. Anonymous surveys are most common. Other information should be requested only if it
is clearly needed. Often, a review of the literature will verify whether or no
particular characteristics will yield useful information. Also, the more categorie
generated by the analysis matrix, the smaller will be the number of cases in any single
cell; this instance may necessitate a larger sample size.

12. Finally, imagine various outcomes that might result from the survey, including
surprising ones. This step helps to anticipate gaps or shortcomings in the approach
and may indicate the need for more background information about the respondents
or additional questions. Nevertheless, this first step is not to open a floodgate;
instead, it is aimed at catching crucial oversights that would otherwise subtract from
the usefulness of the findings.

Types of Surveys

1. *Survey of Records.* These sources of data differ from those in the other survey types
because they are nonreactive; i.e., they do not involve a direct response from people.
Although this circumstance can be an advantage to the objectivity of the information,
there are other problems with how and why records are kept that can offset this:

Advantages	Disadvantages
a. Records are nonreactive.	a. May involve confidential restrictions.
b. They are inexpensive.	b. Are often incomplete, inaccurate, and out-of-date.
c. Records often allow historical comparisons and trend analysis.	c. Changing rules for keeping records often makes year-to-year comparisons invalid.
d. If records are accurate and up-to-date, they provide an excellent baseline for comparisons.	d. Can be misleading unless knowledgeable person can explain how the records were compiled.
	e. Purpose of records usually is unrelated to purpose of surveys.
	f. Factual data only (no input on values or attitudes) are present.

2. *Mailed Questionnaires.* This appearance is the most commonly used survey method
and often the most sterile or misleading, unless the following disadvantages are
heeded and offset:

Advantages	Disadvantages
a. Are inexpensive.	a. Low response rate can occur, especially with less educated and older addressees inviting a nonrepresentative return.
b. Are wide-ranging.	
c. Can be well designed, simple and clear.	b. No assurance the questions were understood.
d. Are self-administering.	
e. Can be made anonymous.	c. No assurance addressee actually was the one who answered.

Note: Questionnaires should be carefully field tested to eliminate ambiguous or biased items and to improve format, both for ease of understanding and facility in analyzing results. Response rates can be improved with stamped return envelopes, follow-up reminders, advance contacts and publicity campaign, personalized letters of transmittal and, when a handful of questions with simple answers is sufficient, a preprinted return postcard can serve as the instrument.

3. *Telephone Surveys.* These are widely used in place of face-to-face interviews by professional pollsters for reasons under "advantages." In general, they tend to achieve similar results.

Advantages	Disadvantages
a. Is less costly than face-to-face interviews.	a. Unlisted telephones (as high as 25%; schools, however, tend to have telephone numbers available).
b. Can be conducted daytime or evenings.	b. Not everyone has a phone, particularly lower income homes.
c. Permits unlimited callbacks.	c. Can be viewed as intrusive into home privacy and can be confused with a disguised sales pitch.
d. Respondent is at ease in own home and tends to be more candid.	
e. Extended geographical coverage and WATS line availability makes feasible state or national samples, if appropriate.	d. Rules out many face-to-face advantages, including visual impressions of home environment.

4. *Group Interview.* Although the "interview" is normally a one-to-one relationship, for many purposes interviewing in groups is appropriate. Not only does it save time, but, if the behavior one is trying to understand takes place in a group interaction setting, the group interview will yield a better picture of this phenomenon.

Advantages	Disadvantages
a. Is more efficient and economical than one-to-one interviews.	a. May intimidate and suppress individual differences.
b. Results reflect group behavior and consensus.	b. Fosters conformity.
c. Reveals group interaction patterns.	c. Intensifies group loyalties and can rigidly polarize opinions.
d. As with brainstorming, can stimulate productivity of others.	d. Is vulnerable to manipulation by an influential and skillful member.

5. *Individual Interviews.* This approach is the conventional method of collecting data face-to-face. It not only can be helpful as the principal method, but also can be especially useful to explore a problem area about which insufficient information exists–for example, as a pilot study on which to base a more extensive questionnaire.

Advantages	Disadvantages
a. Is personalized.	a. Is expensive and time-consuming.
b. Permits in-depth, free responses.	b. May intimidate or annoy respondents with a racial, ethnic, or socio-economic background different from the interviewer.
c. Is flexible and adaptable.	
d. Allows impressions of respondent's gestures, tone of voice, home environment, etc.	c. Is open to overt manipulation or the subtle biases of the interviewer.
	d. Is vulnerable to personality conflicts.
	e. Requires skilled and trained interviewers.
	f. May be difficult to summarize findings.

Sampling Consideration

Whenever practical, especially if a survey touches on controversial matters or will lead to an important decision or conclusion, it is well to include all possible respondents. Otherwise, when this use of a total group is not feasible or sufficiently consequential, sampling is both appropriate and scientifically sound, as long as certain established procedures are followed. The key condition is that the sample must represent, in all important respects, the parent population. Many excellent references are available on the subject of sampling, for when there are a variety of approaches. In practice, the most common technique is to sample at random, such that each respondent in a population of respondents has an equal chance of being selected. There are two principal variations of this technique: (1) *simple random sampling:* e.g., a lottery-like drawing, taking every nth name in an alphabetical listing, or going to a table of random numbers; and (2) *stratified random sampling:* where various "strata" are designated, such as sex, age, socio-economic levels, or grade levels in school, and predetermined proportions of respondents are then randomly selected from each stratum.

REFERENCES

Borg, W. R., & Gall, M. D. (1989). *Educational research: An introduction* (5th ed.). White Plains, NY: Longman.

Borg, W. R., Gall J. P., & Gall, M. D. (1993). *Applying educational research: An introduction* (3rd ed.). New York: Longman. (See Chapters 9 and 10.)

Campbell, A. A., & Katona, G. (1953). The sample survey: A technique for social science research. In L. Festinger and D. Katz (Eds.). *Research methods in the behavioral sciences* (pp. 15-55). New York: Dryden Press.

Webb, E. J., Campbell, D. T., Schwartz, R. D., & Sechrest, L. (1966). *Unobtrusive measures: Nonreactive research in the social sciences.* Chicago, IL: Rand McNally. (See especially Chapter 1.)

Weiss, C. H. (1975). Interviewing in evaluation research. In E. L. Struening and M. Guttentag (Eds.). *Handbook of evaluation research* (Vol. 1) (pp. 355-395). Beverly Hills, CA: Sage Publications.

Worthen, B. R., & Sanders, J. R. (1987). *Educational evaluation: Alternative approaches and practical guidelines.* White Plains, NY: Longman.

THE MAILED QUESTIONNAIRE[1, 2]

1. This is the single most widely used technique in education. It requires a careful, clear statement of the problem underlying the questionnaire. Otherwise, ambiguity and misinterpretation will invalidate the findings.

2. Constructing the questionnaire:
    a. Questionnaires tend to be planned poorly and overdone. To overcome "consumer resistance," they must be expertly designed and skillfully introduced and justified.
    b. State the reason for the questionnaire and explain how the information will be analyzed. Avoid wordiness and ambiguity.
    c. Objectivity is important. Lengthy subjective, open-ended answers are difficult for the respondent to write and for the investigator to evaluate. If the possible categories of responses can be anticipated, these should be offered as alternatives to an objective question. For example:

    Do you have a systematic program for identifying
    gifted children in your school? YES ☐ NO ☐

    If yes, what means of identification do you use?
    ☐ a. Group intelligence test
    ☐ b. Individual intelligence test
    ☐ c. Achievement battery
    ☐ d. Aptitude battery
    ☐ e. Teacher ratings
    ☐ f. Other (specify) ————————————————

    d. One of the best ways of developing good objective questions is to administer an open-ended form of the question to a small sample of subjects representative of the population in which you are interested. These more lengthy answers provide the data from which objective-type answers are derived. (Note: if your topic does not lend itself to this treatment, perhaps you should consider the interview which is far more adaptable to open-ended questions.)
    e. Questions should be asked in such a way that they minimize the evaluation task, eliminating unnecessary processing steps and interpretation problems.
    f. Avoid questions that are threatening to the respondents, exposing them to criticism or placing them in an awkward position. (Sometimes counteracted by assurances of "anonymity.")

---

[1]Adapted from Borg, W. R. (1963). *Educational research* (pp. 204-221). New York: David McKay. By permission. [See also, Borg, W. R., & Gall, M. D. (1989). *Educational research: An introduction* (5th ed.) (pp. 415-469). White Plains, NY: Longman.]
[2]See also: Oppenheim, A. N. (1966). *Questionnaire design and attitude measurement.* New York: Basic Books, Inc.

    g. Avoid questions which evoke predictable response biases and obscure objective information.

    h. Avoid leading questions.

    i. Pretest the questionnaire (see page 143).

3.   The letter of transmittal (see pages 143-144).

4.   The follow-up letter. A few days after the deadline established in the letter of transmittal, a follow-up letter should be sent to the nonrespondents. It should assume the tone that the respondent had intended to return the questionnaire but had perhaps overlooked doing so. It should reaffirm the importance of the study and the value of the individual's contribution to this important study. The Research Division of the National Education Association reports the following results in the return rates of questionnaires:

5.   Nonresponding subjects—implications. In any questionnaire survey there will always be a percentage of nonresponding subjects, as evidenced in the above graph published by the NEA Research Division. The question must be asked, "How would the results have been changed if all subjects had returned the questionnaire?" Ordinarily, percentages under 20% can be reasonably ignored. Percentages over 20%, however, raise increasingly serious questions about the "hold-outs" and what they are withholding. For example, a common sampling bias arises when persons having a good program are more likely to respond than persons having a poor program. An effective correction technique is to select randomly a small sample of the nonrespondents and personally interview them to obtain the missing information. This will reveal any common trend among the nonrespondents that might prove important. The disadvantage of this technique is obvious—it is likely to be time-consuming, inconvenient, and expensive.

6.   The effect of "anonymity." In order to encourage honest and frank answers, some surveys are designed to be returned anonymously. This is more likely to occur where the survey is getting at highly personal or controversial information. The disadvantage is that it usually conceals certain information about the respondent that might be of interest in the analysis, (e.g., sex, age, geographic location, organization, and position). Studies of common questionnaires returned either anonymously or with identification indicate that there is very little difference on most items. Adults tend to answer questions the same in either case.[1]

[1]Adapted from Borg, W. R. (1963). *Educational research* (pp. 204-221). New York: David McKay. By permission.

PRETESTING A QUESTIONNAIRE[1]

1. Select a sample of individuals who are representative of the population toward which the questionnaire is eventually intended.

2. Provide space on the trial questionnaire for the respondents to make reactions and suggested changes.

3. Administer the pretest under conditions comparable to those anticipated in the final study.

4. Check the percent of responses as an estimate of what will occur in the final run; then, examine the returned trial questionnaires for trouble signs—items left blank or yielding no useful information, misinterpretations, and ambiguities. Check the comments for similar indications.

5. Analyze the results to assess the effectiveness of the trial questionnaire to yield the information desired.

6. Make appropriate additions, deletions, and modifications to the questionnaire. (For examples, if answers to a particular question show sharp disagreements or raise further questions, additional clarifying questions may be necessary.)

7. Overall reaction of subjects to the questionnaires—what did they like, dislike, or want modified?

LETTER OF TRANSMITTAL[2]

1. Purpose: to elicit a maximum number of *returned* questionnaires.

2. General characteristics: a clear, brief, yet adequate statement of the purpose and value of the questionnaire.

3. Effectiveness:
   a. It must provide good reason for subjects to respond. It should involve them in a constructive and appealing way. Their sense of professional responsibility, intellectual curiosity, and personal worth, are typical of response appeals.
   b. It should establish a reasonable, but firm, return date.
   c. An offer to send respondent a report of the findings is often effective, though it carries with it the ethical responsibility to honor such a pledge.
   d. If possible, use a letterhead and a signature that will lend prestige and official status to the letter of transmittal.

[1,2]Adapted from Borg, W. R. (1963). *Educational research* (pp. 204-221). New York: David McKay. By permission. [See also, Borg, W. R., & Gall, M. D. (1989). *Educational research: An introduction* (5th ed.) (pp. 436-438). White Plains, NY: Longman.]

(Sample letter of Transmittal)[1]

WESTERN STATE UNIVERSITY
Anytown, California

College of Education
I. V. Tower, Dean

June 11, 1995

Mr. John A. Ford
Superintendent of Schools
Centercity, California

Dear Sir:

The attached questionnaire concerned with procedures used in selecting elementary school principals is part of a statewide study being carried on cooperatively by the State Department of Public Instruction and Western State University. This project is concerned specifically with determining the present status of principal selection in our state. The results of this study will help to provide preliminary criteria to be used for developing better selection procedures and for improving the administrator training program at Western State University.

We are particularly desirous of obtaining your responses because your experience in principal selection will contribute significantly toward solving some of the problems we face in this important area of education. The enclosed questionnaire has been tested with a sampling of school administrators, and we have revised it in order to make it possible for us to obtain all necessary data while requiring a minimum of your time. The average time required for administrators trying out the questionnaire was 9½ minutes.

It will be appreciated if you will complete the questionnaire prior to February 20 and return it in the stamped, special delivery envelope enclosed. Other phases of this research cannot be carried out until we complete analysis of the questionnaire data. We would welcome any comments that you may have concerning any aspect of principal selection not covered in the questionnaire. We will be pleased to send you a summary of questionnaire results if you desire. Thank you for your cooperation.

Sincerely yours,

I. V. Tower, Dean

Enc.
iv:ld

---

[1]Adapted from Borg, W. R. (1963). *Educational research* (pp. 214-215). New York: David McKay. By permission. [See also, Borg, W. R., & Gall, M. D. (1989). *Educational research: An introduction* (5th ed.) (p. 439). White Plains, NY: Longman.]

THE RESEARCH INTERVIEW[1]

1. *Advantages* (over questionnaire):
   a. Permits greater depth.
   b. Permits probing to obtain more complete data.
   c. Makes it possible to establish and maintain rapport with respondent or at least determine when rapport has not been established.
   d. Provides a means of checking and assuring the effectiveness of communication between the respondent and the interviewer.

2. *Disadvantages:*
   Interviews are costly, time-consuming, and inconvenient. If the researcher takes advantage of the interview's adaptability the problem of subjectivity and personal bias can be introduced. Eagerness of the respondent to please the interviewer, a vague antagonism that sometimes arises between the interviewer and the respondent, and the tendency of the interviewer to seek out answers that support preconceived notions all complicate this method. The thorough training required of the interviewer to offset these disadvantages becomes an additional burden, increasing the cost and time factors.

3. *Interview structure (Reliability increases with objectivity):*
   a. Unstructured interviews—The client-centered counseling technique of Carl Rogers illustrates the unstructured approach, giving the respondents broad freedom to express themselves in their own way and in their own time. The interviewer may have a general or specific objective which can best be met without imposing a structure on the respondent. Usually the information involved is of a highly personal and potentially threatening nature. Of the three interview structures, this one is the most vulnerable to subjective bias or errors of inexperience.
   b. Semistructured interviews—These are built around a core of structured questions from which the interviewer branches off to explore in depth. Again, accurate and complete information is desired with the additional opportunity to probe for underlying factors or relationships which are too complex or elusive to encompass in more straight-forward questions. Semistructured interviews require more training and skill both to probe at significant points and to avoid biasing tendencies.
   c. Structured interviews—The interviewer follows a well-defined structure resembling the format of an objective questionnaire, allowing clarification and elaboration within narrow limits. These tend to be factually oriented, aimed at specific information, and relatively brief. Structured interviews are suitable when accurate and complete information from all respondents is important and when the type of information sought fits readily into a structured inquiry.

4. *Planning an interview study:*
   a. Define the purpose of the study—its background, theoretical basis, general goals, possible applications of results, and reasons for using the interview method.
   b. Translate the general goals into *detailed* and *specific objectives* which can be fitted to the particular interview pattern you plan to follow, constructing questions yielding useful information.
   c. Develop a tentative guide to be used during the interview, exploiting the advantages of the interview technique.

---

[1]Adapted from Borg, W. R. (1963). *Educational research* (pp. 221-233). New York: David McKay. By permission. [See also, Borg, W. R., & Gall, M. D. (1989). *Educational research: An introduction* (5th ed.) (pp. 446-450). White Plains, NY: Longman.]

    d.   Develop a satisfactory method of coding and/or recording responses. Generally, responses can be pre-categorized in a pilot study to anticipate the most frequent response patterns. Only responses falling outside these general categories would need to be written out. Tape recording of the interview may offer advantages, unless the nature of the interview is highly personal and produces guarded response. A generally poor technique is a written summary of information recorded during or following the interview. Because of the pace of an interview, the act of writing either slows the interview unnecessarily or causes the interviewer to be selective in the kind and amount of information recorded, at the risk of introducing bias.

5.   *Framing questions for the interview:*
    a.   Questions must be framed in language that insures effective communication between the interviewer and the respondent. Omit all ambiguous vocabulary.
    b.   Make certain respondent appreciates the purpose of each question asked. Avoid arousing any suspicion or resistance.
    c.   Ascertain whether the population from which the respondents have been selected actually has the information sought by the interview and that the questions permit the reasonable recovery of this information.
    d.   Avoid leading questions (questions which suggest a desirable or preferred answer).
    e.   Insure that the frame of reference surrounding each question is clear so that each respondent hears the question in the same way, avoiding misinterpretation.
    f.   Pretest the interview in a pilot study to eliminate weaknesses and experiment with alternative items or techniques.

6.   *Overall fault of questionnaire/interview techniques:* Their retrospective nature which introduces memory errors and contamination because of intervening events and biasing factors which increase with time. These should be checked out by comparing questionnaire/interview results against direct observations.[1]

GUIDELINES FOR INTERVIEWS AND INTERVIEW SCHEDULES[2]

1.   *Direct or Indirect?*—Most data-collection methods in behavioral research are direct or moderately indirect. Highly indirect means are rarely used. The direct approach is more efficient and effective for the purposes. The indirect approach is more useful where anxiety of conformity pressures are apt to conceal true response tendencies.

2.   Interview techniques are especially appropriate for children.

3.   Main shortcoming of the interview technique: Time-consuming and expensive.

4.   Three main purposes of the interview:
    a.   An exploratory device to help identify variables and relations, to suggest hypotheses, and to guide other phases of the research.
    b.   A main instrument in research.
    c.   A supplement to other methods: To follow up unexpected results, to validate other methods, and to go deeper into the motivations of respondents and their reasons for responding as they do.

---

[1]Adapted from Borg, W. R. (1963). *Educational research* (pp. 221-233). New York: David McKay. By permission. [See also, Borg, W. R., & Gall, M. D. (1989). *Educational research: An introduction* (5th ed.) (pp. 451-460). White Plains, NY: Longman.]
[2]Adapted from Kerlinger, F. N. (1986). *Foundations of behavioral research* (3rd ed.). New York: Holt Rinehart, and Winston.

5. Usefulness of the interview depends upon the following considerations:
    a. Can data for the research be obtained in an easier or better way? In other words, how suitable is the interview technique for any given problem and relevant information required.
    b. To insure reliability, interviewers must be trained and questions must be pretested and revised to eliminate ambiguities and inadequate wording.
    c. To insure validity, it is essential to eliminate interviewer bias; questions must be tested for hidden biases.

6. *Structured or Unstructured?* (standardized or unstandardized)—which format to use depends upon the nature of the problem. Where straightforward, factual information is involved, a structured approach is most efficient. Where highly complex or elusive questions are being raised, the unstructured approach is more fruitful.

7. Three types of schedule items:
    a. Fixed-alternative (closed) items. E.g., opinion polls (Do you, or don't you...?) *Advantages:* greater uniformity and reliability; easy to code responses and manipulate data. *Disadvantages:* superficial, artificial; furthermore, its forced-choice nature may irritate or threaten respondents.
    b. Open-ended items. *Advantages:* Gives respondent a frame-of-reference with which to react, without placing any constraint on the reaction. Allows flexibility, depth, clarification, and probing. Enables interviewer to assess respondent's degree of sophistication and knowledge, encourages cooperation and establishment of rapport. Allows unexpected responses which may reveal significant information not anticipated by the research design. *Disadvantages:* More time-consuming, more interviewer skill required, more subject to biasing influences, more difficult to record responses accurately and sufficiently.
    c. Scale items (respondents indicate their answer as a position along some scale). *Advantages:* Objectivity; uniformity; reliability; easier to code responses and manipulate data; also, adds dimension of degree not reflected in the fixed-alternative item. *Disadvantages:* Still tends to be somewhat artificial; the scale positions may irritate respondents. Also, scales are subject to the "over-rater set" and the "under-rater set"—the respondents who are unrealistically but consistently biased in being favorably or unfavorably disposed in their ratings.

8. Criteria for question-writing:
    a. Is the question related to the research problem and objective?
    b. Is the type of question the right and appropriate one?
    c. Is the item clear and unambiguous?
    d. Is the question in any way leading?
    e. Does the question demand knowledge and information that the respondent does not have?
    f. Does the question demand personal or sensitive information that the respondent may resist?
    g. Is the question loaded with social desirability?

9. The self-administered instrument (e.g., mailed questionnaire):
    a. *Advantages:*
        (1) When using well-constructed and pretested closed-type items, allows greater uniformity of response and greater reliability.
        (2) Allows anonymity (if desired), encouraging frankness and honesty if highly personal or threatening information is involved.

(3) Can be distributed to a large number of persons with relative ease; e.g., it can be mailed.
(4) Economical.
b. *Disadvantages:* (These tend to outweigh the advantages.)
(1) Low percentage or returns, raising serious questions about the nature of the nonrespondents and sampling bias.
(2) Does not insure the uniformity of interpretation of each question.
(3) If closed-type items are used, see item 7a, previous page.
(4) If open-ended items are used, respondent may object to writing out answers and resistances may be created that reduce the number of participants in the sample; or may give a superficial and misleading answer to save time and vent annoyance.[1]

ATTITUDE SCALING[2]

General—All *methods of observation* are inferential, varying in the degree of objectivity they possess. Objective methods of observation prescribe the rules for the assignment of the same numerals to a given object by all raters or judges. In variance terms, observer variance is at a minimum.

A *scale*, essentially, is a measuring device allowing the assignment of symbols or numbers to individuals, or their behaviors, by rule. Such an assignment indicates the individual's possession of a corresponding amount of whatever the scale is claimed to measure.

TYPES OF ATTITUDE SCALES

Likert-type or Summated Rating Scales—These contain a set of items, all of which are considered approximately equal in attitude or value loading. The subject responds with varying *degrees of intensity* on a scale ranging between extremes such as agree-disagree, like-dislike or accept-reject. The scores of the position responses for each of the separate scales are summed, or summed and averaged, to yield an individual's attitude score.

Summated rating scales seem to be the most useful in behavioral research. They are easier to develop and yield about the same information as the more laboriously constructed equal-appearing interval scale. The main advantage of a summated scale lies in the greater variance obtained. The disadvantage, as with all scales, is the vulnerability of this variance to biasing response sets (e.g., the over-rater or the under-rater. See page 90).

1.	Capital punishment is a necessary penalty	SA	A	U	D	SD*
2.	Most pupils can handle an independent study program		SA	A	D	SD
3.	"School". . . . . . . Like __:__:__:__:__:__:__ Dislike**					

* *Strongly Agree — Agree — Undecided — Disagree — Strongly Disagree*
The scale can be expanded to seven, or more, positions, although five positions are most common. Item 2 illustrates a forced choice achieved by eliminating the Undecided category.
** Adapted from the semantic differential technique. See pages 152-153.

[1]Adapted from Kerlinger, F. N. (1986). *Foundations of behavioral research* (3rd ed.). New York: Holt Rinehart, and Winston.
[2]The third type of scale (Guttman or Cumulative) is also appropriate for cognitive scaling (measuring aptitudes or achievement).

Thurstone-type or Equal-appearing Interval Scales—These not only place the individual somewhere along an agreement continuum for a given attitude but also scale the attitude items themselves. Each item is assigned a *scale value* indicating the strength of attitude for an agreement response to the item. The items in the scale are assumed to be differentially ordered, rather than equal. It is more difficult to construct than the summated scale and yields similar results.

1. This district treats its teachers better than any other district	(10.2)★★★
2. Doing it all over again, I'd still teach for this district.	(8.5)
3. The teachers and the district take equal advantage of each other	(5.0)
4. If you don't have "pull" around here, you're dead.	(2.3)

★★★This is the scaled value for the item. The person taking this test simply checks the items with which they agree; the points corresponding to those items are totaled and then divided by the number of answered items to yield an average scaled value.

Steps in the construction of an equal-appearing interval scale:
a. Collect a series of short, concise statements reflecting attitudes of all shades toward a particular object or event.
b. Have a group of judges, working individually, sort these statements into a series of eleven piles, *A* through *K*, according to their relative degree of favorableness to unfavorableness.
c. For each item, plot the distribution of scaled values (1-11) assigned by the various judges, locating the *median* of this distribution (its *scaled value*).
d. Eliminate items whose Q value (semi-interquartile range, see page 164) is excessively large, indicating a major discrepancy among the judges.
e. Check for irrelevance by presenting the remaining items to a group of respondents, asking them to mark those statements with which they agreed. Items with poor internal consistency, statistically, are then eliminated.
f. Select from those items remaining the statements whose scale values are equally spaced along the attitude continuum ("equal-appearing interval").

Guttman-type or Cumulative Scales—These consist of a relatively small set of homogeneous items that are supposedly unidimensional, measuring one, and only one, attribute. Such scales get their name from the cumulative relation between items and the total scores of individuals. Items can be ordered in difficulty, complexity, or value-loading (from low to high) so that to answer correctly or approve the last implies success or approval on all the preceding ones; or, to miss or disapprove a middle item implies failure or disapproval on all the subsequent items. When the scale is cumulative and we know a subject's total score, we can predict answering patterns.

Cumulative scales have limited application. They are appropriate where a single clear-cut attribute or stimulus dimension is involved. A well-constructed scale may yield reliable measures of a number of psychological variables: Cognitive complexity, tolerance, conformity, group identification, acceptance of authority, or permissiveness. Furthermore, these scales may be particularly useful with children because of their simplicity and brevity. They also may be adapted as a rating device for an observer rather than a subject.

I want to ask you some questions about a person known to have been a convicted criminal and to have served time in a state penitentiary.*
1. Would you object to such a person living in your community?
2. Would you object to the person working where you are employed?
3. Would you object to inviting the person into your home socially?
4. Would you object to the person marrying a member of your family?

*Answering "Yes" to item 1 predicts "Yes" answers to items 2, 3, and 4; a "No" answer to item 4 predicts "No" answers to items 3, 2, and 1; a "No" answer to item 1 but "Yes" to item 2 predicts "Yes" answers for items 3 and 4.

1. What is 3 x 5?	The four multiplication problems at the left illus-
2. What is 7 x 9?	trate achievement items ordered according to diffi-
3. What is 4 x 23?	culty or complexity level with similar implications
4. What is 15% of 160?	if an item is passed or failed.

REFERENCES

For a comprehensive reference with over 200 exhibits, see : Shaw, M. E., & Wright, J. M. (1967). *Scales for the measurement of attitudes*. New York: McGraw-Hill.
For a guide to the construction of attitude scales, see: Edwards, A. L. (1957). *Techniques of attitude scale construction*. New York: Appleton-Century-Crofts.

GRAPHIC RATING SCALES

One of the most commonly used measures in the behavioral sciences and in business and industry has been the graphic rating scale that typically consists of four to nine steps representing intensity or degree to which certain personal qualities or characteristics have been demonstrated by the ratee. It is desirable that the characteristic being evaluated be stated in behavioral or operational terms whenever possible. Also important is that the various steps reflecting the intensity or amount of the characteristic either be stated operationally or be expressed in terms of words that reflect psychologically equal distances along the scale. An example of a graphic rating scale would be the following:

Place a mark at the appropriate point on the scale that most nearly, accurately reveals the overall competence of this person in his or her current job.

Unsatisfactory–	Poor–shows	Satisfactory–	Superior–meets	Outstanding–
Fails to meet	inconsistency	meets most	all requirements	consistently
even the minimum	in performance;	requirements	well virtually	exceeds all
requirements	needs to improve	most of the time	all of the time	expectations

The expressions of *unsatisfactory, poor, satisfactory, superior,* and *outstanding* represent what are known as response anchors for the rating scale. There is the obvious concern in a quantitative analysis of the data generated from the assignment of values of 1, 2, 3, 4, or 5 to the response anchors whether the distances are equal from one response anchor to another in a psychological sense. Scaling techniques are available which permit an empirical determination of anchors that constitute a scale of approximately equal ntervals of psychological intensity. In the table below, 20 response anchors have been cited that have been subjected to sophisticated scaling analyses. In this table, response anchors are indicated which are psychologically equidistant for scales with five-, six-, or seven-points or steps. These recommended response anchors have been derived from a consensus of the results of five studies as reported in a 1989 article by Schriesheim and Novelli.

It should be pointed out that despite the approximate equality of psychological distances from one response anchor to another, the same previously indicated rating errors associated with the halo effect, central tendency, leniency, and severity still exist. It is advisable to rate all individuals in a group on one characteristic at a time.

AVERAGE SCALE VALUES FOR 20 FREQUENCY EXPRESSIONS DERIVED FROM FIVE MAGNITUDE ESTIMATION STUDIES ALONG WITH RECOMMENDED RESPONSE ANCHOR EXPRESSIONS FOR 5-, 6-, AND 7-POINT RATING SCALES

Response Anchor	Mean Scale Value	Anchors for Scales With		
		5 points	6 points	7 points
Always	100.00	X	X	X
Constantly	92.67			
Continually	88.82			
Frequently if not always	79.07		X	X
Very often	74.27	X		
Quite often	68.01			X
Often	59.98		X	
Rather frequently	59.48			
Fairly many times	53.45	X		X
Sometimes	33.38		X	X
About as often as not	28.88			
Now and then	28.42			
Occasionally	26.70	X		
Once in a while	18.15		X	
Not very often	15.30			X
Not often	14.32			
Seldom	9.16			
Not at all	.50			
Never	.38			
None of the time	.11	X	X	X

Reproduced with permission from an article by Schriesheim, C. A., & Novelli, L. Jr. (1989). A comparative test of the interval-scale properties of magnitude estimation and case III scaling and recommendations for equal-interval frequency response anchors. *Educational and Psychological Measurement, 49,* 70.

THE SEMANTIC DIFFERENTIAL

The semantic differential is a method for measuring the meaning of concepts. In practice, it has had two applications: (1) To measure objectively the *semantic properties* of words and concepts in a tri-dimensional semantic space; and, more commonly and simply, (2) as an *attitude scale*, restricting its focus to the *affective domain* (see page 229) on the *evaluative dimension* (see below).

A semantic differential scale has three elements: (1) The *concept* to be evaluated in terms of its semantic or attitudinal properties, (2) the *polar adjective pair* anchoring the scale, and (3) a series of *undefined scale positions* which, for practical purposes, is not less than five or more than nine steps, with seven steps as the optimal number in the experience of Osgood, its originator.

Osgood, et al.,[1] wanted a method of objectively measuring the semantic properties of words and concepts and factor analyzed 76 pairs of polar adjectives (opposite in meaning). They found three principal factors accounting for most of the semantic loadings:

1. Evaluative (e.g., "good-bad")
2. Potency (e.g., "hard-soft")
3. Activity (e.g., "fast-slow")

Pairs of these polar adjectives are then selected according to the purposes of the research and then arranged at opposite ends of a series of seven-point scales. The concept to be rated is then presented at the top of the combined scale. For example:

School

good	___	: ___	: ___	: ___	: ___	: ___	bad
slow	___	: ___	: ___	: ___	: ___	: ___	fast
large	___	: ___	: ___	: ___	: ___	: ___	small
ugly	___	: ___	: ___	: ___	: ___	: ___	beautiful
active	___	: ___	: ___	: ___	: ___	: ___	passive
light	___	: ___	: ___	: ___	: ___	: ___	heavy
clean	___	: ___	: ___	: ___	: ___	: ___	dirty
weak	___	: ___	: ___	: ___	: ___	: ___	strong
sharp	___	: ___	: ___	: ___	: ___	: ___	dull
delicate	___	: ___	: ___	: ___	: ___	: ___	rugged
dark	___	: ___	: ___	: ___	: ___	: ___	bright
rounded	___	: ___	: ___	: ___	: ___	: ___	angular

The subjects are instructed to rate the concept "school" according to how they perceive it or feel toward it at the moment by placing an "X" somewhere along each of the seven point scales anchored by the polar adjective pairs. In the above example, the resulting twelve individual scale responses can be converted to numerical quantities (scale positions 1-negative, weak, inactive—through 7-positive, strong, active) and treated statistically.

[1]Osgood, C. E., Suci, G. J., & Tannenbaum, P. H. (1957). *The measurement of meaning*. Urbana, IL: University of Illinois Press.

Steps in scale construction:
1. Select the concepts or other stimuli to be rated. These should be relevant to the research problem and sensitive to differences or similarities among the comparison groups.
2. Select the polar adjective pairs with which to anchor the various scales. Where attitudes are concerned, adjective pairs with high evaluative loadings are often appropriate, although the selection of polar adjectives on simply their "face value" for a given situation is acceptable. (See page 154 for sample lists of polar adjective pairs.) The *relevance* of adjective pairs to evaluate particular concepts can only be verified empirically. Apparently "irrelevant" pairs can yield significant information and apparently "relevant" pairs can prove disappointing.
3. Arrange the polar adjective pairs so that the favorable, potent, or active end of the scale is randomly placed in a right or left position to avoid position habits in the response pattern.

Analysis and evaluation of scaled data:
The semantic differential yields a large amount of data with a minimum of effort. By converting the scale positions to numerical values, various statistical assessments can be made:

good   7 : 6 : 5 : 4 : 3 : 2 : 1   bad

In variance terms, there are three main sources of variance: *concepts, scales,* and *subjects.* Thus, the score can be analyzed for differences between concepts, between scales, between subjects, or any combination thereof. Some data analysis options are:
1. Compute a *t* test or a Median test of the significance of a difference between group means or medians for individual scales or for all scales summed.
2. *Profile analysis,* using the sign test. By plotting the profiles of mean (or median) response patterns between comparison groups down a set of scales, similarities or differences in the profiles can be observed. If there are consistently greater means for one group than for another (such that their profiles tend to stand apart), the statistical probability of such a consistent difference can be tested by referring to a Binomial Probability Table. An example of this analysis, along with a binomial probability table, appears on page 155.

3. *Distance-cluster analysis of semantic space.* Given Osgood's three axes of semantic space (evaluative, potency, activity), it is possible to derive a measure of distance along each axis for each concept. The D statistic used for this purpose, along with its application, is described by Osgood, Suci, and Tannenbaum in their book, THE MEASUREMENT OF MEANING (see footnote, opposite page).

4. For additional information on analysis techniques see, Kerlinger, F. N. (1965). *Foundations of behavioral research* (pp. 564-580). New York: Holt, Rinehart, & Winston; Nunnally, J. C. (1962). The Analysis of Profile Data, *Psychological Bulletin, 59,* 311-319; and Snider, J. G., & Osgood, C. E. (Eds.). (1969). *Semantic differential technique.* Chicago, IL: Aldine.

Note: a principal limitation inherent in this or any other scale which depends on a subjective judgment s *interpretation:* even though statistically significant differences between groups can be established, it is difficult to pin down either the theoretical or utilitarian meaning of this difference.

POLAR ADJECTIVE PAIRS

Excerpts from Osgood's Factor Analyzed List [1,2]

Other Suggested Listings [4]

Evaluative		Factor Loading: Evaluative	Potency	Activity
1. good	bad	1.00	.00	.00
2. complete	incomplete	.32	.05	.05
3. sociable	unsociable	.42	−.19	.18
4. kind	cruel	.52	−.28	.00
5. clean	dirty	.45	−.26	.02
6. light	dark	.38	−.30	.01
7. graceful	awkward	.38	−.23	.05
8. pleasurable	painful	.37	−.25	.07
9. beautiful	ugly	.52	−.29	−.02
10. successful	unsuccessful	.51	.08	.29
11. important	unimportant	.38	.04	.31
12. true	false	.50	−.03	.01
13. positive	negative	.48	.00	.07
14. wise	foolish	.57	.06	.11
15. interesting	boring	.40	−.09	.22
Potency				
16. hard	soft	−.24	.97	.00
17. strong	weak	.30	.40	.10
18. severe	lenient	−.25	.43	.04
19. constrained	free	−.16	.21	−.04
20. constricted	spacious	−.16	.26	.04
21. heavy	light	−.20	.48	−.02
22. serious	humorous	.01	.23	.09
23. large	small	.09	.21	−.05
24. masculine	feminine	−.14	.47	.03
Activity				
25. active	passive	.17	.12	.98
26. excitable	calm	−.15	.03	.26
27. hot	cold	.12	.09	.26
28. fast	slow	.01	.26	.35
29. complex	simple	.17	.05	.25

Understandability [3]

predictable-unpredictable
understandable-mysterious
familiar-strange
simple-complicated
clear-confusing

Miscellaneous
(situational)

traditional-progressive
permissive-restrictive
authoritarian-democratic
structured-unstructured
formal-informal
accepting-rejecting
flexible-rigid
original-stereotyped
systematic-unsystematic
responsible-irresponsible
easy-difficult
happy-sad
empty-full
work-fun
open-closed
rich-poor
fresh-stale
near-far
relaxed-tense
genuine-false
deep-shallow
thick-thin
tender-tough
bright-dull
approach-avoid
pleasure-pain

[1] Osgood, C. E., Suci, G. J., & Tannenbaum, P. H. (1957). *The measurement of meaning.* Urbana, IL: University of Illinois Press.
[2] Jenkins J. J., Russell, W. A., & Suci, G. J. (1958). An atlas of semantic profiles for 360 words. *The American Journal of Psychology, 71,* 688-699.
[3] Nunnally, J. C. (1961). *Popular conceptions of mental health* (Chapter 4). New York: Holt, Rinehart, and Winston.
[4] Snider, J. G., & Osgood, C. E. (Eds.) (1969). *Semantic differential technique.* Chicago, IL: Aldine.

PROFILE COMPARISON OF MEAN RESPONSES OF EIGHTH GRADE ACHIEVERS AND NONACHIEVERS TO THE CONCEPT 'SCHOOL';

● ———— ● Achievers
○ – – – – ○ Nonachievers

The Sign Test of the Profile Pattern: The probability that all of the response means of the *Achiever* group would consistently fall to one side of all of the response means of the *Nonachiever* group (no cross-over patterns) is $P = .001$; an occurrence of 9 out of 10 is $P = .011$; an occurrence of 8 out of 10 is $P = .055$. See the table below to confirm these observations.

TABLE OF ONE-TAILED PROBABILITIES ASSOCIATED WITH VALUES AS SMALL AS OBSERVED VALUES OF X IN THE BINOMIAL TEST (DOUBLE ALL ENTRIES FOR TWO-TAILED TESTS):[1,2]

N \ x	0	1	2	3	4	5	6	7	8	9	10	11	12	13	14	15
5	031	188	500	812	969	*										
6	016	109	344	656	891	984	*									
7	008	062	227	500	773	938	992	*								
8	004	035	145	363	637	855	965	996	*							
9	002	020	090	254	500	746	910	980	998	*						
10	001	011	055	172	377	623	828	945	989	999	*					
11		006	033	113	274	500	726	887	967	994	*	*				
12		003	019	073	194	387	613	806	927	981	997	*	*			
13		002	011	046	133	291	500	709	867	954	989	998	*	*		
14		001	006	029	090	212	395	605	788	910	971	994	999	*	*	
15			004	018	059	151	304	500	696	849	941	982	996	*	*	*
16			002	011	038	105	227	402	598	773	895	962	989	998	*	*
17			001	006	025	072	166	315	500	685	834	928	975	994	999	*
18			001	004	015	048	119	240	407	593	760	881	952	985	996	999
19				002	010	032	084	180	324	500	676	820	916	968	990	998
20				001	006	021	058	132	252	412	588	748	868	942	979	994
21				001	004	013	039	095	192	332	500	668	808	905	961	987
22					002	008	026	067	143	262	416	584	738	857	933	974
23					001	005	017	047	105	202	339	500	661	798	895	953
24					001	003	011	032	076	154	271	419	581	729	846	924
25						002	007	022	054	115	212	345	500	655	788	885

* 1.0 or approximately 1.0

Where N = number of observations; x = number of exceptions (for example, out of twelve scales (N = 12), if ten are more favorable for a given group but two are less favorable, then x = 2.)

From Siegel, S. S. (1956). *Nonparametric statistics* (p. 250). Copyright, New York: McGraw-Hill. Used by permission of McGraw-Hill Book Co.

For a discussion of one-tailed and two-tailed tests, see page 193.

KINDS OF TESTS AND MEASUREMENTS COMMONLY USED

Purpose	Typical Examples
A. Cognitive Assessment	
1. Aptitude	Standardized, norm-referenced scholastic aptitude and intelligence tests
2. Achievement	Standardized: (a) norm-referenced tests–both general achievement batteries and specific content area tests; and (b) criterion-referenced tests–specific to a given content area
	Nonstandardized: Grade Point Averages, awards, honors
B. Affective Assessment	Inventories, rating scales, adjective checklists,
1. Preferences/interests	Q-Sort devices, sociometric methods,
2. Attitudes/beliefs	projective instruments, questionnaires,
3. Emotional/social attributes	interviews, opinion polls, unobtrusive measures
C. Perceptual-Motor Assessment	Miscellaneous aptitude tests and batteries
1. Aptitude	Specific performance-based tests (e.g., typing
2. Skills	proficiency, telephone repair proficiency, etc.)
D. Personality/Character Assessment	Miscellaneous instruments and projective devices
E. Behavior/Conduct Assessment	Miscellaneous observation techniques and self-report instruments
F. Environmental/Physical Assessment	Demographic and socio-economic indicators, physical facility and materials inventories, staffing and miscellaneous resources

THE ROLE OF MEASUREMENT IN PROGRAM EVALUATION: SOME PERSPECTIVES

The Tyranny of the Instrument. An instrument, whether it is a test, scale, observation procedure, questionnaire, or interview schedule, only measures what it measures – nothing more, nothing less. One should take a long look at any instrument, once it is in place in an evaluation design, to be clear regarding what it can and cannot register. Beware of the "naming fallacy"[1] – giving a name to a test or other instrument such as "intelligence," "motivation," "attitude" and thereby maintaining that is what it measures. For example, on close inspection, many so-called achievement tests are sensitive to a very narrow range of content actually covered in instruction. Classroom activities

---

[1]Brigham, C. C. (1930). Intelligence tests of immigrant groups. *Psychological Review, 37,* 158-165.

outside this range, however meritorious and worthwhile, will contribute little to the measured outcome. The issue raised is the validity of the instrument. It should be a key consideration in its selection in the first place. Nevertheless, the restrictions inherent in any instrument should be kept in the forefront of attention in designing and evaluating any program.

The Law of Consequences. Program design traditionally sets objectives, plans strategies and activities to achieve these objectives, and then assesses progress toward their attainment. If satisfactory movement toward the objectives is not achieved, the program is then appropriately modified. An entirely new perspective emerges if, instead, one attends to *consequences*. Rather than looking for progress in terms of the objectives, one looks for effects, whatever their source, intended or not. The evaluator asks: What consequences do I observe; what goes with what; under what conditions; and with what outcomes? Not far removed from serendipity, the observer keeps an open mind and looks for effects, planned or not, that yield information of value to understanding and improving programs. The boldest approach to gain this stance is Michael Scriven's *goal-free* evaluation strategy[1] where the evaluator intentionally is shielded from the stated purposes and objectives of the program – the better not to see what is expected, but what is, in fact, happening. Such an unbiased perspective is likely to uncover unforeseen consequences and relationships that, in the long run, could have major significance.

The Backwards Approach. The straightforward conduct of program evaluation is, first, to determine the objectives, and then to select or develop appropriate measures by which their attainment will be assessed. Beginning with an existing measurement because it is conveniently available or has apparent face validity, strictly speaking, is putting the cart before the horse. Nevertheless, there are occasions when it is either impractical or ineffective to follow this sequence. This event happens when the outcome measure is so well established that to depart from it would challenge the credibility of the evaluation or when the complexity or subjectivity of the variables underlying the objectives makes the identification of a given measurement procedure arbitrary across a range of defensible options. It is also true that for the majority of measurement situations, the options are often few in number. An example of the first instance would be the use of a publisher's norm-referenced achievement battery to evaluate a school's instructional program. An example of the second instance would be the use of pupil attendance records as an unobtrusive measure of attitudes toward school. In settings where credibility and practicality have, in effect, predetermined the outcome measures, it is the better part of wisdom to begin at the end – that is, with the outcome measures themselves and work backwards to setting program objectives that aim at these measures.

---

[1]Scriven, M. (1970). Goal-free evaluation. In E. R. House (Ed.), *School evaluation*. Berkeley, CA: McCutchan.

MULTIPLE CRITERION MEASURES FOR EVALUATION OF SCHOOL PROGRAMS: METFESSEL AND MICHAEL[1]

I. *Indicators of Status or Change in Cognitive and Affective Behaviors of Students in Terms of Standardized Measures and Scales.*
   1. Standardized achievement and ability tests, the scores on which allow inferences to be made regarding the extent to which cognitive objectives concerned with knowledge, comprehension, understanding, skills, and applications have been attained.
   2. Standardized self inventories designed to yield measures of adjustment, appreciations, attitudes, interests, and temperament from which inferences can be formulated concerning the possession of psychological traits (such as defensiveness, rigidity, aggressiveness, cooperativeness, hostility, and anxiety).
   3. Standardized rating scales and checklists for judging the quality of products in visual arts, crafts, shop activities, penmanship, creative writing, exhibits for competitive events, cooking, typing, letter writing, fashion design, and other activities.

II. *Indicators of Status or Change in Cognitive and Affective Behaviors of Students by Informal or Semiformal Teacher-made Instruments or Devices.*
   1. Incomplete sentence technique: categorization of types of responses, enumeration of their frequencies, or rating of their psychological appropriateness relative to specific criteria.
   2. Interviews: frequencies and measurable levels of responses to formal and informal questions raised in a face-to-face interrogation.
   3. Peer nominations: frequencies of selection or of assignment to leadership roles for which the sociogram technique may be particularly suitable.
   4. Questionnaires: frequencies of responses to items in an objective format and numbers of responses to categorized dimensions developed from the content analysis of responses to open-ended questions.
   5. Self-concept perceptions: measures of current status and indices of congruence between real self and ideal self—often determined from use of the semantic differential or Q-sort techniques.
   6. Self-evaluation measures: student's own reports on perceived or desired level of achievement, on perceptions of personal and social adjustment, and on future academic and vocational plans.
   7. Teacher-devised projective devices such as casting characters in the class play, role playing, and picture interpretation based on an informal scoring model that usually embodies the determination of frequencies of the occurrence of specific behaviors, or ratings of their intensity or quality.
   8. Teacher-made achievement tests (objective and essay), the scores on which allow inferences regarding the extent to which specific instructional objectives have been attained.
   9. Teacher-made rating scales and checklists for observation of classroom behaviors; performance levels of speech, music, and art; manifestation of creative endeavors, personal and social adjustment, physical well being.
   10. Teacher-modified forms (preferably with consultant aid) of the semantic differential scale.

---

[1]Metfessel, N. S., & Michael, W. B. (1967). A paradigm involving multiple criterion measures for the evaluation of the effectiveness of school programs. *Educational and Psychological Measurement, 27*, 931-943.

MULTIPLE CRITERION MEASURES FOR EVALUATION OF SCHOOL PROGRAMS: METFESSEL AND MICHAEL, cont'd.

III. *Indicators of Status or Change in Student Behavior Other than Those Measured by Tests, Inventories, and Observation Scales in Relation to the Task of Evaluating Objectives of School Programs.*

1. Absences: Full-day, half-day, part-day and other selective indices pertaining to frequency and duration of lack of attendance.
2. Anecdotal records: Critical incidents noted including frequencies of behaviors judged to be highly undesirable or highly deserving of commendation.
3. Appointments: Frequencies with which they are kept or broken.
4. Articles and stories: Numbers and types published in school newspapers, magazines, journals, or proceedings of student organizations.
5. Assignments: Numbers and types completed with some sort of quality rating or mark attached.
6. Attendance: Frequency and duration when attendance is required or considered optional (as in club meetings, special events, or off-campus activities).
7. Autobiographical data: Behaviors reported that could be classified and subsequently assigned judgmental values concerning their appropriateness relative to specific objectives concerned with human development.
8. Awards, citations, honors, and related indicators of distinctive or creative performance: Frequency of occurrence or judgments of merit in terms of scaled values.
9. Books: Numbers checked out of library, numbers renewed, numbers reported read when reading is required or when voluntary.
10. Case histories: Critical incidents and other passages reflecting quantifiable categories of behavior.
11. Changes in program or in teacher as requested by student: Frequency of occurrence.
12. Choices expressed or carried out: Vocational, avocational, and educational (especially in relation to their judged appropriateness to known physical, intellectual, emotional, social, aesthetic, interest, and other factors).
13. Citations: Commendatory in both formal and informal media of communication such as in the newspaper, television, school assembly, classroom, bulletin board, or elsewhere (see Awards).
14. "Contacts": Frequency or duration of direct or indirect communications between persons observed and one or more significant others with specific reference to increase or decrease in frequency or to duration relative to selected time intervals.
15. Disciplinary actions taken: Frequency and type.
16. Dropouts: Numbers of students leaving school before completion of program of studies.
17. Elected positions: Numbers and types held in class, student body, or out-of-school social groups.
18. Extracurricular activities: Frequency or duration of participation in observable behaviors amenable to classification such as taking part in athletic events, charity drives, cultural activities, and numerous service-related avocational endeavors.
19. Grade placement: The success or lack of success in being promoted or retained; number of times accelerated or skipped.
20. Grade point average: Including numbers of recommended units of course work in academic as well as in noncollege preparatory programs.
21. Grouping: Frequency and/or duration of moves from one instructional group to another within a given class grade.
22. Homework assignments: Punctuality of completion, quantifiable judgments of quality such as class marks.
23. Leisure activities: Numbers and types of; times spent in; awards and prizes received in participation.
24. Library card: Possessed or not possessed; renewed or not renewed.

MULTIPLE CRITERION MEASURES FOR EVALUATION OF SCHOOL PROGRAMS: METFESSEL AND MICHAEL, cont'd.

25. Load: Numbers of units or courses carried by students.
26. Peer group participation: Frequency and duration of activity in what are judged to be socially acceptable and socially undesirable behaviors.
27. Performance: Awards, citations received; extra credit assignments and associated points earned; numbers of books or other learning materials taken out of the library, products exhibited at competitive events.
28. Recommendations: Numbers of and judged levels of favorableness.
29. Recidivism by students: Incidents (presence or absence or frequency of occurrence) of a given student's returning to a probationary status, to a detention facility, or to observable behavior patterns judged to be socially undesirable (intoxicated state, drug addiction, hostile acts including arrests, sexual deviation).
30. Referrals: By teacher to counselor, psychologist, or administrator for disciplinary action, for special aid in overcoming learning difficulties, for behavior disorders, for health defects, or for part-time employment activities.
31. Referrals: By students themselves (presence, absence, or frequency).
32. Service points: Numbers earned.
33. Skills: Demonstration of new or increased competencies such as those found in physical education, crafts, homemaking, and the arts that are not measured in a highly valid fashion by available tests and scales.
34. Social mobility: Numbers of times student has moved from one neighborhood to another and/or frequency with which parents have changed jobs.
35. Tape recordings: Critical incidents contained and other analyzable events amenable to classification and enumeration.
36. Tardiness: Frequency of.
37. Transiency: Incidents of.
38. Transfers: Numbers of students entering school from another school (horizontal move).
39. Withdrawal: Numbers of students withdrawing from school or from a special program (see Dropouts).

IV. *Indicators of Status or Change in Cognitive and Affective Behaviors of Teachers and Other School Personnel in Relation to the Evaluation of School Programs.*
1. Articles: Frequency and types of articles and written documents prepared by teachers for publication or distribution.
2. Attendance: Frequency of, at professional meetings or at inservice training programs, institutes, summer schools, colleges and universities (for advanced training) from which inferences can be drawn regarding the professional person's desire to improve competence.
3. Elective offices: Numbers and types of appointments held in professional and social organizations.
4. Grade point average: Earned in postgraduate courses.
5. Load carried by teacher: Teacher-pupil or counselor-pupil ratio.
6. Mail: Frequency of positive and negative statements in written correspondence about teachers, counselors, administrators, and other personnel.
7. Memberships including elective positions held in professional and community organizations: Frequency and duration of association.
8. Model congruence index: Determination of how well the actions of professional personnel in a program approximate certain operationally-stated judgmental criteria concerning the qualities of a meritorious program.

MULTIPLE CRITERION MEASURES FOR EVALUATION OF SCHOOL PROGRAMS: METFESSEL AND MICHAEL, cont'd.

9. Moonlighting: Frequency of outside jobs and time spent in these activities by teachers or other school personnel.
10. Nominations by peers, students, administrators or parents for outstanding service and/or professional competencies: Frequency of.
11. Rating scales and checklists (e.g., graphic rating scales or the semantic differential) of operationally-stated dimensions of teachers' behaviors in the classroom or of administrators' behaviors in the school setting from which observers may formulate inferences regarding changes of behavior that reflect what are judged to be desirable gains in professional competence, skills, attitudes, adjustment, interests, and work efficiency; the perceptions of various members of the total school community (parents, teachers, administrators, counselors, students, and classified employees) of the behaviors of other members may also be obtained and compared.
12. Records and reporting procedures practiced by administrators, counselors and teachers: Judgments of adequacy by outside consultants.
13. Termination: Frequency of voluntary or involuntary resignation or dismissals of school personnel.
14. Transfers: Frequency of requests of teachers to move from one school to another.

V. *Indicators of Community Behaviors in Relation to the Evaluation of School Programs.*
   1. Alumni participation: Numbers of visitations, extent of involvement in PTA activities, amount of support of a tangible (financial) or a service nature to a continuing school program or activity.
   2. Attendance at special school events, at meetings of the board of education, or at other group activities by parents: Frequency of.
   3. Conferences of parent-teacher, parent-counselor, parent-administrator sought by parents: Frequency of request.
   4. Conferences of the same type sought and initiated by school personnel: Frequency of requests and record of appointments kept by parents.
   5. Interview responses amenable to classification and quantification.
   6. Letters (mail): Frequency of requests for information, materials, and servicing.
   7. Letters: Frequency of praiseworthy or critical comments about school programs and services and about personnel participating in them.
   8. Participant analysis of alumni: Determination of locale of graduates, occupation, affiliation with particular institutions, or outside agencies.
   9. Parental response to letters and report cards upon written or oral request by school personnel: Frequency of compliance by parents.
   10. Telephone calls from parents, alumni, and from personnel in communications media (e.g., newspaper reports): Frequency, duration, and quantifiable judgments about statements monitored from telephone conversations.
   11. Transportation requests: Frequency of.

The book of nature is written in the mathematical language. Without its help it is impossible to comprehend a single word of it.

Galileo

CHAPTER SIX

STATISTICAL TECHNIQUES AND THE ANALYSIS OF DATA

Good planning in research or evaluation studies anticipates the problem of the analysis of the data. Appropriate statistical techniques are foreseen and the manner of their application is specified. Many excellent texts exist detailing approaches to this task. The purpose of this section is to summarize briefly the more generally used techniques and to provide guidelines regarding the use of statistical techniques.

OVERVIEW OF STATISTICAL METHODS

A. Numbers and Their Use
   1. Nominal Scale—in place of a name (to identify).
   2. Ordinal Scale—to indicate order (to rank).
   3. Interval Scale—to indicate equal intervals (to add and subtract).
   4. Ratio Scale—to indicate ratio (to multiply and divide).

B. Central Tendency ("Averages")
   1. Mean
   2. Median
   3. Mode

C. Distribution (Spread)
   1. Standard Deviation and Variance

   2. Semi-interquartile Range $\left(\dfrac{Q_3 - Q_1}{2} \right)$

   3. Range $\left(\dfrac{\text{Range}}{6} \cong \text{one standard deviation when } N \cong 100) \right)$

D. Comparisons and Relationships between Numbers
   1. *Simple Correlation*—measures the degree of relationship between two variables. May be positive (direct) or negative (indirect or inverse).

   2. *Partial Correlation*—involves the relationship between two variables in a situation where three or more variables are present, holding one or more variables constant and allowing the others to vary.

   3. *Multiple Correlation*—involves the correlation between a dependent variable (or a criterion variable) and an optimally weighted combination of two or more independent (predictor) variables.

   4. *Factor Analysis*—a technique for analyzing patterns of intercorrelation among many variables, isolating the dimensions to account for these patterns of correlation and, in a well-designed study, to allow inferences concerning the psychological nature of the construct represented by the dimension.

   5. *z-Ratio* or *t-Ratio*—test the (null) hypothesis that two samples come from two populations with the same mean and differ only because of sampling error. (z applies to populations with or without equal variances; t assumes the population variances are equal.)

   6. *Analysis of Variance*—tests one or more (null) hypotheses that the means of all groups sampled come from populations with equal means and with equal variances (i.e. from the same population) and differ only because of sampling error. (F test: The technique used in Analysis of Variance which compares the Between-group variance to the Within-group variance.)

   7. *Chi-square*—a measure of squared deviations between observed and theoretical numbers in terms of frequencies in categories or cells of a table, determining whether such deviations are due to sampling error or some interdependence or correlation among the frequencies. It involves a comparison of frequencies of two or more responding groups. Very useful in tables involving frequencies of Yes-No answers or like-undecided-dislike.

MEASURES OF CENTRAL TENDENCY AND VARIABILITY[1]

A. When to use the three averages:
  1. Compute the arithmetic *mean* when:
    a. The greatest reliability is wanted. It usually varies less from sample to sample drawn from the same population.
    b. Other computations, as finding measures of variability, are to follow.
    c. The distribution is symmetrical about the center, and especially when it is approximately normal.
    d. We wish to know the "center of gravity" of a sample.
  2. Compute the *median* when:
    a. There is not sufficient time to compute the mean.
    b. Distributions are markedly skewed. This includes the case in which one or more extreme measurements are at one side of the distribution.
    c. We are interested in whether cases fall within the upper or lower halves of the distribution and not particularly in how far from the central point.
    d. An incomplete distribution is given.
  3. Compute the *mode* when:
    a. The quickest estimate of central value is wanted.
    b. A rough estimate of central value will do.
    c. We wish to know what is the most typical case.

B. When to use the three measures of dispersion:
  1. Use the *range* when:
    a. The quickest possible index of dispersion is wanted.

$$\frac{\text{Range}}{6} \cong \text{one standard deviation when } N \geqslant 100$$

    b. Information is wanted concerning extreme scores.
  2. Use the *semi-interquartile range*, Q (see preceding page) when:
    a. The median is the only statistic of central value reported.
    b. The distribution is truncated or incomplete at either end.
    c. There are a few very extreme scores or there is an extreme skewing.
    d. We want to know the actual score limits of the middle 50 percent of the cases.
  3. Use the *standard deviation* when:
    a. Greatest dependability of the value is wanted.
    b. Further computations that depend upon it are likely to be needed.
    c. Interpretations related to the normal distribution curve are desired.
    (Note: The standard deviation has a number of useful relationships to the normal curve and to other statistical concepts.)

---

[1]From Guilford, J. P. (1965). *Fundamental statistics in psychology and education* (4th ed.). New York: McGraw-Hill. Used with permission.

FREQUENCY DISTRIBUTION

1. The frequency distribution is a table in which all score units are listed in one column and the number of individuals receiving each score appear as *frequencies* in the second column:

Simple Frequency Distributions— When the score range is small (no more than 20 score units), these can be listed in simple rank order from highest to lowest in column one and the frequencies entered in column two:	*Grouped Frequency Distributions—* When the score range is large (more than 20 score units), these are grouped into a hierarchy of *class intervals* of equal width in column one and the corresponding frequencies in column two:

Score	f
15	1
14	0
13	3
12	2
11	6
10	5
9	2
8	4
7	1
6	2
	N = 26

Class Interval	f	Cum. f[1]
42–44	3	120
39–41	11	117
36–38	8	106
33–35	23	98
30–32	35	75
27–29	14	40
24–26	10	26
21–23	9	16
18–20	6	7
15–17	1	1
	N = 120	

2. Rules for constructing *class intervals* in a *grouped frequency distribution:*
   a. In general, there should be *between 10 and 20 class intervals* based on the *optimal number* that will efficiently summarize the data without distorting its shape. Too few compress the data, concealing meaningful changes in its shape; too many stretch out the data creating unnecessary gaps.
   b. The *width of the class interval* is a function of the range of the raw scores and the number of class intervals desired. In the above example, if the raw score range was 49 - 17 = 32 and the researcher wanted about 10 class intervals, then : 32 ÷ 10 = 3.20. Rounded to the nearest whole number, a class interval width of 3 is obtained.
   c. In general, when the *width of the class interval* is less than 10 score units, odd number widths (1, 3, 5, 7, 9) are more convenient since the midpoint of the interval will be a whole number. For interval sizes of 10 and above, multiples of 5 (10, 15, 20, etc.) are recommended.
   d. *"Real" versus "Apparent" limits* for the class interval. In statistical calculations based on grouped data (e.g., see Computing Guide 3, page 173), it is necessary to use the real limit (rather than the apparent limit) of a given class interval. For example, in the above grouped frequency distribution the interval 36-38 has apparent lower and upper limits of 36 and 38. Strictly speaking, however, the real lower and upper limits of the interval 36-38 are 35.5 and 38.5.

---

[1]"Cumulative frequency"—necessary for the construction of a cumulative frequency curve or ogive (see opposite page).

GRAPHIC REPRESENTATIONS OF DATA–
(Examples based on data from preceding page)

A. HISTOGRAM OR BAR GRAPH: B. FREQUENCY POLYGON:

Scores
(Midpoint of class interval)

Scores
(Midpoint of class interval)

1. Histograms or bar graphs and frequency polygons are very similar, both being constructed from frequency distributions.
2. The *scores* are plotted along the horizontal baseline, also called the abscissa or X axis. The *frequencies* (number or percent of cases) are plotted along the vertical axis, also called the ordinate or Y axis.
   a. *For the histogram or bar graph,* the width of each bar corresponds to the *real limits* of the width of each class interval (see next page). In the above example, this fact holds true although the midpoints of each class interval are presented for clearer reading. The height of each bar corresponds to the frequency or percent of cases in that interval.
   b. *For the frequency polygon,* the points are plotted directly over the *midpoints* of each class interval.
   c. For good graphic proportions, the vertical axis should be roughly two-thirds the length of the horizontal axis.

C. CUMULATIVE FREQUENCY CURVE:

1. Cumulative frequency curves represent the graphing of a cumulative distribution and plotted according to procedures similar to the frequency polygon.

2. Using the X and Y axes noted above, points are plotted directly above the *upper real limit* of each interval (see preceding page). This is necessary because the cumulative frequency or cumulative percentage represents the number of percentage of cases,

respectively, that have scores equal to or below the value at that particular upper limit.

3. Cumulative frequency curves are useful when we are primarily interested in determining the position of an individual in a group, rather than the general form of the group performance as in the case of the histogram or frequency polygon.

SCATTER DIAGRAMS, SCATTERGRAMS, OR SCATTER PLOTS

The Graphic Representation of Correlation

1. Using 1.25-inch graph paper, lay out X (horizontal) and Y (vertical) axes representing two correlated variables.
2. On the X axis, or baseline, low scores begin on the left and increase toward the right of the graph. On the Y axis, or vertical, low scores begin at the bottom and increase toward the top of the graph.
3. For each individual, locate the intersection of the X and Y axes equivalent to the scores on the X and Y variables, respectively. Mark this intersection with a dot and repeat the operations for all individuals in the study.

EXAMPLES:

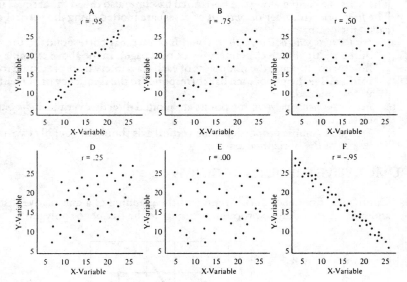

INTERPRETATION: These examples can be interpreted according to the following general principles, given the conditions in steps 1, 2, and 3 above:
1. The slope of the regression line, if it *rises* when moving across the graph from left to right, indicates a *positive correlation* (Example A). If it falls when moving from left to right, this indicates a *negative correlation* (Example F).
2. When all the dots appear to lie very close to the regression line (Example A), the correlation is very high, approaching .90 to 1.00.
3. When the dots scatter around the regression line forming an ellipse midway between a straight line and a full circle (Example C), the correlation is moderate, approaching .50.
4. When the dots scatter around the entire graph more or less equally dispersed in all directions and resembling a full circle (Example E), the correlation is very low, approaching zero.

THE ANALYSIS OF CROSSBREAKS[1]

1. The crossbreak is one of the most graphic displays in data analysis. It can be used with nearly any kind of data and has the graphic power of pointing up similarities and differences in sharp contrast.
    In its most elementary form, it appears as the familiar 2 x 2 contingency table:

	Nonachievers	Achievers
Middle Class	8	22
Lower Class	19	11

2. *Application*—to any data that can be dichotomized into classes or groups. The entries are usually in the form of *frequencies* or *percentages* for their respective variables.

3. *Purpose:*
    a. To facilitate the study and analysis of relations by arranging data into tabular frequencies which clearly display trends and patterns in the relationship.
    b. To facilitate statistical analyses such as the *chi square* test (see Computing Guide 10, page 183) and indices of association such as the *phi coefficient* (see Guilford, J. P. (1965). *Fundamental statistics in psychology and education* (4th ed.) (pp. 333-338). New York: McGraw-Hill.
    c. To study and test a relationship between two variables while controlling for the effects of a third variable, unmasking "spurious" relationships. In other words, it allows us to observe and control for differences in degree of relationships at different levels of a control variable.
    d. To clarify and spell out research problems and the relationships between particular variables in both the problem formulation and data analysis phases of research. Crossbreaks make visible what goes with what in the research design and quickly expose misconceptions or design inadequacies which can be corrected.

---

[1]For an extended discussion on this topic, see Kerlinger, F. N.(1973). *Foundations of behavioral research* (2nd ed.) (Chapter 10). New York: Holt, Rinehart and Winston.

4. *Kinds of crossbreaks*—While the 2 x 2 table is the simplest and most common example of a crossbreak, more complex crossbreaks are frequently used: 2 x 3, 3 x 3, 3 x 4, etc. While there is no theoretical limit to the complexity of these contingency tables, for practical purposes tables in excess of 5 x 5 tend to be unclear, difficult to analyze or interpret, and are rarely reported.

5. *Relationship between crossbreaks and chi square*—Because the chi square test is applied to data in the form of crossbreaks, see pages 184-189 for additional discussion on the use of crossbreaks.

COMPUTING GUIDE 1 - Determining Percentile Equivalents Graphically.[1]

1. Begin with the raw scores (these are scores of 75 ninth-grade boys on Bennett Form AA).

37	43	27	44	27	27	26	31	35	42	50
35	43	36	26	50	47	36	26	32	32	38
36	21	24	40	39	35	38	36	38	21	17
26	35	22	18	50	30	38	50	16	45	8
34	26	34	28	41	27	39	41	30	23	33
22	31	36	40	54	24	22	8	33	42	41
41	31	34	36	32	20	22	34	41		

2. Identify the highest score and the lowest score. If there is a wide range, choose a class interval of 1, 2, 5, 10, 20, etc., and divide the range into classes of equal width. Fifteen or more classes are desirable.

Highest score = 54; lowest score = 8; range = 47. Class interval of 5 will be used. (A smaller interval, such as 2, would be preferable but would be inconvenient in this computing guide.)

3. Tally the number of cases with each score.

4. Write the number of tallies in the Frequency (f) column. Add this column to get N, the number of cases.

5. Begin at the bottom of the column and add frequencies one at a time to determine the cumulative frequency, the number of cases below each division point.

Scores	Tallies	Frequency (f)	Cumulative Frequency	Cumulative Percent
50--54	Ｍ	5	75	100
45–49	//	2	70	93
40–44	Ｍ Ｍ //	12	68	90
35–39	Ｍ Ｍ Ｍ //	17	56	75
30–34	Ｍ Ｍ ////	14	39	52
25–29	Ｍ Ｍ	10	25	33
20–24	Ｍ Ｍ	10	←15[a]	20[b]
15–19	///	3	5[a]	7
10–14		0	2	3
5–9	//	2	2	3
			0	0
		$\overline{75}$ N		

a. 5 cases fall below 19.5; 15 below 24.5; etc.

b. 20 percent of the cases fall below 24.5; 20 is the cumulative percentage corresponding to a raw score of 24.5.

[1]Cronbach, L. J. (1970). *Essentials of psychological testing* (3rd ed.). New York: Harper & Row.

6. Divide the cumulative frequencies by N to determine cumulative percentages.

7. Plot cumulative percentage against score. (In practice, a large sheet of graph paper would be used.)

8. Draw the smooth curve which best fits the points plotted.

9. Determine the percentile equivalent of a score by reading from the curve. (The lines on the chart show how one finds that the percentile equivalent of a raw score of 40 is 74.)

Percentile Equivalents

Raw	%ile	Raw	%ile	Raw	%ile
12	2	24	17	36	60
13	2	25	20	37	64
14	3	26	22	38	67
15	3	27	26	39	71
16	4	28	29	40	74
17	5	29	33	41	77

COMPUTING GUIDE 2 - Determining the Mean and Standard Deviation for Ungrouped Data.[1]

	X	d	d^2
1. Arrange the raw scores in ascending order.	16	5.5	30.25
	14	3.5	12.25
	12	1.5	2.25
	11	.5	.25
	10	−.5	.25
	10	−.5	.25
	9	−1.5	2.25
	9	−1.5	2.25
	8	−2.5	6.25
	6	−4.5	20.25
	$\Sigma X = 105$	$\Sigma d = 0.0$	$\Sigma d^2 = 76.50$

2. To find the mean, sum the raw scores and divide by N, the number of cases:

$$M = \frac{\Sigma X}{N} = \frac{105}{10} = 10.5$$

3. To find the standard deviation:

   a. Subtract the mean from each raw score, obtaining the deviation score, d

   $$X - M = d$$

   b. Square each deviation score, obtaining d^2

   c. Sum the squared deviations, obtaining

   $$\Sigma d^2 = 76.50$$

   d. Obtain the standard deviation by extracting the square root of the sum of the squared deviations divided by N:

   $$\text{s.d.} = \sqrt{\frac{\Sigma d^2}{N}} = \sqrt{\frac{76.50}{10}} = 2.77$$

---

[1]An alternative formula for computing Σd^2 follows where X is the raw score and N is the number of cases. It is useful when a hand calculator is available:

$$\Sigma d^2 = \frac{1}{N} [N\Sigma X^2 - (\Sigma X)^2]$$

and

$$\text{s.d.} = \sqrt{\frac{1}{N^2} [N\Sigma X^2 - (\Sigma X)^2]}$$

COMPUTING GUIDE 3 - Determining the Mean and Standard Deviation for Grouped Data.[1]

1. Begin with the raw scores (these are scores of 75 ninth-grade boys on Bennett Form AA)

37	43	27	44	27	27	26	31	35	42	50
35	43	36	26	50	47	36	26	32	32	38
36	21	24	40	39	35	38	36	38	21	17
26	35	22	18	50	30	38	50	16	45	8
34	26	34	28	41	27	39	41	30	23	33
22	31	36	40	54	24	22	8	33	42	41
41	31	34	36	32	20	22	34	41		

2. Identify the highest score and the lowest score. If there is a wide range, choose a class interval of 1, 2, 5, 10, 20, etc., and divide the range into classes of equal width. Seven to fifteen classes are desirable.

Highest score = 54; lowest score = 8; range = 47. Class interval of 5 will be used. (A smaller interval, such as 2, would be preferable but would be inconvenient in this computing guide.)

Note: The interval 50–54 is, in fact, 5 units wide: *50–51–52–53–54*, or strictly speaking, 49.5–54.5.

3. Tally the number of cases with each score.

4. Write the number of tallies in the Frequency (f) column. Add this column to get N, the number of cases.

5. Select any interval, usually near the middle of the distribution. Call this the arbitrary origin. (Here, the 30–34 interval is used.)

Scores	(f)	d	fd	fd²
50–54 $\mathcal{N}/$	5	4	20	80
45–49 $//$	2	3	6	18
40–44 $\mathcal{N}/ \mathcal{N}/ //$	12	2	24	48
35–39 $\mathcal{N}/ \mathcal{N}/ \mathcal{N}/ //$	17	1	17	17
30–34 $\mathcal{N}/ \mathcal{N}/ ////$	14	0	0	0
25–29 $\mathcal{N}/ \mathcal{N}/$	10	−1	−10	10
20–24 $\mathcal{N}/ \mathcal{N}/$	10	−2	−20	40
15–19 $///$	3	−3	−9	27
10–14	0	−4	−0	0
5– 9 $//$	2	−5	−10	50
	75		+18	290
	N		Σfd	Σfd²

Determine the deviation (d) of each interval from the arbitrary origin.

6. Multiply in each row the entries in the f and d columns, and enter in the fd column.

7. Multiply the entries in the d and fd columns and enter in the fd^2 column. Add the fd and fd^2 columns. (Σ is a symbol meaning "sum of".)

8. Substitute in the following formulas:

$$c \text{ (correction)} = \frac{\Sigma fd}{N} \qquad c = \frac{18}{75} = .24$$

$$M \text{ (mean)} = A.O. + ic* \qquad M = 32.0 + 5(0.24)$$
$$M = 32.0 + 1.20 = 33.20$$

$$\text{s.d.} = i\sqrt{\frac{\Sigma fd^2 - Nc^2}{N-1}} \qquad \text{s.d.} = 5\sqrt{\frac{290 - 75(0.24)^2}{74}} = 5\sqrt{\frac{285.7}{74}}$$

$$= 5\sqrt{3.86} = 5(1.96) = 9.80$$

A.O. is the midpoint of the score-interval selected as arbitrary origin, and i is the width of the interval.

---

[1]Cronbach, L.J. (1960). *Essentials of psychological testing* (2nd ed.) (p. 79). New York: Harper & Brothers.

APPROPRIATE CORRELATIONAL TECHNIQUES FOR DIFFERENT FORMS OF VARIABLES[1,2]

Technique	Symbol	Variable 1	Variable 2	Remarks
Product–moment correlation	r	Continuous	Continuous	The most stable technique
Rank–difference correlation (Rho)	ρ	Ranks	Ranks	Often used instead of product–moment when number of cases is under 30
Kendall's Tau	τ	Ranks	Ranks	Preferable to Rho for numbers under 10
Biserial correlation	r_{bis}	Artificial dichotomy	Continuous	Sometimes exceeds 1—has a larger standard error than r—commonly used in item analysis
Widespread biserial correlation	r_{wbis}	Widespread artificial dichotomy	Continuous	Used when you are especially interested in persons at the extremes on the dichotomized variable
Point–biserial Correlation	r_{pbis}	True dichotomy	Continuous	Yields a lower correlation than r and much lower than r_{bis}
Tetrachoric correlation	r_t	Artificial dichotomy	Artificial dichotomy	Used when both variables can be split at critical points
Phi coefficient	ϕ	True dichotomy	True dichotomy	Used in calculating interitem correlations on multiple choice or two choice items
Contingency coefficient	C	2 or more categories	2 or more categories	Comparable to r_t under certain conditions—closely related to chi-square

[1]Borg, W. R. (1963). *Educational research: An introduction* (p. 157). New York: David McKay. By permission.

[2]Concerning the Variable 1 and Variable 2 categories in the above chart, a *continuous* variable is one representing an underlying continuum tending to be normally distributed. Examples include such variables as height, weight, and ability or achievement as measured by standardized tests. *Artificial*

REFERENCES
SELECTED SOURCES FOR ADDITIONAL COMPUTATIONAL AIDS
AND ACCOMPANYING INTERPRETIVE INFORMATION

The several computational or calculation aids that have been presented in this volume may be supplemented by those in other texts. The so-called cookbook approaches appear in many books, several of which also provide interpretive comments. Typically, step-by-step guidelines in outline form accompany the solution of a statistical or quantitatively oriented research problem in conjunction with summarized interpretive, evaluative, or qualifying information. A few helpful sources include the following:

Bruning, J. L., & Kintz, B. L. (1987). *Computational handbook of statistics* (3rd ed.). New York: Harper Collins.

Dinham, S. M. (1983). *Exploring statistics: An introduction for psychology and education.* Monterey, CA: Brooks & Cole.

Huck, S. W., Cormier, W. H., & Bounds, W. G., Jr. (1974). *Reading statistics and research.* New York: Harper Collins.

Linton, M., Gallow, P. S., Jr., & Logan, C. A. (1975). *The practical statistician: Simplified handbook of statistics.* Monterey, CA: Brooks/Cole.

McCall, R. B. (1994). *Fundamental statistics for the behavioral sciences* (6th ed.). New York: Harcourt, Brace, Jovanovich.

Minium., E. W., King, B. M., & Bear, G. (1993). *Statistical reasoning in psychology and education* (3rd ed.). New York: Wiley.

Siegel, S. S. (1988). *Nonparametric statistics for the behavioral sciences* (2nd ed.). New York: McGraw-Hill.

Welkowitz, J., Ewen, R. B., & Cohen, J. (1990). *Introductory statistics for the behavioral sciences* (4th ed.). New York: Harcourt, Brace, Jovanovich.

Wilson, J. A. R., Robeck, M. C., & Michael, W. B. (1974). *Psychological foundations of learning and teaching* (2nd ed.) (Chapter 19). New York: McGraw-Hill.

dichotomies can be constructed by arbitrarily dividing continuous variables into two groups, usually about the center of the data. Examples include such classifications as achiever-nonachiever, above average-below average, pass-fail, and warm-cold on an attitude scale. *True dichotomies* involve relatively clear-cut (though not necessarily absolute) differences, allowing the data to be categorized into two groups. Examples include such dichotomies as male-female, living-dead, teacher-nonteacher, drop-out-nondropout, and smoker-nonsmoker. Other variables that can be treated *as if* they were true dichotomies for the purposes of computing, for example, a point-biserial correlation coefficient, include: color blind-noncolor blind, alcoholic-nonalcoholic, and right-wrong responses with respect to a particular test item in item analysis (see example, page 178.) The distributions underlying true dichotomies, if not absolute differences, tend to be bimodal and/or relatively discontinuous. For a more complete discussion of these problems, see the references cited above.

COMPUTING GUIDE 4 – The Product-Moment Correlation Coefficient (Pearson r).

1. Begin with the pairs of raw scores to be correlated (X and Y) and arranged in table format, completing the table by calculating the respective values for each column entry:

Student	IQ X	GPA Y	X^2	Y^2	XY
1	111	1.8	12,321	3.24	199.8
2	113	1.7	12,769	2.89	192.1
3	119	1.3	14,161	1.69	154.7
4	120	2.2	14,400	4.84	264.0
5	123	2.7	15,129	7.29	332.1
6	126	1.9	15,876	3.61	239.4
7	128	2.7	16,384	7.29	345.6
8	131	2.1	17,161	4.41	275.1
9	134	3.3	17,956	10.89	442.2
10	135	2.7	18,225	7.29	364.5
11	136	3.1	18,496	9.61	421.6
12	138	2.6	19,044	6.76	358.8
	1,514	28.1	191,922	69.81	3,589.9

2. Resolve the following equation using values in the above table:

$$r = \frac{\Sigma xy - \dfrac{(\Sigma x)(\Sigma y)}{N}}{\sqrt{\left[\Sigma x^2 - \dfrac{(\Sigma x)^2}{N}\right]\left[\Sigma y^2 - \dfrac{(\Sigma y)^2}{N}\right]}}$$

$$r = \frac{44.62}{\sqrt{[\,905.7\,]\,[\,4.01\,]}}$$

$$r = \frac{44.62}{\sqrt{3,631.857}}$$

$$r = \frac{3589.9 - \dfrac{(1514)(28.1)}{12}}{\sqrt{\left[191,922 - \dfrac{(1514)^2}{12}\right]\left[69.81 - \dfrac{(28.1)^2}{12}\right]}}$$

$$r = \frac{44.62}{60.26}$$

$$r = \frac{3589.9 - 3545.28}{\sqrt{[\,191,922 - 191,016.3\,]\,[\,69.81 - 65.8\,]}}$$

$$r = 0.74$$

Note: To determine the statistical significance of the obtained r, see Table D, page 251.

COMPUTING GUIDE 5- Rank-Difference Correlation[1] (Spearman rho).

		Example
1.	Begin with the pairs of scores to be studied.	Man A ($x = 30$; $c = 25,000$)
		Man A has ranks 4, 6
2.	Rank men from 1 to N (number of men) in each set of scores. (Note that the lowest man must have rank N, unless he ties with someone.)	$N = 10$ In case of tied scores, see footnote 2 below.
3.	Subtract the rank in the right-hand column from the one in the left-hand column. This gives the difference D. (As a check, make sure that this column adds to zero.)	Man A: 4–6 = -2
4.	Square each difference to get D^2.	Man A: $(-2)^2 = (-2)(-2)$ $= 4$
5.	Sum this column to get ΣD^2.	
6.	Apply the formula: $$\rho \text{ (rho)} = 1 - \frac{6(\Sigma D^2)}{N(N^2 - 1)}$$	$\rho = 1 - \dfrac{6(36)}{10(100 - 1)}$
7.	To determine the statistical significance of this coefficient, see Table E, page 252. In this instance r is significant at the 5% level, but not significant at the 1% level.[3]	$= 1 - \dfrac{216}{990}$ $= 1 - .218$ $\rho = .782$

Man	Scores Test	Scores Criterion (c)	Ranks Test	Ranks Criterion	Rank Difference (D)	Squared Difference (D^2)
A	30	$25,000	4	6	-2	4
B	34	38,000	2	2	0	0
C	32	30,000	3	4	-1	1
D	47	40,000	1	1	0	0
E	20	7,000	9	10	-1	1
F	24	10,000	7	9	-2	4
G	27	22,000	5	7	-2	4
H	25	35,000	6	3	3	9
I	22	28,000	8	5	3	9
J	16	12,000	10	8	2	4
					$\Sigma D = 0$	$\Sigma D^2 = 36$

Cronbach, L. J. (1970). *Essentials of psychological testing* (3rd ed.) (p. 129). New York: Harper & Row.
In many sets of data, two or more scores will be tied. Simply assign the *mean* rank to all the tied scores based on the span of rank positions equal to the number of tied scores. E. g., if two scores are tied for ranks 7 and 8, both are ranked as 7.5 and will be flanked by ranks 6 and 9. If three scores are tied for ranks 10, 11, 12, all three are ranked as 11 and will be flanked by ranks 9 and 13, etc. In this way, the number of ranks are balanced for all cases of ties and the total number of ranks equals N.
Item 7 added to Cronbach's Computing Guide for this Handbook only.

COMPUTING GUIDE 6 - The Point-biserial Correlation Coefficient for data where one variable is a true dichotomy and the other variable is continuously distributed.[1,2]

1. Compute the standard deviation for the total set of scores on the continuous variable, designating this value as σ_t.

   See Computer Guide 2 or 3.

2. Divide the data into two subgroups based on the dichotomized variable and compute their respective means on the continuous variable. Designate the mean of the subgroup with the higher performance or ability as M_p and the mean of the subgroup with the lower performance or ability as M_q.

   M_p = higher subgroup

   M_q = lower subgroup

3. Determine the proportion of cases in each of the subgroups. Let p = proportion of cases in the higher subgroup and q = proportion of cases in the lower subgroup.

   p = number of cases in the higher subgroup divided by the total number of cases in both subgroups.

   $q = 1.00 - p$

4. Solve for r_{pbis}:

   $$r_{pbis} = \frac{M_p - M_q}{\sigma_t} \sqrt{pq}$$

EXAMPLE: In the item-analysis of a particular test, it is useful to know the relationship between the response patterns of Right or Wrong on a specific test item and the performances on the overall test scores. Suppose those scoring Right on the item in question also score higher on their total test scores than the group whose answers to this item are Wrong. If we are given the following statistical information about these two groups, coded according to the above notations, a point-biserial correlation coefficient can be derived:

Given:

$\sigma_t = 12.4$
$M_p = 134.6$
$M_q = 125.8$
$N_p = 29$
$N_q = 31$

Then:

$$r_{pbis} = \frac{M_p - M_q}{\sigma_t} \sqrt{pq} = \frac{134.6 - 125.8}{12.4} \sqrt{(.483)(.517)} =$$

$$\frac{8.8}{12.4} \sqrt{.249711} = (.7097)(.4997) = .35$$

---

[1] See discussion regarding continuous and dichotomous data in footnote no. 2, page 174-175.

[2] A test of statistical significance for this correlation coefficient is equivalent to a *t*-test of the difference between the two means.

COMPUTING GUIDE 7 - Use of the Spearman-Brown Formula to estimate reliability after a test is lengthened or shortened.[1]

1. Suppose that a test has a known reliability. The Spearman–Brown Formula, given at right, estimates the reliability of the score from a similar test n times as long with homogeneous content.

$$r_n = \frac{nr}{1 + (n - 1)r}$$

where

r is the original reliability; r_n is the reliability of the test n times as long

2. To predict the reliability of a test twice as long as the original test, substitute in the formula $n = 2$.

If r is .40, $r_2 = \dfrac{2(.40)}{1 + (1)\,.40}$

$$= \frac{.80}{1.40} = .57$$

3. Suppose the original test is to be reduced to only half its original length. The reliability of the short test is estimated using $n = \frac{1}{2}$.

$$r_{\frac{1}{2}} = \frac{\frac{1}{2}(.40)}{1 + (\frac{1}{2} - 1)(.40)}$$

$$= \frac{.20}{1 - \frac{1}{2}(.40)} = \frac{.20}{.80}$$

$$= .25$$

The Spearman-Brown Formula permits us to estimate what reliability that the scores on a test would have if it were lengthened or shortened. The formula assumes that when we change the length of the test, we do not change its nature. Extreme increases in test length, however, introduces boredom and may reduce reliability. Added items or added periods of observation may not confer the same behavior or ability as the original test.

Note: An increase in test length has a great effect on reliability but a much smaller effect on validity.

COMPUTING GUIDE 8 - Item Score Matrix of a Four-Item Total Test Preliminary to Obtaining an Internal-Consistency Estimate of Reliability.

Person j (N = 10)	Item i (i = 1, 2, 3, 4, or 5) Items (k = 4) 1	2	3	4	Person's Score X_j on Total Test	Deviation Scores x_t	x_t^2
A	0	0	0	0	0	-2	4
B	1	0	0	0	1	-1	1
C	0	1	0	0	1	-1	1
D	1	1	0	0	2	0	0
E	1	0	1	0	2	0	0
F	1	1	0	0	2	0	0
G	1	0	0	1	2	0	0
H	1	1	1	0	3	+1	1
I	1	1	1	0	3	+1	1
J	1	1	1	1	4	+2	4
Sums Np	8	6	4	2	20 = ΣX;		$12 = \Sigma x_t^2$
p_i	.80	.60	.40	.20	$\Sigma p_i = 2.0 = M_t$	$\sigma_t^2 = \dfrac{\Sigma x_t^2}{N} = \dfrac{12}{10} = 1.20$	
q_i	.20	.40	.60	.80			
p_iq_i	.16	.24	.24	.16		$\sigma_t = \sqrt{1.2} = 1.095^+$	
KR-20							

$$r_{tt} = \frac{k}{k-1} \cdot \frac{\sigma_t^2 - \Sigma p_i q_i}{\sigma_t^2} = \frac{4}{4-1} \cdot \frac{1.20 - .80}{1.20} = \frac{4}{3} \cdot \frac{.40}{1.20} = .44$$

Note: In ordinary practice it is not necessary to present an item score matrix. All that is needed in the calculation of KR formula 20 estimates is the number of items k, the variance of the test scores σ_t^2 and the $\Sigma p_i q_i$ across all items.

[1] Cronbach, L. J. (1960). *Essentials of psychological testing* (2nd ed.) (p. 76). New York: Harper & Brothers.

COMPUTING GUIDE 9 - Hypothetical Item Score Matrix of 8 Examinees (A, B, . . ., H) in a Five-Item Attitude Scale Involving Five Levels of Response (1, 2, 3, 4, or 5) Preliminary to Obtaining an Internal-Consistency Estimate of Reliability.

(Coefficient Alpha)

Person j (N = 8)	Items i (k = 5) 1 2 3 4 5	Person j's Score X_{jt} on Total Scale	Squared Deviation Scores $\chi_{jt}^2 = (X_{jt} - \overline{X}_t)^2$
A	2 2 3 4 5	16	1
B	1 2 4 4 4	15	0
C	1 1 2 3 3	10	25
D	2 3 3 5 4	17	4
E	2 2 4 4 4	16	1
F	2 2 3 4 4	15	0
G	3 2 2 4 3	14	1
H	3 2 3 4 5	17	4
Sum	16 16 24 32 32	$120 = \Sigma x_{jt}$	36
Mean	2 2 3 4 4	$\overline{X}_t = \dfrac{120}{8} = 15.00$	
Σx_i^2	4 2 4 2 4	$\sigma_t^2 = \dfrac{36}{8} = 4.5$	
σ_i^2	.50 .25 .50 .25 .50		
$\Sigma \sigma_i^2$		$\Sigma \sigma_i^2 = .50 + .25 + .50 + .25 + .50 = 2.00$	

$$\alpha = \frac{k}{k-1} \; \frac{\sigma_t^2 - \Sigma \sigma_i^2}{\sigma_t^2}$$

$$= \frac{5}{4} \; \frac{4.50 - 2.00}{4.50}$$

$$= \frac{5}{4} \; \frac{2.50}{4.50} = \frac{12.50}{18.00} = .694$$

COMPUTING GUIDE 10 - The z test,* or Critical Ratio, to determine a significant difference between two sample means.[1] (Large Samples).[2]

Note: z assumes the two samples come from two populations with equal means but not necessarily equal variances.

1. Determine the means and standard deviations for *each* of the two samples in question.	See Computing Guide 2 or 3.
2. Determine the z-ratio.	$z = \dfrac{M_1 - M_2}{\sqrt{\dfrac{\sigma_1^2}{N_1 - 1} + \dfrac{\sigma_2^2}{N_2 - 1}}}$

3. Enter Table A, page 248, to determine whether the z-ratio indicates a significant difference between the two sample means.

z values at the .05 and .01 levels for one-tailed and two-tailed tests:[3],**

	One-tailed test	Two-tailed test
.05	≥ 1.65 or ≤ -1.65	≥ 1.96 or ≤ -1.96
.01	≥ 2.33 or ≤ -2.33	≥ 2.58 or ≤ -2.58

***Note:* Concerning negative numbers, -1.70 is *less than* -1.65.

EXAMPLE: Achievement test scores for an experimental and control group.

See Mnemonic Table for Null Hypothesis, p. 195.

Although no hard and fast rule exists as a dividing line between large and small samples, in practice a sample size greater than 30 typically is considered large and one of 30 or less is considered small.

One-tailed tests predict a difference in only one direction, either plus (but not minus) or minus (but not plus); two-tailed tests predict a difference simultaneously in either direction. See pages 192-194 for further implications of hypothesis testing.

Step	Experimental (Sample 1)	Control (Sample 2)
1	Given: $N_1 = 44$ $M_1 = 78.09$ $\sigma_1 = 17.44$	Given: $N_2 = 49$ $M_2 = 68.14$ $\sigma_2 = 18.03$

2

$$z = \frac{M_1 - M_2}{\sqrt{\dfrac{\sigma_1^2}{N_1 - 1} + \dfrac{\sigma_2^2}{N_2 - 1}}} = \frac{78.09 - 68.14}{\sqrt{\dfrac{(17.44)^2}{43} + \dfrac{(18.03)^2}{48}}}$$

$$= \frac{9.95}{\sqrt{\dfrac{304.15}{43} + \dfrac{325.08}{48}}} = \frac{9.95}{\sqrt{7.07 + 6.77}}$$

$$= \frac{9.95}{\sqrt{13.84}} = \frac{9.95}{3.72} = 2.67$$

3   Entering Table A, page 248, a z value of 2.67 corresponds to a point on the normal curve above which 0.38 percent of the area lies. Presuming a one-tailed test of significance for the research hypothesis that the mean ($\overline{M}_1$) of the experimental population is greater than the mean ($\overline{M}_2$) of the control population ($\overline{M}_1 - \overline{M}_2 > 0$), the null hypothesis that a difference between the first and second population means ($\overline{M}_1 - \overline{M}_2$) is negative or at most equal to zero can be rejected at the .01 level. The null hypothesis of no difference ($\overline{M}_1 - \overline{M}_2 = 0$) also would be rejected for a two-tailed test at the .01 level, had that been the case.

COMPUTING GUIDE 11 - The t test* to determine a significant difference between two sample means. (Satisfactory for Large Samples; particularly appropriate for Small Samples).[1]

1.	Determine the *means* and *sum of squares*, Σd^2, for each of the two samples in question.	See Computing Guide 2 or 3.
2.	Determine the *t*-ratio.	$$t = \frac{M_1 - M_2}{\sqrt{\left(\dfrac{\Sigma d^2_1 + \Sigma d^2_2}{N_1 + N_2 - 2}\right)\left(\dfrac{N_1 + N_2}{N_1 N_2}\right)}}$$
3.	Determine degrees of freedom, *df*.	$df = N_1 + N_2 - 2$
4.	Enter appropriate table to determine whether the *t*-ratio indicates a significant difference between the two sample means.	a. If *df* is greater than 30, use Table A, page 248, where the values at the .05 and .01 levels for one-tailed and two-tailed tests are;[2]

	One-tailed test	Two-tailed test
.05	≥ 1.65 or ≤ -1.65	≥ 1.96 or ≤ -1.96
.01	≥ 2.33 or ≤ -2.33	≥ 2.58 or ≤ -2.58

b. If *df* is 30 or less, Use Table B, page 246.

*Note: *t* assumes the two samples come from two populations with equal means *and* equal variances. Concerning negative numbers, -1.70 is *less than* -1.65.

In general the power of *t* is enhanced when the sample sizes and the variances underlying the two samples are equal, or nearly equal. Departures from these two conditions tend to compromise the use of *t*.

See footnote no. 3, page 181, regarding one-tailed and two-tailed tests.

EXAMPLE: Two groups of children have been taught spelling using two teaching strategies: Method A or spaced practice and Method B or massed practice. The research hypothesis predicts that spaced practice is superior to massed practice, as measured by a selected spelling test.

Step	Method A—Spaced Practice	Method B—Massed Practice

1	Given: $N_1 = 10$ $M_1 = 25.5$ $\Sigma d^2_1 = 168.50$	Given: $N_2 = 10$ $M_2 = 22.0$ $\Sigma d^2_2 = 178.00$

2 $$t = \frac{M_1 - M_2}{\sqrt{\left(\dfrac{\Sigma d^2_1 + \Sigma d^2_2}{N_1 + N_2 - 2}\right)\left(\dfrac{N_1 + N_2}{N_1 N_2}\right)}} = \frac{25.5 - 22}{\sqrt{\left(\dfrac{168.50 + 178.00}{10 + 10 - 2}\right)\left(\dfrac{10 + 10}{(10)(10)}\right)}}$$

$$t = \frac{3.5}{\sqrt{\left(\dfrac{346.50}{18}\right)\left(\dfrac{20}{100}\right)}} = \frac{3.5}{\sqrt{3.85}} = \frac{3.5}{1.96} = 1.786$$

3   Since df is $N_1 + N_2 - 2$, or 18, we enter Table B, page 249, finding that a t-value of plus 1.786 for a one-tailed test as predicted by the research hypothesis is significant at the .05 level.

CHI SQUARE

Chi square is a means of answering questions about data existing in the form of frequencies, rather than as scores or measurements along some scale. Typically, the question we want answered when we have such frequency data is *whether the frequencies observed in our sample deviate significantly from some theoretical or expected population frequencies.* The frequencies refer to the categories with which we have classified our data. Examples of the latter include such common classifications as male or female, yes or no, agree or disagree, pass or fail, or achiever or nonachiever.

If, for example, we want to know whether or not there is a significant difference in the proportions of students from either *higher* or *lower socio-economic* backgrounds who *complete high school* or who become *dropouts,* the chi square test would be the appropriate statistical tool to apply. We simply select an unbiased sample of students from the two defined populations (higher and lower socio-economic backgrounds), determine whether or not they completed high school or became dropouts (being careful to avoid contaminating factors which might bias our interpretation), and apply the chi square test. Classification patterns with more than two dimensions are possible with chi square. For example: high, average, or low achievers; freshmen, sophomores, juniors, or seniors; or the letter grade categories of A, B, C, D, or F.

Restrictions on the Use of Chi Square:

1. Chi square can be used only with frequency data. (Note that data normally reported as scores along some scale of measurement such as IQ's, or achievement test scores can be categorized into frequency form; for example, high, average, and low scoring ranges.)

2. Chi square requires that the individual events or measures are independent of each other. In other words, each response must be free of any influence upon the nature of any other response in the set of responses being compared.

3. In general, no theoretical frequency should be smaller than 5.[1] (In this event, for 2 x 2 table, use Fisher's Test of Exact Probability. See Siegel, S. S. (1956). *Nonparametric statistics* (p. 94). New York: McGraw-Hill.

4. There must be some logical or empirical basis for the way the data are categorized.

5. The sum of expected and the sum of observed frequencies must be the same.

6. The algebraic sum of the discrepancies between the observed and the corresponding expected frequencies will be zero.

COMPUTING GUIDE 12 - Chi Square for a 2 x 2 Table.[2]

1. Arrange data in a 2 × 2 table: (*Note:* Cells are assigned letter values to facilitate calculation.)

B	A	A + B
D	C	C + D

$$B + D \qquad A + C \qquad \underline{N}$$

2. Compute chi square:

$$\chi^2 = \frac{N(AD - BC)^2}{(A+B)\ (C+D)\ (A+C)\ (B+D)}$$

3. Determine whether a one-tailed or two-tailed test is involved.

4. In Table C, page 250, chi square values for 1 degree of freedom (number of rows—1 times number of columns − 1) are listed both for one-tailed and two-tailed tests. A chi square value as large as 3.84 is significant at the .05 level for a two-tailed test and at the .025 level for a one-tailed test.

EXAMPLE: A test of whether or not there is a significant difference between the proportions of girls or boys who prefer either listening to the radio or reading a book in their free time; equivalent to determining whether there is a relationship between sex membership and activity preference.

---

[1]The theoretical frequency for any cell is the product of the two marginal totals common to that cell divided by the total number of cases, *N*.

[2]Siegel uses a formula involving a *correction for continuity* for a 2 x 2 table (*df* = 1). Optional when *N* > 100; desirable when *N* < 100. See Siegel, S. S. (1956). *Nonparametric statistics* (p. 107). New York: McGraw-Hill.

$$\chi^2 = \frac{N(AD - BC)^2}{(A + B)(C + D)(A + C)(B + D)} = \frac{206[(62)(58) - (47)(39)]^2}{(109)(97)(101)(105)} = \frac{640,282,814}{112,126,665} = 5.71$$

From information given in Item 3 above, (or Table C, page 250), we conclude that there is a significant difference between boys and girls in their preference for listening to the radio or reading a book in their free time. This difference is significant at the 5% level but is not large enough to be significant at the 1% level.

$$\chi^2 = \frac{N\left[(AD - BC) - \dfrac{N}{2}\right]^2}{(A + B)(C + D)(A + C)(B + D)}$$

COMPUTING GUIDE 13 - Median Test for a difference between two medians.[1]

Many times data are available that do not permit mathematical operations involved in calculating the mean and standard deviation. Typically, such data either are markedly skewed or represent an ordinal (rank-ordered) scale of measurement. In place of either a *z* test or *t* test for a significance of the difference between two sample *means*, we use the median test which asks whether there is a significant difference between the *medians* of two samples.

The median test turns out to be nothing more than a *chi square* calculation using the median as a dividing point to form frequency categories. It is a procedure for testing

1. Combine the two sets of ranks or scores from the two samples into a single rank-ordered distribution, determining the *new combined median*. Keep track of which of the two original samples each score represents.

2. Using the new combined median as the dividing point, cast these data into a 2 × 2 table:

	Group I	Group II
No. of scores above combined median:	B	A
No. of scores below combined median:	D	C

3. Follow the procedure for finding chi square for a 2 x 2 table given in Computing Guide 12, on the preceding page, using the formula in the footnote, corrected for continuity.

[1]When *N* for the sum of both samples is less than 30 (small sample), see Siegel, S. S. (1956). *Nonparametric statistics for the behavioral sciences* (pp. 96-104 and pp. 111-112). New York: McGraw-Hill, as the Fisher exact probability test may be necessary.

whether it is probable that two independent groups (not necessarily the same size) have been drawn from populations with the same median.

EXAMPLE: A counselor in a high school obtains two samples of percentile ranks and wants to know if they are significantly different:
   Sample I: 17, 23, 23, 28, 31, 34, 37, 39, 42, 47, 56, 58, 61
   Sample II: 23, 26, 35, 40, 43, 44, 44, 47, 52, 56, 59, 65, 70, 72, 77
   Putting together the two sets of scores, the new combined median is 43.5. The resulting frequencies are cast into a 2 x 2 table and we obtain these results:

	Sample I	Sample II	
No. of scores above combined median:	4 B	A	10
No. of scores below combined median:	9	D C	5

Then:
$$= \frac{N\left[(AD - BC) - \dfrac{N}{2}\right]^2}{(A + B)(C + D)(A + C)(B + D)} = \frac{28[56]^2}{(14)(14)(15)(13)} = \frac{87,808}{38,220} = 2.297$$

According to Table C, page 250, a chi square value of 2.297, for one degree of freedom and a *two-tailed* test (since only a difference was sought), is *not* significant and the null hypothesis must be accepted (fails to be rejected).

COMPUTING GUIDE 14 - Chi Square for Categories Exceeding a 2 x 2 Table.

1. Arrange data in an appropriate table format (e.g., 2 × 3, 3 × 3, 3 × 4, 4 × 4, etc.) based on categories used in your study.   See EXAMPLE on page 188.

2. Apply the chi square formula: $\chi^2 = \Sigma \dfrac{(0 - E)^2}{E}$

3. Determine degrees of freedom: df = number of columns (k) − 1 *times* number of rows (r) − 1.

4. Enter Table C, page 250, for appropriate df to determine significance.   See EXAMPLE on page 188.

EXAMPLE:[1] Is there a significant relationship between the responses of persons with membership in one of four groups representing different socio-economic levels and their responses to the question, "Is your family more prosperous (better off) today than two years ago, less prosperous, or the same?" Group A is the highest socio-economic level; Group D, the lowest.

Group	More	Same	Less	Uncertain	Total
A	115 (120)	245 (229.5)	125 (131)	15 (19.5)	500
B	375 (360)	690 (688.5)	375 (393)	60 (58.5)	1500
C	460 (480)	920 (918)	540 (524)	80 (78)	2000
D	250 (240)	440 (459)	270 (262)	40 (39)	1000
Column Total	1200	2295	1310	195	5000

O	E	$O-E$	$(O-E)^2$	$\dfrac{(O-E)^2}{E}$
115	120	−5	25	.208
375	360	15	225	.625
460	480	−20	400	.833
250	240	10	100	.417
245	229.5	15.5	240.25	1.047
690	688.5	1.5	2.25	.003
920	918	2	4	.004
440	459	−19	361	.786
125	131	−6	36	.275
375	393	−18	324	.824
540	524	16	256	.489
270	262	8	64	.244
15	19.5	−4.5	20.25	1.038
60	58.5	1.5	2.25	.038
80	78	2	4	.051
40	39	1	1	.026
				$\chi^2 = 6.908$

Computational steps:

1. Arrange data for *observed frequencies* in 4 x 4 table format (four groups—A, B, C, and D; four types of responses—"more," "same," "less," "uncertain").

2. Compute values for the *expected frequencies* (in parentheses) by multiplying the *column total* times the *row total*, for each cell in the table and dividing this product by N. For example, in the first cell in row A with an observed frequency of 115:

$$\frac{(1200)\ (500)}{5000} = 120$$

3. In each cell subtract the theoretical frequency from the observed frequency to obtain the deviation: $O - E$.

---

[1]Data taken from Spence, J. T., Underwood, B. J., Duncan, C. P., & Cotton, J. W. (1968). *Elementary statistics* (p. 204). New York: Appleton-Century-Crofts.

4. Square the deviation: $(O - E)^2$

5. Divide each squared deviation by the theoretical frequency of each cell:

$$\frac{(O - E)^2}{E}$$

6. Determine chi square by summing the resulting quotients:

$$\chi^2 = \Sigma \; \frac{(O - E)^2}{E} \; = 6.908$$

7. Determine degrees of freedom (*df*): Number of columns – 1, times number of rows – 1, equals 9.

8. Enter Table C, page 250, for 9 *df* to determine whether a chi square value as large as 6.908 is statistically significant. Since a chi square value of at least 16.92 must be obtained to be significant at even the 5% level of significance, we accept (fail to reject) the null hypothesis of no relationship and conclude that whatever differences appear to exist in the data, they are probably due to chance. In other words, the observed differences in the sample data are not statistically significant and may be attributed to chance.

ANALYSIS OF VARIANCE

The *z* test or *t* test (Computing Guides 10 and 11) answer the question: Is the difference between *two* sample means statistically significant? Typically, one mean represents an experimental group receiving some treatment condition and the other mean represents a control group. Many research problems in education, however, involve more than two groups and yield more than two means. For example, we may want to study the effects of two methods of teaching in relationship to two levels of intelligence upon achievement test scores—a 2 x 2 design involving four group means:

	Low IQ	High IQ
Method A	M_2	M_1
Method B	M_4	M_3

Or, consider the more complex investigation of three teaching strategies in conjunction with three age levels of children compared to the child's sex—a 3 x 3 x 2 design involving 18 group means. The advantages of these factorial designs are important: they yield information about the *main effects* of particular variables by themselves (e.g., the effect of method alone, intelligence alone, or age level alone) and they also yield information about *interactions* between variables (e.g., method *and* intelligence, or method *and* age level).[1]

---

[1] See "FACTORIAL DESIGNS," pp. 82-85; and "THE ANALYSIS OF CROSSBREAKS," pp. 169-170.

The task of *pairing up* all relevant combinations of two sample means and computing individual z or t tests soon becomes burdensome. Furthermore, if none of these tests happens to be statistically significant, a great deal of effort is spent in this determination. Also, when dealing with a large number of such individual tests, *chance alone* allows 5% of the difference between pairs of sample means to reach the .05 level of significance. A single composite test to compare all sample means simultaneously and to tell us whether or not a statistically significant difference exists somewhere in the data overcomes these disadvantages. It has the additional advantage of a more nearly accurate estimate of the population variance since it could base this estimate on all the sample data taken together, rather than just two samples, as in the case of the z or t test. Carrying out either of these tests after an F-test can be a hazardous undertaking; correct procedures are described in most of the works in statistics and in experimental design cited near the end of this chapter.

Analysis of variance is the statistical tool having these characteristics. It answers the question: Is the variability *between* groups large enough in comparison with the variability *within* groups to justify the inference that the means of the populations from which the different groups were sampled are not all the same? In other words, if the variability between groups means is large enough, we can conclude they probably come from different populations and that there is a statistically significant difference present in the data. The particular statistical test yielding the answer is the F ratio:

$$F = \frac{\text{Between Group Variance}}{\text{Within Group Variance}}$$

While *analysis of variance* is the first step in the analysis of these more complex designs, it is only a preliminary and exploratory tool. If a significant F ratio is obtained, the researcher only knows that somewhere in the data something other than chance is probably operating. Researchers must attempt to isolate the presence, nature, and extent of this non-chance influence. In many instances the researcher will then proceed with either z or t tests, now that the investigator has established the worth of such an effort, although the hazards referenced previously should be investigated. Many procedures exist for testing significance of difference between pairs of numbers that control for making erroneous inferences. These individual tests also are strengthened by a more nearly accurate estimate of the population variance gained in the analysis of variance calculation.

Underlying assumptions—Guilford (see "References" on page 213) notes four principal assumptions underlying analysis of variance as a parametric technique:
1. The contributions to variance in the total sample must be additive.
2. The observations within sets must be mutually independent.
3. The variances within experimentally homogeneous sets must be approximately equal.
4. The variations within experimentally homogeneous sets should be from normally distributed populations.

The general strategy to follow in meeting these assumptions is (1) random sampling within sets and (2) use of a good metric scale. To the extent that the above assumptions are compromised, the F ratio tends to be less significant than it appears.

Some sources of information on analysis of variance—Analysis of variance is a complex tool with many limitations, applications, and variations in form. Since it cannot realistically be reduced to a series of Checklists or Computing Guides, the investigator must consult the standard texts on this subject (see pages 213-215) and, if possible, seek expert assistance in its application.

ANALYSIS OF COVARIANCE

Many times in studies of the type suitable for analysis of variance, there will be initial differences between groups on pretest criteria that arise either by chance or, more likely, because of the inability of the educational researcher to select subjects at random. This includes sets of data that are not independent, involving correlated means. *Analysis of covariance* adjusts for initial differences between groups and for the correlation between means. In effect, it permits the comparison of groups on one variable when information is available on another variable correlated with it, or on several such variables. It is generally preferable to *matching* subjects for the same purpose. Random assignment is recommended.

ANALYSIS OF VARIANCE AND COVARIANCE AND COMPUTER PROGRAMS

Because of the speed and capacity of computers and the availability of computer programs, many research data using analysis of variance and/or covariance are processed in this way. Investigators should make use of data processing facilities in their community. If operational programs are available, the cost is very nominal.

MULTIVARIATE STATISTICAL PROCEDURES

During the past several years large-scale advances have been made in treating statistically large numbers of independent and dependent variables in a variety of contexts. In particular, multiple regression techniques, simple and multiple discriminant function analyses, canonical correlation methods, and factor analytic approaches have been widely applied largely because of the increased capabilities of computers. An overview section on these multivariate procedures is included near the end of this chapter along with a substantial number of relevant references that the reader may consult.

HYPOTHESIS TESTING AND STATISTICAL SIGNIFICANCE

1. *The Research (Alternative) Hypothesis and the Null Hypothesis*
   a. The *research hypothesis*— states the expectations of the researcher in positive terms. It identifies the variables or conditions which, in causal relationship, will be advanced to account for the results and is often derived from a theory.
   b. The *null hypothesis*—the hypothesis of "no relationship or difference"—is the one actually tested statistically. It is an arbitrary convention hypothesizing that any relation or difference in the findings is due to chance or sampling error and puts this supposition to a probability test. Theoretically, it is an hypothesis set up for possible *rejection* and though the degree of relationship or margin of difference need not be zero, it frequently is.

2. *Stating the Null Hypothesis*–four alternatives, using the example of the difference between two sample means:[1]
   a. There is no difference between the means of the two populations from which the two samples were drawn at random.
   b. The two means in the two populations from which the samples were respectively drawn at random are equal.
   c. The mean of the sampling distribution of differences between an infinite number of pairs of means of randomly drawn samples equals zero.
   d. Any difference between two sample means drawn randomly from their respective populations is due to sampling error—that is, such differences can readily be attributed to chance.

3. *Accepting or Rejecting the Null Hypothesis—What it Means*
   Testing the null hypothesis results in one of two outcomes:
   a. *Accepting (failing to reject)* the null hypothesis as true, in which case it is concluded that any differences in the results are:
      (1) not statistically significant, therefore are probably
      (2) due to sampling error or chance.
   b. *Rejecting* the null hypothesis as false, in which case it is concluded that the differences in the results are:
      (1) statistically significant, therefore are probably
      (2) due to some determining factor or condition, other than chance.

Accepting the null hypothesis also means that the corresponding research hypothesis is not supported or is disconfirmed. Rejecting the null hypothesis also means the corresponding research hypothesis has survived a test of disconfirmation and, in that sense, is supported. More precisely, the differences in the data reasonably cannot be attributed to chance and the causal factors stated in the research hypothesis may possibly explain the difference, but not necessarily so as long as there are *plausible rival hypotheses* also to account for the data. Obviously, the more tests of disconfirmation a given research hypothesis can survive, the stronger is the evidence in its support.

---

[1]Adapted from notes for a seminar presented by William B. Michael. This material is essentially the same as that appearing in Wilson, J. A. R., Robeck, M. C., & Michael, W. B. (1974). *Psychological foundations of learning and teaching* (2nd ed.). New York: McGraw-Hill.

4. *Accepting or Rejecting the Null Hypothesis—Two Types of Errors*
   a. *Type I (Alpha) Error*—to reject the null hypothesis of no differences when it is true. In other words, to conclude falsely that a difference exists in the data when in fact it does not. Since such an error is particularly embarrassing to scientists (saying something exists when it does not), they tend to avoid risking this error and choose a conservative level of significance which minimizes it.

   b. *Type II (Beta) Error*—to accept the null hypothesis of no differences when it is false. In other words, to conclude falsely that a difference does not exist in the data when in fact it does.

   c. *The decision between risks*—Whether to run the risk of a Type I or Type II error, since the probability of one increases as the other decreases, is a question of utility. Which is preferable in a given situation: (1) a Type I *fine screen* designed to eliminate chance differences at the expense of throwing away some genuine differences in the process? or (2) a Type II *coarse screen* that lets through some of the unwanted chance differences to insure that most of the genuine differences are kept? When the consequences of mistaking a chance difference for a genuine difference are too costly and the risk of such an error must be minimized, a conservative level of significance is set, avoiding the Type I error. When, on the other hand, there is a search for all promising leads and no genuine prospect can be overlooked, a liberal level of significance is selected, avoiding the Type II error. *Note: To avoid the probability of either error, increase the sample size, N.*

5. *Rejecting the Null Hypothesis and Theory-Building*[1]
   The task of theory-building and data analysis is to *reject* inadequate hypotheses. Experimental findings never confirm or prove a theory. Rather, the successful theory is tested and escapes being disconfirmed and the more tests of this nature it survives, the stronger it stands. Strictly speaking, the null hypothesis can never be accepted—it can only be rejected or fail to be rejected.

6. *One-tailed and Two-tailed Tests of the Null Hypothesis*
   When a particular research hypothesis simply predicts that a *difference* will exist in the data and allows this difference to be in *either direction* (larger or smaller), it is a two-tailed test of its null hypothesis counterpart, since the difference can fall in either tail of this sampling distribution. If, on the other hand, the research hypothesis predicts the direction of the difference (*either* larger *or* smaller), it is a one-tailed test of the corresponding null hypothesis.

7. *The Power of a Statistical Test*
   The power of a statistical test is defined as the probability of rejecting the null hypothesis of no differences when it is actually *false*. In other words, differences really do exist, and the null hypothesis should be rejected:

$$\text{Power} = 1 - \text{probability of Type II error}$$

The power of a statistical test is a function of:
   a. The underlying assumptions of the test: Parametric tests make stronger assumptions than nonparametric tests.
   b. Whether the test is one-tailed (often more powerful in a certain region of admissible alternative hypotheses of interest) or two-tailed (less powerful in that same region).

---

[1] Based on a discussion by Campbell, D. T., & Stanley, J. C. (1966). *Experimental and quasi-experimental designs for research.* Chicago, IL: Rand McNally.

c. Sample size N: As N increases, power usually increases. *Power efficiency* refers to the increase in sample size necessary to make test X as powerful as a second test Y.

8. *Level of Significance and Replications*[1]
While the conventional level for rejecting the null hypothesis is $p = .05$ or .01 (5 percent and 1 percent, respectively), significance levels of 10 to 20 percent are tolerable in preliminary investigations, *with replication*. Note: If two successive findings are each significant at the 10-percent level, this is roughly equivalent to a single finding at the 1-percent level since the two kinds of outcomes are about equally probable. Moreover replication provides empirically stronger evidence than a single occurrence and justifies the more liberal test of the null hypothesis, avoiding the Type II error.[2]

9. *Statistical Significance versus Practical Significance*
In the researchers' zeal to obtain statistically significant findings, they often overlook the more relevant question: Is it educationally significant? Is the difference large enough to be practical? Are the gains important enough to be worth the cost and effort to obtain them? This question gets at the trade-off factor in educational decision-making and involves the problem of accountability in cost effectiveness economics. Even when these practical matters are settled or in the background, there are valuable considerations of social and psychological nature that frequently override a choice based solely on statistical significance.

---

[1]Based on notes taken at a Field Studies Workship given by staff members of the Far West Regional Laboratory, Berkeley, CA, 1968.

[2]For another consideration of this problem, see Guilford, J. P. (1965). *Fundamental statistics in psychology and education* (4th ed.) (pp. 248-250). New York: McGraw-Hill.

Mnemonic Table for Null Hypothesis: Two-Tailed Test of Significance of Differences Between Means for Large-Sample Approach

z-Value (Critical Ratio)	Associated Probability Value (P)	Acceptance or Rejection of Null Hypothesis	Conclusion regarding Null Hypothesis (NH)	Conclusion regarding Statistical Significance	Conclusion regarding Research Hypothesis (RH)*	Tail-area Picture relative to z Value
$z < 1.96$ (z less than 1.96)	$P > .05$ (P greater than .05)	Accepted (tenable)	The NH is supported. It is not unreasonable to believe that the two samples come from two populations with equal means.	Not significant (NS). The difference between the two means is statistically not significant.	RH not supported	Less than 95% — Large tail area (relatively low confidence level—less than 95%)
$1.96 \leq z < 2.576$ (z greater than, or at least equal to, 1.96, but less than 2.576)	$.01 < P \leq .05$ (P less than, or at most equal to .05, but greater than .01)	Rejected at .05 level, but accepted at .01 level (untenable at .05 level but tenable at .01 level)	The NH is probably not supported. It is reasonable to believe that the two samples come from two populations with different means.	Significant at .05 level, but not at .01 level (S). The difference between the two means is statistically significant at .05 level (but not at .01 level)	RH supported	Between 95 and 99% — Small tail area (relatively high confidence level—between 95 and 99%)
$z \geq 2.576$ (z greater than, or at least equal to, 2.576)	$P \leq .01$ (P less than, or at most equal to, .01)	Rejected at .01 level as well as at .05 level (untenable at both .05 and .01 levels)	The NH is very probably not supported. It is very reasonable to believe that the two samples come from two populations with different means.	Very significant at or beyond .01 level (as well as at .05 level) (VS). The difference between the two means is statistically significant at or beyond .01 level—very significant.	RH very strongly supported	At least 99% — Very small tail area (relatively very high confidence level—at least 99%)

* If research hypothesis is positively stated.

From Wilson, J. A. R., Robeck, M. C., & Michael, W. B. (1969). *Psychological foundations of learning and teaching* (p. 556). New York: McGraw-Hill. Used with permission of McGraw-Hill Book Co.

THE SEARCH FOR PROMISING PRACTICES: AVOIDING THE TYPE II ERROR[1]

Traditional research as a form of educational inquiry stresses principles of rigorous design in order to maximize both internal and external validity (particularly internal validity). Customarily, conservative standards of statistical significance are employed relative to which the probability for the rejection of the null hypothesis is set at or below .05. The logic of this approach has been to avoid the Type I error–namely concluding that a treatment makes a difference between the means of one or more experimental groups and a comparison group when, in fact, it does not or that an association exists between two variables when indeed it does not.

On the other hand, such a rigorous approach may tend to be counterproductive in an educational setting in which learning outcomes can be the result of many complex factors acting independently and jointly in addition to the one under investigation. In educational and psychological research, differences between the means of groups or the magnitudes of correlation coefficients obtained are likely to be low at best. This circumstance is further compounded when the sample sizes are quite small, as is often the case in research with human subjects. The risk that the researcher now faces is likely to be one associated with Type II error–concluding that the treatment has not yielded a difference or observable effect when, in fact, it has or that two variables are not related when indeed they are.

A pragmatic solution to this dilemma has been proposed by N. L. Gage, Professor of Education and Psychology at Stanford University. In its most rudimentary form, the solution ignores standards of meticulous design and statistical significance on the grounds that neither design rigor nor statistical significance is necessarily crucial. Specifically, research on any variable when it actually is of consequence usually will yield outcomes suggestive of genuine effects or relationships with or without elegant designs or statistical precision. In any given study by itself such an implied assumption would not be warranted. By examining several investigations concerned with a common treatment variable–especially when each study differs from the other in terms of particular design weaknesses–one can simply count the number of times relative to which the results are favorable. If there is a preponderance of findings in the anticipated or hypothesized direction, the effect of the independent variable in question would be supported. This level of support would be reinforced by the fact that the common treatment variable had yielded results holding across nearly all studies, whereas support for each of the rival hypotheses challenging the effect of the common treatment variable arises from particular design weaknesses and varies from one study to another. It follows that if one has to shift from one criticism to a different one to call the common treatment variable into question as each of several studies is being examined that circumstance in itself indirectly supports the possible influence of the common treatment variable.

Consistent with this orientation of evaluating the probable impact of a treatment variable is use of a statistical significance test such as the nonparametric sign test (based on applying the binomial distribution) that would indicate in a set of experiments how many times the results favored the common treatment variable. For example, if in 18 investigations in which the outcome was registered as being present or absent in relation to the occurrence of a common treatment variable researchers noted an anticipated

[1]Based on an article by: Gage, N. L. (1978). The yield of research on teaching. *Phi Delta Kappan, 59,* 229-235.

effect 13 times, they could infer that the probability of that number of so-called favorable events was less than .05 provided that the various research studies could be assumed to be independent of one another.

Expanding upon this approach, Gage has offered a second procedure which makes use of somewhat complex techniques. This procedure requires the investigator to take into account both the sample sizes and the magnitudes of the statistical significance levels associated with the reported differences or with observable relationships in a given set of studies. The result of this process can afford even a stronger means than that provided by the first approach in concluding that a selected treatment variable has, in fact, registered an effect when viewed across several independent studies. The reader who wishes to pursue these points at greater length will find the article by Gage that has been cited in the footnote to be of considerable interest.

SAMPLING

1. When we *sample*, we are drawing from some *population* of possible cases.

2. The sample will deviate from the true nature of the defined population by a certain amount due to chance variations in drawing the sample's few cases from the population's many possible cases. This deviation is called *sampling error* and is distinguished from non-chance variations due to *determining factors* (e.g., biased sampling procedures, effects of independent variables, research conditions, and other causal agents or circumstances).

3. The problem that sampling error presents to sampling statistics occurs in two important settings:
   a. *When we wish to generalize from a sample to a particular population.* In doing so, we must estimate the size of the sampling error. If it is sufficiently small, we reasonably can conclude that any difference between the sample mean and the estimated population mean is due to chance—therefore, the sample is representative of the population and allows generalizations about the population. If it is too large to assign to chance variations, we must conclude that the sample is not representative of the defined population and we should avoid generalizations.
   EXAMPLE: In a consumer survey, a researcher draws a sample of consumer opinions about alternative packaging procedures for a new product, from which inferences are made about the *population* of all possible consumers.
   b. *When we wish to determine whether two or more samples were drawn from the same, or different populations.* Instead of making generalizations from a single sample to some population, we now are asking whether two or more samples are sufficiently different to rule out chance and point to some determining (causative) agent or condition; or, whether they are sufficiently similar to attribute any differences to chance alone. We are asking, in other words, is there a systematic (nonchance) difference between the two samples, supporting the conclusion that each represents a different population? EXAMPLE: A research psychologist investigates the effect of a drug on the maze-learning behavior of rats using two samples of rats, an experimental group receiving the drug and a control group not receiving the drug.
   Typically, in setting 3a we hope to attribute differences to chance so that we can generalize about the population. In setting 3b, however, we hope to rule out chance so that we can attribute differences to determining factors and causal relationships.

4. **Two Modes of Sampling from a Population of Possible Cases:**

   a. *Random sampling*—Selecting cases or subjects in such a way that all have an equal probability of being included and the selection of one case has no influence on the selection of any other case. Drawing names from a hat, taking every tenth name from an alphabetical listing, or entering a table of random numbers are typical methods of sampling at random.

   b. *Stratified random sampling*—When there are two or more ways of classifying the data—sex, age, educational level, intelligence level, socio-economic status, or ethnic membership—and it is important to insure that each category is *proportionately represented* in the sample, the population is subdivided into the appropriate strata and then a predetermined quota of cases is drawn *at random* from each substratum.

5. **Small or Large Samples?**
   Between the economy and convenience of small samples and the reliability and representativeness of large samples lies a trade off point balancing practical considerations against statistical power and generalizability.
   Some of the merits of small samples are listed on page 101. In addition, small samples are more appropriate for in-depth case studies or where complex techniques of eliciting or evaluating behavior are involved, such as psychodrama, role playing, intensive counseling or interviewing procedures, or projective instruments.
   Nevertheless, it remains true that the larger the sample, the smaller the sampling error and, other things being equal, it is preferable to increase the sample size wherever practical. Large samples, moreover, often are essential when the following factors are present:[1]

   a. *When a large number of uncontrolled variables are interacting unpredictably* and it is desirable to minimize their separate effects by sampling from a large variety of situations representing different amounts and combinations of these variables. The result is to mix them together randomly, cancelling out chance imbalances. Example: A study involving two teaching methods sampling equally from twenty teachers, rather than two. This minimizes the possible source of interaction between one of the methods and a highly effective teacher, where the difference is more attributable to this one teacher than to the method.

   b. *When the total sample is to be divided into several subsamples* and these subsample categories are the actual units of comparison. Obviously, it is the size of the subsample that is critical in estimating the sampling error, not the size of the total sample. Example: When studying the interaction between a given curriculum innovation and such organismic variables as age, grade level, sex, socio-economic status, ethnic membership, and the school attended, breaking down the overall sample into smaller comparison groups based on these classifications.

   c. *When the population is made up of a wide range of variables and characteristics* and a small sample would run a high risk of missing or misrepresenting many of these differences. Example: A census study to determine the nature of a city, state, or national population.

---

[1]Adapted from Borg, W. R. (1963). *Educational research: An introduction* (pp. 171-174). New York: David McKay. [See also, Borg, W. R., & Gall, M. D. (1989). *Educational research: An introduction* (5th ed.) (pp. 233-236). White Plains, NY: Longman.]

d. *When differences in the results are expected to be small* and it is important to insure against losing these differences in the "noise" background of the inevitable error variance. Example: A school district wants to evaluate the effect of a new lighting system on student attitude and achievement. Assuming that the lighting change is a minor improvement, it would be unrealistic to anticipate large increments of gain on the student variables and the district would be satisfied to demonstrate any gain at all.

6. *Pitfall in Sampling: The Volunteer*—Many studies, knowingly or unknowingly, build in a *volunteer* factor in the selection of participants. Questionnaire or interview studies depending on the voluntary cooperation of the respondent or a research investigation permitting some teachers to select themselves into one or more of the treatment groups illustrate this problem. The pitfall is the likelihood that volunteers differ from nonvolunteers, compromising the interpretation and generalizability of the results. See page 68, item 6 and page 69, item 1, for relationship to internal and external validity, respectively.

ESTIMATING SAMPLE SIZE REQUIRED FOR MAKING INFERENCES ABOUT MAGNITUDES OF POPULATION PROPORTIONS

When one is preparing to select a sample from a population of known size (finite population), how large must the sample be before reliable inferences can be made about the proportion of individuals in the population who would be responding in a designated manner? If one assumes that the population proportion P of individuals answering "yes" or "agree" is .50 and the proportion Q, or $1-P$ in the population replying "no" or "disagree" is also .50, it is possible to determine how large a sample size S would be needed when the sample is randomly chosen from a population of size N so that the probability would be .95 that the sample proportion p would fall within .05 (5 percentage points) of the population proportion P. In other words, in randomly drawing 100 samples all of the same size S, 95 out of 100 would yield a proportion p within .05 units of the true population proportion P. It should be mentioned that the selection of a value of .50 for P is a conservative approach that will tend to overestimate the size of the interval within which a designated probability of occurrence of sample proportions would fall if P is less than .50 or greater than .50.

In the table that follows this discussion, entries for the required sample size S are provided in a column immediately to the right of that portraying corresponding finite populations of given size N. These values for S are those that would be necessary to provide the outcome discussed in the previous paragraph. As an illustration, the sample size S of 278 cases would be needed from a finite population with N equal to 1,000 cases so that there would be a 95-percent level of confidence that the sample proportion p would be within an amount of .05 of the population value of .50 for P. It should be emphasized that all samples are assumed to have been drawn at *random*. Moreover, if P differed slightly from .50, a somewhat smaller sample could be used than that specified in the table.

In their 1970 article in *Educational and Psychological Measurement* (which has been referred to in the footnote at the bottom of the table to follow) Krejcie and Morgan have provided the following formula for estimating the sample size S needed relative to (a) population of a known size, (N), (b) a specified confidence level (e.g., .95) associated with a chi square statistic for one degree of freedom, and (c) the designated degree of accuracy as reflected by the amount of sampling error d that can be tolerated. (Thus, for the tabular entries d was set at .05–a value equivalent to $\pm$ 1.96 times the standard error of the proportion σ_p. The formula is as follows:

$$S = \frac{\chi^2 \, NP \, (1-P)}{d^2 \, (N-1) + \chi^2 P \, (1-P)} \text{, in which}$$

$S =$ required sample size

$N =$ the given population size

$P =$ population proportion that for table construction has been assumed to be .50, as this magnitude yields the maximum possible sample size required

$d =$ the degree of accuracy as reflected by the amount of error that can be tolerated in the fluctuation of a sample proportion p about the population proportion P–the value for d being .05 in the calculations for entries in the table, a quantity equal to $\pm$ 1.96 σ_p.

$\chi^2 =$ table value of chi square for one degree of freedom relative to the desired level of confidence, which was 3.841 for the .95 confidence level represented by entries in the table

TABLE FOR DETERMINING NEEDED SIZE S OF A RANDOMLY CHOSEN SAMPLE FROM A GIVEN FINITE POPULATION OF N CASES SUCH THAT THE SAMPLE PROPORTION p WILL BE WITHIN ± .05 OF THE POPULATION PROPORTION P WITH A 95 PERCENT LEVEL OF CONFIDENCE[1]

N	S	N	S	N	S
10	10	220	140	1200	291
15	14	230	144	1300	297
20	19	240	148	1400	302
25	24	250	152	1500	306
30	28	260	155	1600	310
35	32	270	159	1700	313
40	36	280	162	1800	317
45	40	290	165	1900	320
50	44	300	169	2000	322
55	48	320	175	2200	327
60	52	340	181	2400	331
65	56	360	186	2600	335
70	59	380	191	2800	338
75	63	400	196	3000	341
80	66	420	201	3500	346
85	70	440	205	4000	351
90	73	460	210	4500	354
95	76	480	214	5000	357
100	80	500	217	6000	361
110	86	550	226	7000	364
120	92	600	234	8000	367
130	97	650	242	9000	368
140	103	700	248	10000	370
150	108	750	254	15000	375
160	113	800	260	20000	377
170	118	850	265	30000	379
180	123	900	269	40000	380
190	127	950	274	50000	381
200	132	1000	278	75000	382
210	136	1100	285	100000	384

Note: N is population size; S is sample size.

[1]Krejcie, R. V., & Morgan, D. W. (1970). Determining sample size for research activities. *Educational and Psychological Measurement, 30,* 607-610.

WAYS OF INTERPRETING CORRELATION COEFFICIENTS

1. In its simplest form, a correlation coefficient is a number indicating the degree of relationship between two variables. It measures to what extent variations in one go with variations in the other:

    1.00   A perfect positive correlation: Changes in one variable are accompanied by equivalent changes in the *same* direction in the other variable, without exception.

    .00   No correlation: Changes in one variable have no relationship, or are randomly related, to changes in the other variable.

    -1.00 A perfect negative correlation: Changes in one variable are accompanied by equivalent changes in the *opposite* direction in the other variable, without exception.

2. A correlation coefficient requires two sets of measurements on the same groups of individuals, or on matched pairs of individuals, and cannot be computed on one person alone.

3. *Coefficient of Determination, r^2*
    The correlation coefficient, r, is a measure of the strength of relationship between two variables. It does not represent a percentage of the determinants they have in common unless it is squared and becomes an estimate of variance called the coefficient of determination. When the latter is multiplied by 100, it indicates the percentage of variance held in common by the two variables, X and Y, assuming linear regression. It answers the question: How much of the variance in Y is accounted for, associated with, or determined by the variance in X? The following table summarizes the relationship between r and r^2, expressing the latter as a percentage to the nearest whole unit ($100r^2$ and rounded):

r	Percent of Variance $100r^2$	r	Percent of Variance: $100r^2$
.00	0%	.55	30%
.05	0	.60	36
.10	1	.65	42
.15	2	.70	49
.20	4	.75	56
.25	6	.80	64
.30	9	.85	72
.35	12	.90	81
.40	16	.95	90
.45	20	.98	96
.50	25	.99	98

The implications of this table can be illustrated by the relationship between grade point average (GPA) and intelligence (IQ) which, in the general population, fluctuates about an r of .50. This suggests that, in variance terms, 25 percent of factors accounting for GPA can be attributed to factors also accounting for IQ; therefore, 75 percent of the determinants of GPA are independent of the IQ. Furthermore, an r of .7071 is necessary before 50 percent of the underlying variance is held in common between two measures.

4. The practical significance of a correlation coefficient in making accurate predictions is revealed in the following table by Thorndike and Hagen:[1]

ACCURACY OF PREDICTION FOR DIFFERENT VALUES OF THE CORRELATION COEFFICIENT
(1000 cases in each row or column)

r = .00

Quarter on Predictor	Quarter on Criterion			
	4th	3rd	2nd	1st
1st	250	250	250	250
2nd	250	250	250	250
3rd	250	250	250	250
4th	250	250	250	250

r = .60

Quarter on Predictor	Quarter on Criterion			
	4th	3rd	2nd	1st
1st	45	141	277	537
2nd	141	264	318	277
3rd	277	318	264	141
4th	537	277	141	45

r = .40

Quarter on Predictor	Quarter on Criterion			
	4th	3rd	2nd	1st
1st	104	191	277	428
2nd	191	255	277	277
3rd	277	277	255	191
4th	428	277	191	104

r = .70

Quarter on Predictor	Quarter on Criterion			
	4th	3rd	2nd	1st
1st	22	107	270	601
2nd	107	270	353	270
3rd	270	353	270	107
4th	601	270	107	22

r = .50

Quarter on Predictor	Quarter on Criterion			
	4th	3rd	2nd	1st
1st	73	168	279	480
2nd	168	258	295	279
3rd	279	295	258	168
4th	480	279	168	73

r = .80

Quarter on Predictor	Quarter on Criterion			
	4th	3rd	2nd	1st
1st	6	66	253	675
2nd	66	271	410	253
3rd	253	410	271	66
4th	675	253	66	6

From this table a number of conclusions can be reached. For instance, if the correlation between a Predictor and a Criterion happens to be .50, then out of the 1000 cases falling in the fourth, or lowest, quarter on the Criterion, on the Predictor only 73 (7.3 percent) scored in the first quarter, 168 (16.8 percent) scored in the second quarter, 279 (27.9 percent) scored in the third quarter, and 480 (48.0 percent) scored in the fourth quarter.

It is also clear that the higher the correlation, the fewer the errors in prediction. The diagonal entries represent cases that fall in the same quarter on both Predictor and Criterion. Note that the further out from the diagonal, the greater the discrepancy between the two variables; also, the higher the correlation, the fewer the discrepancies when moving out from the respective diagonals.

[1]Thorndike, R. L., & Hagen, E. (1969). *Measurement and evaluation in psychology and education* (3rd ed.) (p. 173). New York: Wiley. By permission.

5. The size of *r* increases directly with the variability of the measurements. The more variable the measurements, the higher the correlation coefficient, other things being equal. The problem of *restriction of range* is illustrated by the finding that, when dealing with normal range of variability in the general population, there is an *r* of about .50 between IQ and the achievement. When this range is restricted, as among students qualifying for graduate school, this correlation approaches zero.

6. *Correlation and Causation*
Science is ultimately concerned with identifying cause-and-effect relationships. Since such relationships are always correlated, there is a strong tendency to reverse the process and infer cause-and-effect status between two or more variables based on an established correlation coefficient. The danger is clear: *Correlation does not necessarily imply causation.* Two variables simply may be correlated with a third variable, as in the case of a positive correlation between water temperature and the incidence of drownings along the coast of California. It is incorrect to conclude that warm ocean water is more dangerous and the explanation lies in the obvious fact that more people go swimming when the water is warm, an activity increasing the exposure factor.

A perusal of research on teaching convinces one that the causal interpretation of correlational data is overdone rather than underdone and that plausible rival hypotheses are often overlooked. Furthermore, to establish the temporal antecedent-consequent nature of a causal relationship, observations extended in time, if not experimental intrusion of the treatment variable, are essential. For example, where teacher and pupil behavior are correlated, we would almost never consider the viewpoint that the pupil behavior was causing the teacher behavior, but the other way round. The causal interpretation of a simple or a partial correlation depends upon both the presence of a compatible plausible causal hypothesis and the absence of plausible rival hypotheses to explain the correlation upon other grounds.[1]

7. *Nonlinear or Curvilinear Relationships*
The standard assumption underlying most correlation coefficients is that the relationship between the two variables is linear: As one increases or decreases, so does the other, forming a straight-line regression function. Certain relationships, however, are not this consistent. Chronological age and achievement, for example, increase rapidly in childhood and youth; then level off in the twenties, typically declining with advancing years, creating a U-shaped regression line. A linear correlation study between these two variables using a large age span (age 5 to 65) would probably yield an *r* of zero. In fact, there is a sizeable relationship that simply changes rate and direction with age. Another example would be the relationship between IQ and job performance requiring average ability. Job performance will generally increase between an IQ range of 90 to 110; beyond these limits performance falls off due either to lack of aptitude for lower scores or boredom and lack of challenge for higher scores. Such a relationship is described as *curvilinear*, since high Criterion ratings only occur within an optimum range on the Predictor and decreases in both directions beyond this range:
The simplest procedure for detecting nonlinear trends in correlation data is to construct a scatter diagram (see page 168), inspecting the shape of the plots for bends and curves in the regression line departing from a straight-line function. For a statistical test of linearity-nonlinearity and the most commonly used correlation technique for nonlinear data, the *correlation ratio*, see first entry in item eight, on the following page.

---

[1]Adapted from Campbell, D. T., & Stanley, J. C. (1966). *Experimental and quasi-experimental designs for research.* Chicago, IL: Rand McNally.

8. *Special Correlation Problems and Methods*[1]
Nonlinear regression. The most widely used statistical test to assess the curvature in a regression line is the *F* test of linearity. The statistical method to determine a correlation coefficient with nonlinear data is the *correlation ratio.*

Data where both sets vary along a continuous scale of measurement but one set is arbitrarily dichotomized. Example: A correlation study between IQ and a pass-fail outcome of a driver's license examination. Use the *biserial correlation method.*

Data where one set varies along a continuous scale of measurement but the other set is a true dichotomy. Example: A correlation study between achievement test scores and the dichotomy, male-female. Use the *point-biserial correlation method.*

Data where both sets vary along a continuous scale of measurement but both are arbitrarily dichotomized. Example: A correlation study between achievement test scores and IQ levels when both variables are dichotomized about their respective medians. Use the *tetrachoric correlation method.*

Data where both sets are true dichotomies. Example: A correlation study between residential status (resident-nonresident) and marital status (married-single). Use the *phi coefficient correlation method.*

9. *Other Special Correlation Problems and Methods*
For problems involving more than two variables, such as partial correlation, multiple correlation, and factor analysis, consult Guilford[1] or other advanced treatments of correlation methodology.

10. *Two Final Precautions*
A major weakness of the correlation method is its encouragement of the *"shotgun" approach* to research, devouring all data in sight indiscriminately. Such data are extremely difficult to interpret and mostly useless. Also, the *reliability* of a correlation coefficient varies directly with the sample size.

---

[1]Guilford, J. P. (1965). *Fundamental statistics in psychology and education* (4th ed.) (Chapter 14). New York: McGraw-Hill.

THE PROBLEM OF HITS AND MISSES IN PREDICTIVE VALIDITY:[1]

Many decisions ask for a prediction of success or failure on some future behavior called the *Criterion Variable*, basing the prediction on a *Predictor Variable:* for example, selecting college applicants by predicting their future grade point average (criterion variable) basing the prediction on scores obtained on the College Board Examination (predictor variable).

Since the correlation coefficient between these two variables is imperfect, some of the predictions will be correct (hits) and others will be incorrect (misses). The hits include those correctly predicted to be either successful (*True Positives*) or unsuccessful (*True Negatives*). The misses include those wrongly predicted to be successful (*False Positives*)—those who passed the examination but were unsuccessful in college; and those wrongly predicted to be unsuccessful (*False Negatives*)—those who scored too low on the examination to qualify for admission yet would have succeeded if given the opportunity.

Consider the following Fourfold Table superimposed on a correlation surface (scattergram) representing the distribution of scores between the Predictor Variable and the Criterion Variable:

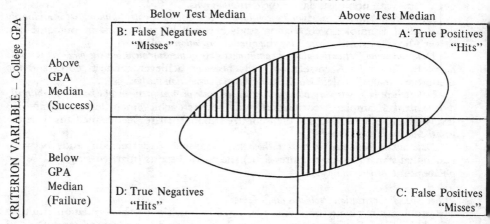

The symbols *B, A, D,* and *C* stand for the numbers of individuals in the first, second, third, and fourth quadrants, respectively. The following statements can then be made:

Let $H = \dfrac{A + D}{N}$ = the proportion of individuals in the total population of size N who are correctly placed (hits).

Let $E = \dfrac{A + D}{N}$ -.5000 = the proportion of correctly placed individuals in excess of the chance proportion of .50 which is associated with an *r* of zero.

---

[1]Adapted from Michael, W. B. (1966). An interpretation of the coefficients of predictive validity and of determination in terms of the proportions of correct inclusions or exclusions in cells of a fourfold table. *Educational and Psychological Measurement, 26*, 419-425.

$$\text{Let } I = \frac{100\left(\dfrac{A + D}{N}\right) - .5000}{.5000} =$$ the percentage of improvement in correct placements relative to the proportion of .50 for an r of zero.

Note: When r is negative, similar definitions are formed using $B + C$ in place of $A + D$.

Three Indices Explaining Predictive Validity for Various Values in r and r^2 when a Correlation Surface is Subdivided at the Median in Both the Predictor and Criterion Variables

r	r^2	H	E	I
.00	.0000	.5000	.0000	0.00
.05	.0025	.5159	.0159	3.18
.10	.0100	.5319	.0319	6.38
.15	.0225	.5479	.0479	9.59
.20	.0400	.5641	.0641	12.82
.25	.0625	.5804	.0804	16.09
.30	.0900	.5970	.0970	19.40
.35	.1225	.6138	.1138	22.76
.40	.1600	.6310	.1310	26.20
.45	.2025	.6486	.1486	29.72
.50	.2500	.6667	.1667	33.33
.55	.3025	.6854	.1854	37.07
.60	.3600	.7048	.2048	40.97
.65	.4225	.7252	.2252	45.05
.70	.4900	.7468	.2468	49.36
.75	.5625	.7699	.2699	53.99
.80	.6400	.7952	.2952	59.03
.85	.7225	.8234	.3234	64.68
.90	.8100	.8564	.3464	71.29
.95	.9025	.8989	.3989	79.78
1.00	1.0000	1.0000	.5000	100.00

Using the above table, the relationships between the indices $H, E,$ and I to both r and r^2 are quickly ascertained. For example, when $r = .60$ and $r^2 = .36$, the Proportion of Correct Placements, H, is .7048, meaning that about 7 out of 10 individuals are being correctly predicted on the criterion. The Proportion of Incorrect Placements, $1 - H$, would be .2952 (the proportion of misses). The index E has a value of .2048, reflecting the proportion in the total population accurately placed in excess of the chance proportion of .5000 when $r =$ zero. This value corresponds to an improvement index I of 40.97 percent in correct placements over that obtainable by chance when $r =$ zero.

Note that when $r = .71$, r^2 is nearly .50 and H approaches .75—an improvement of about 50 percent of correct placements over chance. Since .71 is close to the upper limit of predictive validities in most selection programs, in a situation using *median splits* where chance allows 2 out of 4 correct placements, the Predictor Variable would yield 3 out of 4 correct placements. With smaller selection ratios (.10 to .25),[1] this yield will increase to as much as 4 out of 5, or higher.

---

[1]"Selection ratio" indicates the proportion of individuals in an applicant group who are chosen because they fall above a certain cutting score.

META-ANALYSIS AND EFFECT SIZE[1, 2, 3]

In reviewing the literature to determine the impact of a particular variable of interest one often finds a sizeable number of studies with a range of results, performed with different subjects, under a variety of conditions, and executed with varying degrees of expertise. A problem arises in coming to a summary of conclusions about the variable in question based on the assortment of findings.

Gene Glass and his associates developed a technique called meta-analysis to come to terms with such otherwise elusive information. First, it converts the findings of all the associated studies to a common statistic called effect size (Δ). For studies comparing experimental to control groups, the effect size is computed by subtracting the mean of the control group on the dependent variable from the experimental group mean and dividing by the control group standard deviation. For other inferential statisitics such as F-ratios, percentages, and correlation coefficients, equivalent conversions have been developed. The mean of the effect sizes is then calculated for all the studies reviewed to provide an estimate of average effect of the variable of interest.

Although there are advantages and disadvantages to this technique, it remains the single best method to distill the essence of accumulated research findings. Its major shortcoming is the fact that it makes no distinction between well conducted or poorly conducted studies, methodologically speaking, as meta-analysis treats them uniformly as one body of information. It is argued that the poor studies typically have outcomes similar to the good studies and that there is more to be gained than lost by taking in all the data. On the cautious side, however, it would be important to examine the data – in particular, data from the poor studies – for signs of a systematic bias that, undetected, would mislead the results of meta-analysis.

EFFECT SIZE

In searching for ways of improving student performance, educational researchers are constantly looking for interventions that promise to make a difference. Herbert Walberg and his colleagues analyzed nearly 3,000 such studies to identify interventions and their impact on various measures of academic achievement. The chart on the following page summarizes the results.[4]

The first column lists the interventions studied, each being the subject of numerous investigations. The second column is a statistic called effect size.[5] This statistic describes in a quantitative manner how well the average student receiving the intervention performed relative to the average student not receiving the intervention. An effect size

[1]Glass, G. V. (1976). Primary, secondary, and meta-analysis of research. *Educational Researcher 5*, 3-8.

[2]Glass, G. V., McGraw, B., & Smith, M. L. (1981). *Meta-analysis in social research*. Beverly Hills, CA: Sage.

[3]Borg, W. R., & Gall, M. D. (1989). *Educational research* (5th ed.) (pp. 172-174). White Plains, NY: Longman, Inc.

[4]Data from Walberg, H. J. (1984). Improving the productivity of America's schools. *Educational Leadership, 41*, Table: Reproduced from Borg, W. R., & Gall, M. D. (1989). *Educational research* (5th ed.) (p. 7). White Plains, NY: Longman, Inc.

[5]See discussion under meta-analysis for its calculation.

of 0 indicates no difference between the two. Positive effect sizes indicate that the intervention is making a positive difference and the larger the effect size, the more powerful is the intervention. Researchers consider effect sizes greater than .33 to have a practical significance that is large enough to make a practical difference.

The third column lists percentile equivalency to clarify further the meaning of effect size. The percentile equivalents for each intervention predict where an average student scoring at the 50th percentile on a given achievement instrument prior to receiving the intervention would score following the intervention. For example, before receiving reinforcement a student scoring at the 50th percentile, once given reinforcement, would move to the 88th percentile on that same achievement measure.

EFFECTS OF INSTRUCTIONAL FACTORS ON STUDENT LEARNING OUTCOMES

Method	Size	Percentile
1. Reinforcement	1.17	88
2. Acceleration	1.00	84
3. Reading training	.97	83
4. Cues and feedback	.97	83
5. Science mastery learning	.81	79
6. Graded homework	.79	79
7. Cooperative learning	.76	78
8. Reading experiments	.60	73
9. Class morale	.60	73
10. Personalized instruction	.57	72
11. Home interventions	.50	69
12. Adaptive instruction	.45	67
13. Tutoring	.40	66
14. Instructional time	.38	65
15. Home environment	.37	64
16. Individualized science	.35	64
17. Higher-order questions	.34	63
18. Diagnostic prescriptive methods	.33	63
19. Individualized instruction	.32	63
20. Individualized mathematics	.32	63
21. New science curricula	.31	62
22. Teacher expectations	.28	61
23. Assigned homework	.28	61
24. Socio-economic status	.25	60
25. Computer-assisted instruction	.24	59
26. Peer group	.24	59
27. Sequenced lessons	.24	59
28. Advanced organizers	.23	59
29. New mathematics curricula	.18	57
30. Inquiry biology	.16	56
31. Homogeneous groups	.10	54
32. Class size	.09	54
33. Programmed instruction	-.03	49
34. Television	-.05	48
35. Mainstreaming	-.12	45

Source: Data from Walberg, H. J. (1984). Improving the productivity of America's schools. *Educational Leadership, 41.* Reproduced from Borg, W. R., & Gall, M. D. (1989). *Educational research* (5th ed.). White Plains, NY: Longman, Inc.

MULTIVARIATE STATISTICAL PROCEDURES

Although this volume is an introductory one, an extremely brief overview of four widely-employed multivariate techniques is presented. The interested reader can find additional information of varying levels of complexity in the following section of references dealing with multivariate statistical procedures (at the very end of this chapter).

MULTIPLE REGRESSION ANALYSIS

In multiple regression analysis two important objectives are (a) to determine the degree of relationship given by an index number known as the multiple correlation coefficient between a customarily continuous criterion measure (dependent variable) and an optimally weighted combination of two or more predictor (independent) variables that are usually continuous and (b) to predict the standing of individuals in a sample on the criterion variable from scores earned in a weighted linear combination of predictor variables along with an indication of an expected margin of error. Occasional instances do arise in which the criterion variable is dichotomous or trichotomous rather than strictly continuous. Numerous procedures are available for selection of predictor variables to maximize the degree of relationship between the criterion measure and a weighted composite of predictors and correspondingly to minimize the errors of prediction. Typically, the most efficient prediction and highest degree of multiple correlation occurs when each predictor variable shows a modest to high correlation with the criterion measure, but a low or preferably zero correlation with every other predictor. The multiple correlation coefficient obtained for a given sample is likely to be inflated in value as a function of favorable sampling errors that entered into the selection of the predictors. Hence, it is important that the regression equation or prediction equation derived from one sample be applied to another to ascertain how much shrinkage in the multiple correlation has occurred. Known as a cross-validation procedure, the observed scores in the criterion measure for the new sample are correlated with the predicted scores of the new sample as derived from the regression equation obtained from the first sample.

Multiple regression techniques have been widely employed in the selection of personnel in business and industry and in the civil and military services of the nation. Multiple regression techniques have been particularly effective in decision making concerning which of several measures should be included in a test battery for selection of personnel. The multiple correlation coefficient is an indicator of the validity of a battery or combination of tests—a validity coefficient that typically exceeds the value of the zero-order coefficient associated with a single predictor.

DISCRIMINANT FUNCTION ANALYSIS

Whereas multiple regression analysis is often employed for selection purposes, discriminant analysis is used primarily to classify individuals into two or more categories such as occupational groups, college majors, or personality types. A simple discriminant analysis is concerned with the prediction of membership in one of two categories of a dependent variable from scores on two or more predictor variables, and a multiple discriminant analysis is directed toward prediction of membership in one of three or more categories in a dependent variable from scores on a similar composite of two or more predictor variables. In the instance of a dichotomous criterion measure to which values of one or zero could be assigned, the simple discriminant analysis equation will register weights proportional to those found for the multiple regression equation and thus will afford a comparable solution in the prediction process. Accuracy of prediction in discriminant analysis is often evaluated in terms of the frequencies of correct and incorrect placements in the criterion categories as predicted in relation to the actual frequencies of placement in the same categories. As in multiple regression analysis, it is important to carry out cross-validation procedures, as once again, predictor variables are often chosen for inclusion in the discriminant equation on the basis of patterns of correlation coefficients that have been distorted by sampling error.

CANONICAL ANALYSIS

Representing in effect an extension of multiple regression analysis, a canonical analysis permits the estimation of the maximum degree of association (canonical correlation) between a linear set or weighted combination of two or more criterion variables with a corresponding linear set or weighted combination of two or more predictor variables. Typically, both criterion and predictor measures are continuous. The canonical solution provides (a) first a choice of an initial pair of dimensions (a linear combination of variables)–one from the group of criterion measures and the other from the group of predictor variables–that affords the highest possible degree of association or correlation and (b) the progressive selection of remaining pairs of dimensions until non-chance or reliable variance in scores has been almost entirely extracted. However, never more dimensions can be identified than the number of variables in the smaller set of criterion or predictor measures. The successive canonical correlations between each criterion set and predictor set do not necessarily show a progressive diminution in value. As implied earlier, each canonical coefficient portrays the maximum possible amount of association between two canonical variates within a given pair of dimensions. In short, the weights assigned to members of the predictor composite (a canonical variate for the set of independent variables) yields the most nearly correct potential prediction of standing on the optimally but differently weighted members of the criterion composite (a canonical variate for the group of dependent variables).

It has been the writers' experience that canonical correlations and associated analyses do not provide for nearly so meaningful psychological interpretability of behavioral data as do alternative multivariate methodologies such as those found in multiple regression analysis, simple or multiple discriminant analysis, or factor analysis. However, it is possible to square the canonical correlation coefficient to identify what proportion of variance is shared by the pair of extracted dimensions.

This squaring of a correlation coefficient in the instance of multiple regression analysis furnishes a means of ascertaining what proportion of variance in the criterion measure is accounted for by the composite of optimally weighted predictor variables. Moreover, a technique known as commonality analysis applied to multiple regression data permits an identification of what proportion of variance each independent variable contributes by itself and in combination with other predictor variables to the variance in the criterion measure. This approach has been described at length and illustrated in the 1989 text by Kerlinger and Pedhazur that is cited in the references at the conclusion of this chapter.

FACTOR ANALYSIS

Factor analysis is a statistical procedure that affords an explanation of how the variance common to several intercorrelated measures can be accounted for in terms of a small number of dimensions with which the variables are correlated. In addition to describing a parsimonious structure in the covariation present among many variables in terms of a relatively small number of common factors, the technique provides a means for testing of hypotheses regarding anticipated structures and for generating new hypotheses to account for unanticipated dimensions that may emerge.

The correlation of a variable (typically a test) with a statistically isolated dimension is called a factor loading for that variable. Customarily, at least three (test) variables must register correlations or loadings on a factor so that it can be given a psychologically meaningful interpretation. It is not uncommon to find clusters or groupings of variables that will yield modest to high correlations on just one factor or possibly two factors, but virtually zero loadings with other dimensions. Once the factor solution has been found that is psychologically interpretable, an improved understanding of the constructs represented by the variables often results.

As a rule, one can identify about one third as many dimensions as there are correlated variables. From the loadings that these variables display on the factor dimensions, it is possible to reproduce rather closely the initial matrix of correlations among all the variables.

It should also be pointed out that the factor dimensions may or may not be correlated with one another. Many factor analysts prefer to work (for reasons of simplicity of interpretation and of mathematical computations) with independent factor dimensions that are said to be orthogonal to one another. The presence of correlated dimensions is said to be associated with an oblique solution. Test variables also register loadings on oblique factors, although the magnitudes of these loadings will differ from those found in the orthogonal solution. In summary it may be mentioned that three kinds of potential correlations exist: (a) correlations among pairs of the initial variables (typically tests), (b) correlations between each test and a factor dimension (orthogonal or oblique), and (c) correlations among the dimensions themselves (correlations which are zero in the orthogonal case). Mathematical procedures exist for determining these correlations from raw score data that can be entered into computers for processing. Despite the existence of relatively objective statistical procedures, the output may be difficult to interpret psychologically particularly in the absence of a careful design for the selection of variables (within a well defined and carefully delineated test domain) that are congruent with the constructs of at least a rudimentary theory or model.

The meaningful use of factor analysis depends upon a considerable amount of training and psychological insight. The references set forth in the concluding section of this chapter should be helpful to the interested readers who wish to expand their horizons in a challenging and useful methodology.

REFERENCES
General References in Statistics

Dinham, S. M. (1983). *Exploring statistics: An introduction for psychology and education.* Monterey, CA: Brooks & Cole.

Dixon, W. J., & Massey, F. J., Jr. (1983). *Introduction to statistical analysis* (4th ed.). New York: McGraw-Hill.

Ferguson, G. A., & Takane, Y. (1989). *Statistical analysis in psychology and education* (6th ed.). New York: McGraw-Hill.

Glass, G. V., & Hopkins, K. D. (1995). *Statistical methods in education and psychology.* Englewood Cliffs, NJ: Prentice Hall.

Guilford, J. P., & Fruchter, B. (1978). *Fundamental statistics in psychology and education* (6th ed.). New York: McGraw-Hill.

Hays, W. L. (1988). *Statistics* (4th ed.). New York: Holt, Rinehart and Winston.

Hinkle, D. E., Wiersma, W., & Jurs, S. G. (1994). *Applied statistics for the behavioral sciences* (3rd ed.). Geneva, NY: Houghton Mifflin.

Hopkins, K. D., & Hopkins (in press). *Basic statistics for the behavioral sciences.* Englewood Cliffs, NJ: Prentice Hall.

Hurlburt, R. T. (1994). *Comprehending behavioral statistics.* Monterey, CA: Brooks & Cole.

Kirk, R. E. (1990). *Statistics: An introduction* (3rd ed.). New York: Harcourt, Brace, Jovanovich.

Lehman, R. S. (1994). *Statistics in the behavioral sciences: A conceptual introduction.* Monterey, CA: Brooks & Cole.

McCall, R. B. (1994). *Fundamental statistics for the behavioral sciences* (6th ed.). New York: Harcourt, Brace, Jovanovich.

McNemar, Q. (1975). *Psychological statistics* (5th ed.). New York: Wiley.

Minium, E. W., King, B. M., & Bear, G. (1993). *Statistical reasoning in psychology and education* (3rd ed.). New York: Wiley.

Roscoe, J. T. (1975). *Fundamental research statistics for the behavioral sciences* (2nd ed.). New York: Holt, Rinehart and Winston.

Runyon, R. P., & Haber, A. (1991). *Fundamentals of behavioral statistics* (7th ed.). New York: McGraw-Hill.

Runyon, R. P., Haber, A., & Coleman, K. A. (1994). *Behavioral statistics: The core.* New York: McGraw-Hill.

Shavelson, R. J. (1989). *Statistical reasoning for the behavioral sciences* (2nd ed.). Boston: Allyn and Bacon.

Siegel, S. S. (1988). *Nonparametric statistics for the behavioral sciences* (2nd ed.). New York: McGraw-Hill.

Walker, H. M., & Lev, J. (1953). *Statistical inference.* New York: Holt. (Cited for historical importance).

Weinberg, G. H., & Schumaker, J. A. (1981). *Statistics: An intuitive approach* (3rd ed.). Monterey, CA: Brooks & Cole.

Experimental Design

Campbell, D. T., & Stanley, J. C. (1966). *Experimental and quasi-experimental designs for research.* Chicago: Rand McNally.

Cook, T. D., & Campbell, D. T. (1976). The design and conduct of quasi-experiments and true experiments in field settings. In M. D. Dunnette (Ed.), *Handbook of industrial and organizational psychology.* Chicago: Rand McNally.

Cook, T. D., & Campbell, D. T. (1979). *Quasi-experimentation: Design and analysis issues for field settings.* Chicago: Rand McNally.

Edwards, A. L. (1972). *Experimental design in psychological research* (4th ed.). New York: Holt, Rinehart and Winston.

Kirk, R. E. (1994). *Experimental design: Procedures for the behavioral sciences* (3rd ed.). Belmont, CA: Wadsworth.

Winer, B. J., Brown, D., & Michels, K. E. (1991). *Statistical principles in experimental design* (2nd ed.). New York: McGraw-Hill.

Multivariate Statistical Procedures

Bentler, P. M. (1980). Multivariate analysis with latent variables: Causal modeling. In M. R. Rosenzweig and L. W. Porter (Eds.), *Annual review of psychology* (Vol. 31). Palo Alto, CA: Annual Reviews. (A very basic article with excellent bibliography.)

Bentler, P. M. (1989). *EQS structural equations program manual.* Los Angeles, CA: BMDP Statistical Software, Inc.

BMDP (1994). Los Angeles, CA: BMDP Statistical Software, Inc. (Statistical software packages available for PC use.)

Bock, R. D. (1975). *Multivariate statistical methods in behavioral research.* New York: McGraw-Hill. (An advanced book requiring considerable statistical sophistication.)

Cohen, J., & Cohen, P. (1983). *Applied multiple regression/correlation analysis for the behavioral sciences* (2nd ed.). Hillsdale, NJ: Lawrence Erlbaum Assoc, Inc.. (Intermediate difficulty level.)

Comrey, A. L., & Lee, H. B. (1992). *A first course in factor analysis* (2nd ed.). Hillsdale, NJ: Lawrence Erlbaum Assoc. Inc.

Cooley, W. W., & Lohnes, P. R. (1971). *Multivariate data analysis.* New York: Wiley. (Combines general theoretical principles with many computer programs.)

Everitt, B. (1992). *Applied multivariate data analysis.* New York: Oxford University Press.

Ezekiel, M., & Fox, K. A. (1965). *Methods of correlation and regression analysis: Linear and curvilinear.* New York: Wiley.

Gorsuch, R. L. (1989). *Factor analysis.* Hillsdale, NJ: Lawrence Erlbaum.

Guertin, W. H., & Bailey, J. P. (1970). *Introduction to modern factor analysis.* Ann Arbor, MI: Edwards. (Elementary text.)

Harman, H. H. (1967). *Modern factor analysis* (2nd ed.). Chicago, IL: University of Chicago Press. (Authoritative but relatively difficult text.)

Johnson, R. A. (1992). *Applied multivbariate statistical analysis* (3rd ed.). Englewood Cliffs, NJ: Prentice Hall.

Jöreskog, K. G., & Sörbom, D. (1993). *LISREL 8: Structural equation modeling with the SIMPLIS*[TM] *command language.* Hillsdale, NJ: Lawrence Erlbaum Assoc. Inc. (A very basic document affording information for computer programs in causal modeling and confirmatory factor analysis).

Kerlinger, F. N., & Pedhazur, E. J. (1989). *Multiple regression in behavioral research.* New York: Holt, Rinehart and Winston. (A basic text in multiple regression analysis and in associated topics in multivariate analysis that is extremely clearly written with a minimum of mathematical notation.)

Lindeman, R. H., Merenda, P. F., & Gold, R. Z. (1980). *Introduction to bivariate and multivariate analysis.* Glenview, IL: Scott, Foresman. (A well-written text that provides a most favorable balance between a verbalized psychological interpretation of multivariate methods of data analysis and mathematical notation.)

Merrifield, P. R. (1974). Factor analysis in educational research. In F. N. Kerlinger (Ed.), *Review of Research in Education* (Vol. 2.). Itasca, IL: F. E. Peacock.

Meyer, G. E. (1993). *SPSS: A minimalist approach.* New York: Harcourt Brace.

Michael, W. B. (1982). Prediction methods. In H. F. Mitzel, J. H. Best, and W. Rabinowitz (Eds.), *Encyclopaedia of Educational Research* (5th ed.). Toronto, Canada: MacMillan.

Nie, N. H., Hull, C. H., Jenkins, J. G., Steinbrenner, K., & Bent, D. H. (1994). *SPSS: Statistical package for the social sciences.* New York: McGraw-Hill. (Basic computer programs available for use in PC applications.)

Nunnally, J. C., & Bernstein, I. H. (1994). *Psychometric theory* (3rd ed.). New York: McGraw-Hill. (Chapters 5, 10, 11, and 12.) (Intermediate difficulty level.)

Rummel, R. J. (1970). *Applied factor analysis.* Evanston, IL: Northwestern University Press. (Relatively easy text to read.)

SAS Institute Inc. (1992). SAS/STAT. Cary, NC: SAS Institute Inc.

Stevens, J. (1992). *Applied multivariate statistics for the social sciences* (3rd ed.). Hillsdale, NJ: Lawrence Erlbaum.

Tabachnick, B. G. & Fidell, L. (1983). *Using multivariate statistics.* New York: Harper & Row.

Tatsuoka, M. M. (1988). *Multivariate analysis: Techniques for educational and psychological research* (2nd ed.). Englewood, Cliffs, NJ: Prentice Hall

Thorndike, R. M. (1978). *Correlational procedures for research.* New York: Gardner Press. (Very clearly written with superb diagrams.)

Timm, N. H. (1975). *Multivariate analysis with applications in education and psychology.* Monterey, CA: Brooks/Cole.

Van de Geer, J. P. (1971). *Introduction to multivariate analysis for the social sciences.* San Francisco: W. H. Freeman.

Weiss, D. J. (1976). Multivariate procedures. In M D. Dunnette (Ed.), *Handbook of industrial and organizational psychology.* Chicago: Rand McNally. (An excellent overview of multivariate methods.)

CHAPTER SEVEN

NATURALISTIC/QUALITATIVE EVALUATION METHODOLOGY[1]

At the onset of the massive federal effort to support education in the 1960's, requirements for program evaluation suffered from at least one major shortcoming. At the time the state-of-the-art for evaluating such programs was largely dependent on traditional experimental paradigms as represented by Campbell and Stanley's classic work in this field (1966). As Stufflebeam (1971) has pointed out, experimental designs have substantial utility for evaluating the attainment of goals and objectives of comprehensive ongoing programs involving measurable products where the focus is on summative or terminal outcomes. They are not intended, however, to address the needs of formative evaluation where the emphasis is upon assessing the process components underlying program development and implementation.

Moreover, experimental paradigms run the risk of creating artificial conditions that are seldom realistic or practical when it comes to the ongoing educational enterprise. They violate the natural context in which classroom (or other real world) activities are normally conducted which often make as much difference as the treatment itself.

To capture this context, as well as to recognize what is going on during the development and implementation stages of a program and its processes, naturalistic methods are appropriate.[2]

This section presents some of the salient highlights of naturalistic program evaluation. Although the proponents of these methodologies have built a persuasive case for their use as independent, stand-alone alternatives in place of the more traditional approaches, it is more likely that they will be used in a complementary manner by combining methods as each study and setting invite.

---

[1]Reprinted from Husen, T., & Postlethwaite, T. H. (1994). The International Encyclopedia of Education (2nd ed.). From Vol. 4 *Evolution of Evaluation Design* by Michael W. B., & Benson, J. with kind permission from Elsevier Science Ltd., The Boulevard, Langford Lane. Kidlington OX5 1CB UK.

[2]Naturalistic methodology is used here as a generic term to include ethnographic and qualitative research methods as well.

NATURALISTIC, ETHNOGRAPHIC, AND QUALITATIVE RESEARCH METHODS DEFINED

The three terms – naturalistic, ethnographic, and qualitative – are often used interchangeably. Although they have much in common, each does have distinguishing features that characterize it. Of the three, naturalistic research is the most encompassing. It is based on the philosophical viewpoint of phenomenology allowing multiple realities arising from natural differences in the development of human perception. This is in contrast to the philosophy of positivism underlying conventional scientific research which presupposes a single reality governed by a finite number of laws to be discovered by investigating cause-and-effect relationships among the variables under controlled conditions. The thrust of naturalistic research is to investigate human behavior in its natural and unique contexts and settings by avoiding the artificial constraints of control and manipulation. Because of its dependence on human perception and multiple realities, it is not concerned at arriving at a final unified system of knowledge, as is most conventional research. It is heavily empirical and ideographic in its outlook.

Ethnographic methodology, by way of anthropology, is a particular application of naturalistic research that focuses upon the study of a culture or community with the intent of a descriptive reconstruction of its characteristic attributes and dimensions. Obviously, it depends heavily on both qualitative and naturalistic principles and methods.

Qualitative methodology addresses the manner of generating data by underscoring its contrast to quantitative methodology that is so pervasive in conventional research. It principally reflects the role of subjective judgment in generating data. Typical examples would be survey research originating in sociology involving the attitudes or opinions of human subjects and observational research involving the judgment of an observer. Common themes within a body of information are sought and interpreted as are discrepancies and inconsistencies.

To avoid redundancy, the discussion that follows will refer to naturalistic research because of its more inclusive scope.

TRADITIONAL AND NATURALISTIC METHODOLOGIES COMPARED[1]

In the planning of evaluation studies there are three factors to anticipate: (1) The precise nature of the information that is needed to answer questions about the effectiveness of the program; (2) The optimal means of obtaining that information; and (3) An ongoing awareness of the primary audience to receive the report to ensure that the methods and types of analyses used will be appropriate and understandable.

Once the information needs have been clearly specified, there are essentially four kinds of designs with which to proceed. The first three are traditional and the fourth is more recently gaining acceptance: experimental, quasi-experimental, survey, and naturalistic.

Experimental design. In its classic form, depends heavily on controlling all potential independent and extraneous variables and on deliberately manipulating the one of

[1]Reprinted from Husen, T., & Postlethwaite, T. H. (1994). *The International Encyclopedia of Education* (2nd ed.). From Vol. 4 *Evolution of Evaluation Design* by Michael W. B., & Benson, J. with kind permission from Elsevier Science Ltd., The Boulevard, Langford Lane. Kidlington OX5 1CB UK.

principal interest called the experimental or dependent variable, with many variations on this theme. A distinctive feature of this method is the random selection of participants and random assignment of treatment conditions to give it maximum protection from sources of bias or contamination. This feature makes it the most rigorous and powerful of the designs in establishing causal relationships among the variables. Its principal weakness is the presence of artificial or unnatural conditions that make its results difficult to generalize to the real world.

Quasi-experimental design recognizes that in most real life or applied settings it is not feasible or even possible to control all the independent or extraneous variables – in particular, to carry out the random selection of subjects and random assignment of treatments as required in its true experimental counterpart. The evaluator proceeds under the best approximations that circumstances allow. Although less rigorous or powerful, the quasi-experimental design allows the evaluator to meet enough of the experimental demands to remain credible. It is further reinforced by such techniques as replication and the use of different cohorts to study program impact.

Survey design, as the term implies, is a systematic means of collecting descriptive information about the characteristics, practices, or attitudes of a defined population of participants. Surveys, which are the most common tool used in applied research, are most often found in the fields of sociology, political science, business, and education to gather factual information necessary for policy decisions. Although their strength is a relatively quick and cost-effective means of gathering data, their weakness lies in the standardization of their questions, and in the risk of making complex issues oversimplified and superficial.

Naturalistic design addresses the overriding weaknesses in the previous three approaches to gathering information – specifically, the artificial nature of experimental designs and the superficiality of surveys. What naturalistic design strives to preserve is the real life context in which events occur and the manner in which the many complex variables interact, with a minimum of intrusion and an absence of any attempt to control or manipulate variables. Case and field methods are, for all practical purposes, closely related terms. What emerges as perhaps the principal limitation of these approaches is the possibility that the unique differences in many such studies will allow a minimal amount of generalization and little opportunity to derive conclusions of casuality.

FIFTEEN ATTRIBUTES OF NATURALISTIC INQUIRY[1]

1. Naturalistic inquiry takes place in a natural setting. The distinctive point of view is that human behavior is best understood in its real-world context. It sees causes and effects as interactive and inseparable. To establish so-called experimental conditions introduces variables that are artificial and misleading.
2. The primary instrument for data collection is the human observer because he or she is the most sensitive, insightful, and wide-ranging source of information where complex phenomena are concerned.
3. Because of its reliance on human perception, naturalistic inquiry leads to multiple realities – the world as seen through the eyes of more than one beholder. This circumstance is illustrated by the contrasting world views constructed by cultures throughout history. The assumption is made that each of these multiple realities is equally legitimate and in that sense each is "real."

---

[1]Adapted from Lincoln, Y. S., & Guba, E. G. (1985). *Naturalistic inquiry.* Beverly Hills: Sage.

4. In addition to propositional knowledge (knowledge directly expressible in language form), naturalistic inquiry relies on tacit or intuitive knowledge to appreciate multiple realities, to tap the subtleties of human interaction, and more accurately to reflect the value patterns of the investigator.

5. Qualitative methods normally are preferred to quantitative ones because they adapt more readily to multiple realities; more appropriately reflect the nature of investigator-respondent interaction, including biases of the former's own perspective; and are more adaptable and sensitive to the variety of influences and value patterns encountered.

6. Purposeful sampling[1] is preferred to random or representative sampling because it brings to light a wider range of cases, the extremes of which are of particular interest. It also increases the likelihood of uncovering the full array of multiple realities as well as maximizing the investigator's accounting for the nature of conditions, interactions, and values that might be useful in assessing transferability.

7. Inductive data analysis is preferred to its deductive counterpart because it is more likely to identify multiple realities in data because it makes the investigator-respondent interaction more nearly clear and more accountable; because its more encompassing description facilitates decisions about transferability; because it is better suited in identifying the interaction or mutually-shaping influences; and it makes values an explicit part of the analytic structure.

8. Grounded theory that emerges from the data is the trademark of naturalistic inquiry, in contrast to a priori theory which cannot anticipate the possible variety of multiple realities that may be forthcoming. This approach preserves the neutrality of the investigator and any prejudgments that a priori theories otherwise impose on data.

9. This emergent research design unfolds as a function of interaction with the social entity under investigation. To proceed in a conventional manner underlying the experimental method would contradict both the letter and the spirit of naturalistic inquiry, which avoids imposing a preordained structure on phenomena. What one would need to know to do otherwise can only be found out through interaction with the entity in question, out of which the data eventually emerge.

10. The research outcomes are the result of negotiations between the researcher and the human sources yielding the data. This result is appropriate, as it is the reality constructions of the latter that the inquirer seeks to reconstruct. Only the providers of this information can verify the authenticity of the data and the associated meanings and interpretations arising in context with local conditions, patterns, and values.

11. The preferred mode of reporting is the case study mode because it is the most adaptable to emergent multiple realities. It is also more adaptable to the nature of the researcher's particular viewpoint and to the manner in which this viewpoint interacts with those of the respondents and their respective values. It lends itself to the generation of so-called "thick descriptions" which attempt to provide detailed reconstructions of the various multiple realities and which lay the foundation on which transferability is judged.

12. Data interpretations are likely to be idiographic (in terms of particulars in each case) rather than nomothetic (in terms of lawlike generalizations across cases). This situation is so because different interpretations are likely to reflect the unique attributes of different realities. Moreover, the idiosyncratic nature of each investigator and each group of respondents, the contextual features distinguishing each setting, and the specific interaction of values representing all relevant participants further incline interpretations accordingly.

---

[1]See pages 223-224.

13. Findings are likely to be regarded by the researcher as tentative because of the uncertainties, making broad application of the results tenuous. The entire combination of factors underlying this inclination includes the multiple nature of realities, their differences, and the extent to which the attributes and interactions within a given research setting and its participants are unique.
14. The boundaries for a given inquiry are likely to be emergent rather than preconceived, inasmuch as the multiple realities are not necessarily known at the onset of any investigation. Such a determination depends upon an intimate knowledge of context and the factors shaping mutual perspectives, interpretations, and values.
15. Trustworthiness of results involves special criteria. The conventional standards of internal and external validity, reliability, and objectivity pose serious problems in a naturalistic setting. In their place, four similar but modified criteria are proposed: credibility, transferability, dependability, and confirmability.

BUILDING TRUSTWORTHINESS INTO NATURALISTIC STUDIES[1]

Conventional methodology puts a major emphasis on four criteria to ensure that research results are sound: (1) internal validity, designed to eliminate rival explanations for the findings in contrast to those advanced by the researcher; (2) external validity, which seeks to generalize research findings from a particular study to other appropriate settings; (3) reliability, which asks whether or not findings in a particular study can be replicated; and (4) objectivity, which strives to eliminate subjective bias by assuring that the methods of obtaining information are public and observable in order to allow agreement across multiple observers.

Naturalistic studies taking place in real life settings and relying primarily on qualitative methods of data collection have a similar need. As with conventional research, four criteria have been proposed to accomplish this need. Although they play a similar role, their characterization is distinctly different: (1) credibility, which aims to produce findings that are believable and convincing; (2) transferability, which attempts to apply findings in one setting to other contextually similar settings; (3) dependability, which addresses the question concerning which findings are consistent with those of other similar investigations; and (4) confirmability, which ensures that both the process and the product are auditable.

CRITERIA FOR ESTABLISHING TRUST AND CONFIDENCE IN RESEARCH RESULTS

Conventional Research	Naturalistic Research
Internal Validity – Did variations in the independent variable produce a change in the dependent variable?	Credibility – Will the methodology and its conduct produce findings that are believable and convincing?
External Validity – Can the results of this investigation be generalized to other settings?	Transferability – To what other contextually similar settings can these findings be applied?
Reliability – Are the results consistent, repeatable, and predictable from one study to another?	Dependability – Within reasonable limits, are the findings consistent with other similar studies?
Objectivity – Are the events under study public and observable so as to allow agreement among investigators?	Confirmability – Are both the process and the product of the data collection and analysis auditable by an outside party?

[1]Adapted from Lincoln, Y. S., & Guba, E. G. (1985). *Naturalistic inquiry*. Beverly Hills: Sage.

OVERVIEW OF NATURALISTIC CRITERIA[1]

Given the relative unfamiliarity and subjectivity of naturalistic methodology, what follows is a brief summary of the four criteria presented in the chart on the previous page. Noteworthy in this overview are the rigor and labor intensive thoroughness of this approach when properly conducted.

Credibility

The key to establishing credibility in naturalistic research is a judgment call by its reviewers in evaluating the quality of the study and its conduct. Five techniques are proposed by Lincoln and Guba in reaching this conclusion:

1. *Integrity of the observations.* This technique involves the following:
   a. Prolonged engagement sufficient to gain an overview of the social entity and its context to minimize sources of misinformation and distortions, and to build trust.
   b. Persistent observation aimed at sorting out the significant from the superfluous, as well as identifying salient features and any noteworthy atypical events.
   c. Triangulation designed to corroborate findings by arriving at them from different directions, using different sources, methods, or investigators.

2. *Peer debriefing.* This technique involves engaging a disinterested outside party to ask searching questions, to play the devil's advocate, and generally to explore the breadth and depth of one's approach by identifying its strengths and weaknesses, as well as its implications, oversights and choice of options. Although this procedure runs the risk of prematurely discouraging further inquiry or inappropriately deflecting its intent, the benefits of enhancing the quality of the study and of avoiding pitfalls outweigh these risks.

3. *Negative case analysis.* This technique is the process of revising a hypothesis through applying hindsight until it accounts for all known cases without exception. In contrast to accepting or rejecting hypotheses statistically, as in conventional research, the task in naturalistic inquiry is to recast hypotheses until they fit the observed reality.

4. *Referential adequacy.* This technique necessitates the recording and setting aside of unanalyzed raw data either through using videotapes or by archiving sections of the data collection process, so that at a later time, when tentative findings are being formulated, these reserve records can be examined for fit with the emerging findings from the principal data sources. Although many drawbacks are present in this approach (loss of data to the main study, the question of their representativeness, and use by reviewers of similar or different frameworks in their analysis), it is an option worthy of serious consideration in the interest of credibility.

5. *Member checks.* This approach is the most crucial technique of the five in establishing credibility. It involves the representativeness of the participants themselves from whom data were originally obtained by testing the authenticity of these data, analytic categories, interpretations, and conclusions. This checking is done both formally and informally, as well as continuously. Although this checking can precipitate problems, without the agreement of those whose reality is being reconstructed, credibility is nil.

---

[1]Adapted from Lincoln, Y. S., & Guba, E. G. (1985). *Naturalistic inquiry.* Beverly Hills: Sage.

Transferability

Transferability asks the question, are there similarities between the original study and its context and any other settings where this conclusion is possible? Although this transferability is not a necessary outcome of naturalistic inquiry, it is a finding that lends credence to its value and utility as a scientific contribution.

Dependability

This criterion of dependability asks the question, if it were done over again, would one arrive at essentially the same findings and conclusions? Lincoln and Guba propose two ways of answering this question. First, is the method of overlap, a variation of triangulation, where the investigator comes at the problem from different angles to determine whether or not the original findings hold up. Second, is an abbreviated version of the audit where an outside person examines both the process and the product of a particular inquiry, including the accuracy and integrity of the data.

Confirmability

The most ambitious and demanding of the four criteria, confirmability involves a full-scale inquiry audit where the auditor agrees to follow the entire sequence of events from beginning to end by checking, reconstructing, and assessing the audit trail of data and records, as well as the nature and adequacy of the overall audit process. The purpose of this comprehensive examination is to establish the extent to which not only sound decisions and judgments were made but if accurate information was recorded. It ultimately leads to a statement by the auditor attesting to the adequacy of the study.

PURPOSEFUL SAMPLING

A method of sampling data that is particularly appropriate for naturalistic research is *purposeful sampling*. It is a series of sampling strategies designed to understand certain select cases in their own right rather than to generalize results to a population, as in the case of random or representative sampling based on probability. The power of purposeful sampling lies in selecting what Patton has called information-rich cases for study in-depth – cases from which one can learn most about issues central to the purpose of the evaluation and the needs of decision makers.[1]

1. *Extreme or deviant case sampling.* It is often informative to examine some of the extreme cases in a population – those performing unusually well or poorly. The logic of this strategy is that one has the most to learn from these two categories as compared to studying average cases. The strategy, when it is economical in the instance of limited resources and time, aims straight at the most promising sources of useful information.
2. *Maximum variation sampling.* This strategy sets out to sample the wide range of diversity that exists in a particular population with the aim of capturing central themes or principal outcomes. This sampling is done by selecting the most diverse characteristics on which to base the sample with two outcomes in mind: (a) High quality and detailed descriptions of each case to document uniqueness; and (b) important shared patterns cutting across cases that assume increased significance because they emerged out of heterogeneity.

---

[1]Adapted from Patton, M. Q. (1990). *Qualitative evaluation and research methods.* Thousand Oaks, CA: Sage.

3. *Homogeneous samples.* In deliberate contrast to maximum variation sampling, is the strategy of picking a small homogeneous sample. By describing some particular subgroup in-depth, especially if that subgroup contains significant or challenging types of individuals, one obtains information that illuminates major program evaluation issues.
4. *Typical case sampling.* In the instance of this form of sampling the intent is to profile what is average or usual when that is the appropriate focus for decision makers or other interested individuals, especially if they are unfamiliar with what is typical. It is important to achieve broad consensus about what is usual so that the selection of cases reflect these criteria.
5. *Critical case sampling.* Sampling critical cases refers to those that can make a point quite dramatically or are particularly important in the scheme of things. This procedure is useful when time and resources are limited and when one or more salient cases exist which somehow sum up the problem in a nutshell or are "make or break" cases in the eyes of decision makers.
6. *Snowball or chain sampling.* The aim of this approach is to locate key informants or information-rich cases that zoom in on significant aspects of a study. The process begins by asking, "Who knows a lot about_____?" One informant leads to another, until the more knowledgeable ones are identified through repeated reference, along with the more significant events.
7. *Criterion sampling.* The logic of this strategy is to study all cases that meet some predetermined criterion of importance. In particular, it sets out to understand cases which are likely to be information rich because they may reveal major system weaknesses (or strengths) leading to program improvement.
8. *Confirmatory or disconfirming cases.* Following the early exploratory phase of qualitative evaluation, when some preliminary patterns and findings have emerged, it is useful to identify confirming or disconfirming cases that either support or call into question the emerging trends and patterns. They add richness, depth, credibility, or raise still further questions or limitations. They often become the key exhibits of an evaluator's work.
9. *Sampling politically important cases.* Because evaluation often takes place in a politically sensitive environment, it is practical to sample politically important or sensitive cases. This approach does not imply any improprieties to "stack the deck" or to gain favor but is grounded in the realistic position that some things are more visible and consequential than others to the body politic. It makes sense both to be informed and forthcoming in their regard.
10. *Convenience sampling.* Finally, comes the strategy that is weakest of the ten: sampling for what is most quickly and easily available. Whereas each of the preceding approaches attempts to sample in a manner that extracts the most useful information with minimum effort, convenience sampling simply takes what involves the least effort. It is, in actuality, neither purposeful nor strategic.

REFERENCES

Denzin, N. K., & Lincoln, Y. S. (1994). *Handbook of qualitative research.* Thousand Oaks, CA: Sage.
Marshall, C., & Rossman, G. B. (1994). *Designing qualitative research* (2nd ed.). Thousand Oaks, CA: Sage.
Miles, M. B., & Huberman, A. M. (1994). *Qualitative data analysis.* Thousand Oaks, CA: Sage.
Walcott, H. F. (1994). *Transforming qualitative data.* Thousand Oaks, CA: Sage.

"When I use a word," Humpty Dumpty said,
"it means just what I choose it to mean—neither more nor less."
"The question is," said Alice, "whether you can make words mean so many different things."
"The question is," said Humpty Dumpty,
"which is to be the master—that's all."

Lewis Carroll

THROUGH THE LOOKING GLASS

CHAPTER EIGHT

STATING COGNITIVE AND AFFECTIVE OBJECTIVES

WRITING BEHAVIORAL OBJECTIVES

Educational *objectives* typically are the offspring of parent goal statements. Educational *goals* are broadly philosophical, global, relatively timeless and nonmeasurable. For example:

- ✓ To prepare students for a life of responsible citizenship
- ✓ To provide students with the basic competencies to survive
- ✓ To enable students to develop a wholesome self-concept

As these statements stand, they lack tangible substance. They can only be evaluated subjectively in terms of impressions or opinions. To assess whether or not the goals have been attained it is necessary to spell out each goal into a set of clear, concrete, measurable objectives. In contrast to goals, *behavioral objectives* are highly specific, discretely quantifiable, and time-bound. They can be operationally defined in terms of the learner activities or performance characteristics that will be visible and manifest when the objective has been reached.

In his pioneering work in this area Mager (1962)[1] specified three necessary elements in a behavioral objective: (1) a statement of the *observable behavior* which will be expected of the student in demonstrating mastery, (2) a description of the *conditions* or the learning task with its constraints under which the student demonstrates competence, and (3) a specification of a *criterion* level of performance. Kibler, Barker, and Miles (1970)[2] added

---

[1]Mager, R. F. (1962). *Preparing instructional objectives.* Palo Alto, CA: Fearon.
[2]Kibler, R. J., Barker, L. L., & Miles, D. T. (1970). *Behavioral objectives and instruction.* Boston, MA: Allyn & Bacon.

two elements to behavioral objectives: (4) the *product* or result of behavior and (5) a *description of the learner.* Integrating these elements, Wilson, Robeck, and Michael (1974)[1] listed these five requirements of well-formulated behavioral objectives:

1. Statement of *conditions or stipulations,* in essence describing the learning task and its constraints (*content*).
2. Designation of the *learner* (such as a fourth-grade pupil or a ninth grade mathematics student).
3. Use of *action verbs* (such as to construct, to define, to order) that indicate observable activities, although sometimes more complex objectives stated as inferred processes (such as to solve, to analyze, to synthesize, or to apply) may be used.
4. Specification of an outcome (product).
5. Specification of the *standard* or *criterion* of an expected or acceptable level of performance with a possible time limitation.

Illustration:

Objective: Given 20 addition problems consisting of 5 two-digit numbers arranged vertically (condition or content), a pupil in the fourth grade (learner) can write (action verb-observable process) the answer (the written answer being the product) to 18 out of 20 problems in not more than 5 minutes (standard or criterion, quantity, and time specified).

When a standard or criterion is specified for a test item that parallels an objective, for example that 80 percent of the students will answer a given item correctly, it is said to be *criterion-referenced.* Tests which consist of several criterion-referenced items are called criterion-referenced tests. Scores on such tests indicate not only the level of student performance, but also the degree to which teachers are considered accountable for having their students meet a standard of performance that may have been set either by the teacher or by administrators. *Domain-referenced* tests refer not only to tests that are criterion referenced but also to the objectives that are organized into broad categories called *domains*, each of which reflects what its underlying sets of objectives share in common. For example, in the area of reading, a domain would be reading comprehension. The particular sets of objectives which define the elements comprising reading comprehension are each spelled out in their respective individual objectives and associated test items.

A practical problem faced by anyone setting out to write behavioral objectives based on goal statements is to know when one has completed the task. Specifically, how many objectives are necessary before the goal has been circumscribed? Mager (1962)[2] suggested reading through the list of objectives and asking oneself: Is there anything else I expect of individuals who have attained this goal? Goal attainment also may be defined as meeting the standard of a certain proportion of the associated objectives, e.g., 80 percent.

[1]Wilson, J. A. R., Robeck, M. C., & Michael, W. B. (1974). *Psychological foundations of learning and teaching* (2nd ed.). New York: McGraw-Hill.
[2]Mager, R. F. (1962). *Preparing instructional objectives.* Palo Alto, CA: Fearon.

CONTRIBUTION OF BEHAVIORAL OBJECTIVES

Although it is possible to find objections, both practical and theoretical, to behavioral objectives, education has been lax about making its objectives specific and measurable. Between the subjectivity of values and the objectivity of facts, a balance is needed that behavioral objectives facilitate. In helping educators pinpoint their intentions, behavioral objectives will encourage better educational management, more effective classroom procedures, superior feedback to the learner, and a more satisfactory accounting to the public.

SOME LIMITATIONS OF BEHAVIORAL OBJECTIVES

1. Complex behaviors involving inferred processes (to comprehend, to analyze, to synthesize, to perceive) are difficult, if not impossible, to define in any precise, observable way. They also omit any reference to the students themselves: their attitudes, motivations, feelings, and thought processes. Unless these aspects of the learner enter into the teaching/learning experience, the learning situation can become mechanical and artificial. Wilson, Robeck, and Michael (1974)[1] proposed the use of *inferred process objectives* as a means of keeping them in perspective with the outcome and product objectives.

2. Behavioral objectives are painstaking and tedious to write. As a consequence, many educators never get around to preparing them. Moreover, once written, they are of little value unless they have matching test items, observation checklists, or scoring criteria and procedures.

3. Michael Polanyi (1966)[2] defended the notion of "tacit knowing"–those unmeasurables which underlie individuals' skills or competencies in real world problem-solving situations and show up in the impressions formed by their associates. This orientation is supported by the inability of a computer program to simulate some aspects of human intelligence because it cannot evaluate what it cannot count, as human beings obviously do.

---

[1]Wilson, J. A. R., Robeck, M. C., & Michael, W. B. (1974). *Psychological foundations of learning and teaching* (2nd ed.). New York: McGraw-Hill.

[2]Polanyi, M. (1966). *Tacit dimensions*. New York: Doubleday.

SUMMARY OF THE TAXONOMY OF EDUCATIONAL
OBJECTIVES–COGNITIVE DOMAIN[1]

1.00 *Knowledge* Remembering something previously encountered.
    1.10 *Knowledge of specifics* Recall of information bits with concrete referents.
       1.11 Knowledge of terminology
       1.12 Knowledge of specific facts
    1.20 *Knowledge of ways and means of dealing with specifics* Includes methods of inquiry, chronological sequences, standards of judgment, patterns of organization within a field.
       1.21 Knowledge of conventions: characteristic ways of testing ideas and phenomena (usage, style, etc.)
       1.22 Knowledge of trends and sequences
       1.23 Knowledge of classifications and categories
       1.24 Knowledge of criteria
       1.25 Knowledge of methodology, methods of inquiry, and problem-solving approaches.
    1.30 *Knowledge of the universals and abstractions in a field*
       1.31 Knowledge of principles and generalizations
       1.32 Knowledge of theories and structures
2.00 *Comprehension* Understanding of material being communicated, without necessarily relating it to other material.
    2.10 *Translation* from one language or form of communication to another
    2.20 *Interpretation* The explanation or summarization of a communication
    2.30 *Extrapolation* Extension of trends beyond the given data
3.00 *Application* The use of abstractions in particular and concrete situations
4.00 *Analysis* Breaking down communication into its parts so that organization of ideas is clear
    4.10 *Analysis of elements* Recognizing assumptions and distinguishing facts from hypotheses
    4.20 *Analysis of relationships*
    4.30 *Analysis of organizational principles* of structure and arrangement
5.00 *Synthesis* Putting elements into a whole
    5.10 *Production of a unique communication*
    5.20 *Production of a plan for operations*
    5.30 *Derivation of a set of abstract relations*
6.00 *Evaluation* Judging the value of material and methods for a given purpose
    6.10 *Judgments in terms of internal evidence* Logical accuracy and consistency
    6.20 *Judgments in terms of external evidence* Consistency with established standards or models

---

[1]After Bloom, B. S., Engelhart, M. D., Furst, E. J., Hill, W. H., & Krathwohl, D. R. (1956). *Taxonomy of educational objectives, Handbook I: Cognitive domain.* New York: David McKay Co. By permission.

SUMMARY OF THE TAXONOMY OF EDUCATIONAL OBJECTIVES–AFFECTIVE DOMAIN[1]

1.0 *Receiving (attending)* The willingness to attend to or receive certain stimuli.

    1.1 Awareness—to be conscious of stimulus events.
    1.2 Willingness to receive—to attend willingly, without avoidance.
    1.3 Controlled or selected attention—to differentiate figure and ground.

2.0 *Responding* Active involvement and participation.

    2.1 Acquiescence in responding.
    2.2 Willingness to respond.
    2.3 Satisfaction in response.

3.0 *Valuing* The worth of a thing, phenomenon, or behavior.

    3.1 Acceptance of a value.
    3.2 Preference for a value.
    3.3 Commitment.

4.0 *Organization* The organization, interrelationship, and ordering of values.

    4.1 Conceptualization of a value.
    4.2 Organization of a value system.

5.0 *Characterization by a value or value complex* The generalization and integration of a total world view or philosophy.

    5.1 Generalized set—one's basic orientation or point of view.
    5.2 Characterization—the peak of the internalization process.

---

[1] After Krathwohl, D. R., Bloom, B. S., & Masia, B. B. (1956). *Taxonomy of educational objectives, Handbook II: Affective domain.* New York: David McKay Co. By permission.

NEWTON S. METFESSEL, WILLIAM B. MICHAEL, & DONALD A. KIRSNER

INSTRUMENTATION OF THE TAXONOMY OF EDUCATIONAL OBJECTIVES: COGNITIVE DOMAIN[1]

Taxonomy Classification	KEY WORDS	
	Examples of Infinitives	Examples of Direct Objects
1.00 Knowledge		
1.10 Knowledge of Specifics		
1.11 Knowledge of Terminology	to define, to distinguish to acquire, to identify, to recall, to recognize	vocabulary, terms, terminology, meaning(s), definitions, referents, elements
1.12 Knowledge of Specific Facts	to recall, to recognize, to acquire, to identify	facts, factual information, (sources), (names), (dates), (events), (persons), (places), (time periods), properties, examples, phenomena
1.20 Knowledge of Ways and Means of Dealing with Specifics		
1.21 Knowledge of Conventions	to recall, to identify to recognize, to acquire	form(s), conventions, uses, usage, rules, ways, devices, symbols, representations, style(s), format(s)
1.22 Knowledge of Trends, Sequences	to recall, to recognize, to acquire, to identify	action(s), processes, movement(s), continuity, development(s), trend(s), sequence(s), causes, relationship(s), forces, influences
1.23 Knowledge of Classifications and Categories	to recall, to recognize, to acquire, to identify	area(s), type(s), feature(s), class(es), set(s), division(s), arrangement(s), classification(s), category/categories
1.24 Knowledge of Criteria	to recall, to recognize, to acquire, to identify	criteria, basics, elements
1.25 Knowledge of Methodology	to recall, to recognize, to acquire, to identify	methods, techniques, approaches, uses, procedures, treatments
1.30 Knowledge of the Universals and Abstractions in a Field		
1.31 Knowledge of Principles, Generalizations	to recall, to recognize, to acquire, to identify	principle(s), generalization(s), proposition(s), fundamentals, laws, principal elements, implication(s)
1.32 Knowledge of Theories and Structures	to recall, to recognize, to acquire, to identify	theories, bases, interrelations, structure(s), organization(s), formulation(s)

---

[1]Metfessel, N. S., Michael, W. B., & Kirsner, D. A. (1969). Instrumentation of Bloom's and Krathwohl's taxonomies for the writing of educational objectives. *Psychology in the Schools, 6,* 227-231. By permission.

INSTRUMENTATION OF BLOOM'S AND KRATHWOHL'S TAXONOMIES

Taxonomy Classification	KEY WORDS Examples of Infinitives	Examples of Direct Objects
2.00 Comprehension		
2.10 Translation	to translate, to transform, to give in own words, to illustrate, to prepare, to read, to represent, to change, to rephrase, to restate	meaning(s), sample(s), definitions, abstractions, representations, words, phrases
2.20 Interpretation	to interpret, to reorder, to rearrange, to differentiate, to distinguish, to make, to draw to explain, to demonstrate	relevancies, relationships, essentials, aspects, new view(s), qualifications, conclusions, methods, theories, abstractions
2.30 Extrapolation	to estimate, to infer, to conclude, to predict, to differentiate, to determine, to extend, to interpolate, to extrapolate, to fill in, to draw	consequences, implications, conclusions, factors, ramifications, meanings, corollaries, effects, probabilities
3.00 Application	to apply, to generalize, to relate, to choose, to develop, to organize, to use, to employ, to transfer, to restructure, to classify	principles, laws, conclusions, effects, methods, theories, abstractions, situations, generalizations, processes, phenomena, procedures
4.00 Analysis		
4.10 Analysis of Elements	to distinguish, to detect, to identify, to classify, to discriminate, to recognize, to categorize, to deduce	elements, hypothesis/ hypotheses, conclusions, assumptions, statements (of fact), statements (of intent), arguments, particulars
4.20 Analysis of Relationships	to analyze, to contrast, to compare, to distinguish, to deduce	relationships, interrelations, relevance, relevancies, themes, evidence, fallacies, arguments, cause-effect(s), consistency/consistencies, parts, ideas, assumptions
4.30 Analysis of Organizational Principles	to analyze, to distinguish, to detect, to deduce	form(s), pattern(s), purpose(s), point(s) of view(s), techniques, bias(es), structure(s), theme(s), arrangement(s), organization(s)

INSTRUMENTATION OF THE TAXONOMY OF EDUCATIONAL OBJECTIVES: AFFECTIVE DOMAIN[1]

Taxonomy Classification	KEY WORDS	
	Examples of Infinitives	Examples of Direct Objects
5.00 Synthesis		
5.10 Production of a Unique Communication	to write, to tell, to relate, to produce, to constitute, to transmit, to originate, to modify, to document	structure(s), pattern(s), product(s), performance(s), design(s), work(s), communications, effort(s), specifics, composition(s)
5.20 Production of a Plan, or Proposed Set of Operations	to propose, to plan, to produce, to design, to modify, to specify	plan(s), objectives, specification(s), schematic(s), operations, way(s), solution(s), means
5.30 Derivation of a Set of Abstract Relations	to produce, to derive, to develop, to combine, to organize, to synthesize, to classify, to deduce, to develop, to formulate, to modify	phenomena, taxonomies, concept(s), scheme(s), theories, relationships, abstractions, generalizations, hypothesis/hypotheses, perceptions, ways, discoveries
6.00 Evaluation		
6.10 Judgments in Terms of Internal Evidence	to judge, to argue, to validate, to assess, to decide	accuracy/accuracies, consistency/consistencies, fallacies, reliability, flaws, errors, precision, exactness
6.20 Judgments in Terms of External Criteria	to judge, to argue, to consider, to compare, to contrast, to standardize, to appraise	ends, means, efficiency, economy/economies, utility, alternatives, courses of action, standards, theories, generalizations
1.0 Receiving		
1.1 Awareness	to differentiate, to separate, to set apart, to share	sights, sounds, events, designs, arrangements
1.2 Willingness to Receive	to accumulate, to select, to combine, to accept	models, examples, shapes, sizes, meters, cadences
1.3 Controlled or Selected Attention	to select, to posturally respond to, to listen (for), to control	alternatives, answers, rhythms, nuances
2.0 Responding		
2.1 Acquiescence in Responding	to comply (with), to follow, to commend, to approve	directions, instructions, laws, policies, demonstrations
2.2 Willingness to Respond	to volunteer, to discuss, to practice, to play	instruments, games, dramatic works, charades, burlesques
2.3 Satisfaction in Response	to applaud, to acclaim, to spend leisure time in, to augment	speeches, plays, presentations, writings

[1]Metfessel, N. S., Michael, W. B., & Kirsner, D. A. (1969). Instrumentation of Bloom's and Krathwohl's taxonomies for the writing of educational objectives. *Psychology in the Schools, 6*, 227-231. By permission.

INSTRUMENTATION OF THE TAXONOMY OF
EDUCATIONAL OBJECTIVES: AFFECTIVE DOMAIN

	KEY WORDS	
Taxonomy Classification	Examples of Infinitives	Examples of Direct Objects
3.0 Valuing		
3.1 Acceptance of a Value	to increase measured proficiency in, to increase numbers of, to relinquish, to specify	group membership(s), artistic production(s), musical productions, personal friendships
3.2 Preference for a Value	to assist, to subsidize, to help, to support	artists, projects, viewpoints, arguments
3.3 Commitment	to deny, to protest, to debate, to argue	deceptions, irrelevancies, abdications, irrationalities
4.0 Organization		
4.1 Conceptualization of a Value	to discuss, to theorize (on), to abstract, to compare,	parameters, codes, standards, goals
4.2 Organization of a Value System	to balance, to organize, to define, to formulate	systems, approaches, criteria, limits
5.0 Characterization by Value or Value Complex		
5.1 Generalized Set	to revise, to change, to complete, to require,	plans, behavior, methods, effort(s)
5.2 Characterization	to be rated high, by peers in, to be rated high by superiors in, to be rated high by subordinates in, and	humanitarianism, ethics, integrity, maturity
	to avoid, to manage, to resolve, to resist	extravagance(s), excesses, conflicts, exorbitancy/ exorbitancies

SOME LIMITATIONS IN ASSESSING OBJECTIVES IN
THE AFFECTIVE DOMAIN

1. The state of the art in devising reliable and valid measurements of objectives associated with such constructs as attitudes, self-concepts, motivation, emotion, and feelings is often marginal. For example, two individuals on a so-called self-concept test may mark the same response position on a rating scale. If it is low, one person actually may feel inferior to others on this item, whereas the second person is self-confident but self-critical on that particular item (the capacity for self-criticism is not the same as having a poor self-concept). If, on the other hand, the two individuals rate themselves high, one could be covering up a feeling of inferiority, whereas the other really feels on top of things. Altogether, these examples bring into question both the reliability and validity of such instruments portraying a sampling of affective objectives.

2. Attitudes and feelings, like the weather, tend to be changeable, unpredictable, and sensitive to many factors, both inside and outside the learning situation. Hence, writing widely applicable and stable affective objectives is correspondingly difficult.

3. The cause-and-effect relationships between attitudes and feelings, on the one hand, and performance and achievement, on the other, are little understood and seldom straight-forward. For example, there is no broad, consistent body of evidence that children who exhibit positive attitudes toward school or self, necessarily tend to work harder or to achieve at a higher level than do those children who show corresponding negative attitudes. Perhaps some children who feel good about things are more secure, relaxed, and less motivated to extend themselves. A recent study on effective teaching, in fact, revealed a tendency for "competent" teachers to have students with higher cognitive achievement indicators but lower affective indicators, whereas the reverse tendency was true for the "incompetent" teachers.[1]

4. There is likely to be a negative relationship at certain stages of development between age and measured attitudes. Young children (age 5-6), for instance, respond very positively to most experiences, but begin to differentiate along a broader range of feelings as they grow older and become more discerning, critical, or analytical. The result is a shift from more positive to less positive responses as time passes. Although this observation suggests a negative shift in attitude resulting from the learning experience itself, especially in longitudinal studies, it is probably a developmental shift in the child's maturity level.

5. Attitudes are sensitive to such factors as newness, novelty, and the "upbeat" nature of a beginning enterprise or fresh start. A shift in a less positive direction is probable as the experience becomes routine and familiar. In a pretest-posttest design, such as the beginning and end of a school year, this measured shift to a lower position on an attitude scale for reasons of adaptation to novelty becomes confounded with the possibility of an actual downturn in attitudes for reasons related to shortcomings in the program or setting. These confounding factors could compromise the validity of attitudinal measures reflecting affective objectives.

---

[1]Coker, H., Medley, D. M., & Soar, R. S. (1980). How valid are expert opinions about effective teaching? *Phi Delta Kappan, 62,* 131-134, 149.

6. Wherever attitudes are involved, individuals in general tend to have predispositions that are more often positive than negative. The predisposition resembles what has been characterized as the "80–20" phenomenon.[1] Other things being equal, something like 80% of the population are prone to be positive and 20% are negative. Data collected in group settings also are influenced by the "bandwagon" or "contagion" effect, or the impact of a dominant personality. The bipolar predisposition just described would make difficult the universal application of measures of selected affective objectives.

7. Last but not least is the *invasion of privacy* question (Family Rights and Privacy Act). Many affective instruments may violate this statute unless carefully screened for objectionable content. Either prior written consent from the participants or their parents/guardians, if the participants are underage, or anonymity may be possible alternatives. As a general rule, the objectives and instrumentation should be restricted to the educational setting, avoiding attitudes and behaviors outside the school environment.

In spite of the foregoing cautions, measurement in the affective domain can provide useful information. Gallup polls, public acceptance or resistance, the act of casting ballots in an election, and an entire gamut of so-called unobtrusive evidence, all reflect this important dimension. In relation to affective objectives in learning the purpose of this section is precautionary, not disclamatory.

REFERENCE

Gronlund, N. E. (1995). *How to write and use instructional objectives* (5th ed.). Englewood Cliffs, NJ: Prentice Hall.

---

[1]First observed in research on suggestibility by Clark Hull in the 1920's. Subjects were attached to sensitive indicators which would register any body movement forward or backward. They were then instructed to stand perfectly still while the investigator repeatedly suggested that they were falling forward. No one stood perfectly still. Eighty percent moved forward and twenty percent actually moved backward.

"A question well-stated is a question half-answered."

Anonymous

CHAPTER NINE

CRITERIA AND GUIDELINES FOR PLANNING, PREPARING, WRITING, AND EVALUATING THE RESEARCH PROPOSAL, REPORT, THESIS, OR ARTICLE

The final, most important question asked of a research or evaluation study is, *What does it mean?* Each previous section has contributed to the foundation on which conclusions must rest. Careful planning, designing, instrumentation, and statistical analysis form a composite prerequisite to reaching sound conclusions.

This chapter is concerned with how one presents the results of an investigation. Criteria and guidelines are included to assist the researcher in planning, preparing, writing, and evaluating the research proposal, report, thesis (dissertation), or professional journal article.

FORM FOR THE EVALUATION OF AN ARTICLE[1,2]

Characteristic	Completely Incompetent (1)	Poor (2)	Mediocre (3)	Good (4)	Excellent (5)
1. Problem is clearly stated					
2. Hypotheses are clearly stated					
3. Problem is significant					
4. Assumptions are clearly stated					
5. Limitations of the study are stated					
6. Important terms are defined					
7. Relationship of the problem to previous research is made clear					
8. Research design is described fully					
9. Research design is appropriate for the solution of the problem					
10. Research design is free of specific weaknesses					
11. Population and sample are described					
12. Method of sampling is appropriate					
13. Data-gathering methods or procedures are described					
14. Data-gathering methods or procedures are appropriate to the solution of the problem					
15. Data-gathering methods or procedures are utilized correctly					
16. Validity and reliability of the evidence gathered are established					
17. Appropriate methods are selected to analyze the data					
18. Methods utilized in analyzing the data are applied correctly					
19. Results of the analysis are presented clearly					
20. Conclusions are clearly stated					
21. Conclusions are substantiated by the evidence presented					
22. Generalizations are confined to the population from which the sample was drawn					
23. Report is clearly written					
24. Report is logically organized					
25. Tone of the report displays an unbiased, impartial scientific attitude					

[1]Wandt, E., California State University, Los Angeles, CA.
[2]Not all of these twenty-five criteria or characteristics are appropriate in the evaluation of a given article.

A RESEARCH PROPOSAL: A CHECKLIST OF ITEMS FOR POSSIBLE INCLUSION[1]

The following is a checklist of items which are typically included in a research dissertation or report. Not all of the suggested categories are necessary or appropriate for all studies, and the order of items within chapters may vary somewhat. These items are intended to serve as a guide:

CHAPTER I: THE PROBLEM
- [ ] Introduction
- [ ] Background of the problem (e.g., educational trends related to the problem, unresolved issues, social concerns)
- [ ] Statement of the problem situation (basic difficulty – area of concern, felt need)
- [ ] Purpose of the study (goal oriented) – emphasizing practical outcomes or products
- [ ] Questions to be answered or objectives to be investigated
- [ ] Conceptual or substantive assumptions (postulates)
- [ ] Rationale and theoretical framework (when appropriate)
- [ ] Delineation of the research problem (explication of relationships among variables or comparisons to be considered)
- [ ] Statement of hypotheses (conceptual rendition subsequently followed by operational statements in Chapter I or in Methodology Chapter)
- [ ] Importance of the study – may overlap with statement of problem situation
- [ ] Definition of terms (largely conceptual here; operational definitions may follow in Methodology Chapter)
- [ ] Scope and delimitations of the study (narrowing of focus)
- [ ] Outline of the remainder of the thesis or proposal

CHAPTER II: REVIEW OF RELATED LITERATURE
- [ ] Organization of the present chapter – overview
- [ ] Historical background (if necessary)

Purposes to be Served by Review of Research Literature
- [ ] Acquaint reader with existing studies relative to what has been found, who has done work, when and where latest research studies were completed, and what approaches involving research methodology, instrumentation, and statistical analyses were followed (literature review of methodology sometimes saved for chapter on methodology)
- [ ] Establish possible need for study and likelihood for obtaining meaningful, relevant, and significant results
- [ ] Furnish from delineation of various theoretical positions a conceptual framework affording bases for generation of hypotheses and statement of their rationale (when appropriate)

Note: In some highly theoretical studies the chapter "Review of Literature" may need to precede "The Problem" chapter so that the theoretical framework is established for a succinct statement of the research problem and hypotheses. In such a case, an advance organizer in the form of a brief general statement of the purpose of the entire investigation should come right at the beginning of the "Review of Literature" chapter.

[1]Michael, J. J. North Carolina State University, Raleigh, NC, & Michael, W. B. University of Southern California.

Sources for Literature Review
- [ ] General integrative reviews cited that relate to the problem situation or research problem such as those found in *Review of Educational Research, Encyclopedia of Educational Research,* or *Psychological Bulletin.*
- [ ] Specific books, monographs, bulletins, reports, and research articles – preference shown in most instances for literature of the last ten years
- [ ] Unpublished materials (e.g., dissertations, theses, papers presented at recent professional meetings not yet in published form, but possibly available through ERIC)
- [ ] Selection and arrangement of literature review often in terms of questions to be considered, hypotheses set forth, or objectives or specific purposes delineated in problem chapter
- [ ] Summary of literature reviewed (very brief)

CHAPTER III: METHODOLOGY OR PROCEDURES
- [ ] Overview (optional)
- [ ] Description of research methodology or approach (e.g., experimental, quasi-experimental, correlational, causal-comparative, or survey)
- [ ] Research design (Spell out independent, dependent and classificatory variables and sometimes formulate an operational statement of the research hypotheses in null form so as to set the stage for an appropriate research design permitting statistical inferences.)
- [ ] Pilot studies (as they apply to the research design, development of instruments, data collection techniques, and characteristics of the sample)
- [ ] Selection of subjects (This is concerned with sample and population.)
- [ ] Instrumentation (tests, measures, observations, scales, and questionnaires)
- [ ] Field, classroom or laboratory procedures (e.g., instructions to subjects or distribution of materials)
- [ ] Data collection and recording
- [ ] Data processing and analysis (statistical analysis)
- [ ] Methodological assumptions
- [ ] Limitations (weaknesses)
- [ ] Possible restatement of conceptual hypotheses from problem chapter in operational form relative to instrumentation and experimental procedure or design followed (operationally stated hypotheses can also be put in null form to furnish an optional third set of hypotheses amenable to statistical testing) – if not done elsewhere.
- [ ] Summary (optional)

CHAPTER IV: FINDINGS (ANALYSIS AND EVALUATION)
- [ ] Findings are presented in tables or charts when appropriate
- [ ] Findings reported with respect to furnishing evidence for each question asked or each hypothesis posed in problem statement
- [ ] Appropriate headings are established to correspond to each main question or hypothesis considered
- [ ] Factual information kept separate from interpretation, inference, and evaluation (one section for findings and one section for interpretation or discussion)

Note: In certain historical, case-study and anthropological investigations, factual and interpretive material may need to be interwoven to sustain interest level, although the text should clearly reveal what is fact and what is interpretation.

- [ ] Separate section often entitled "Discussion," Interpretation," or "Evaluation" ties together findings in relation to theory, review of literature, or rationale
- [ ] Summary of chapter

CHAPTER V: SUMMARY, CONCLUSIONS, RECOMMENDATIONS

☐ Brief summary of everything covered in first three chapters and in findings portion of Chapter IV

☐ Conclusions ("so what" of findings; often the hypotheses restated as inferences with some degree of definitive commitment and generalizability)

☐ Recommendations (practical suggestions for implementation of findings or for additional research)

CRITERIA FOR EVALUATION OF A RESEARCH REPORT, ARTICLE, OR THESIS[1]

I. Title of article or report

   A. Precise identification of problem area, often including specification of independent and dependent variables and identification of target population.

   B. Sufficient clarity and conciseness for indexing of title.

   C. Effective arrangement of words in title.

II. The problem

   A. Description and statement of problem.
     1. Statement of basic (felt) difficulty or problem situation—significance and importance of the problem area in either basic or applied research.
     2. Careful analysis of known and suspected facts and explanation of existing information and knowledge that may have some bearing on problem—the spelling out of specific factors giving rise to the basic difficulty, of their interrelationships, and of their relevance to the problem area.
     3. Soundness of the logic underlying selection of variables or factors to be studied and expression of their relationship to the problem area.
     4. Systematic and orderly presentation of the interrelationships of relevant facts and concepts underlying the problem.
     5. Clear identification of the problem statement through use of an appropriate heading or paragraph caption (the same requirement holding for other major categories of the research).
     6. Succinct, precise, and unambiguous statement of the research problem (including the delineation of independent, dependent, and classificatory variables), of the major questions to be resolved, or of the objectives to be investigated.
     7. Distinction (if required) between problems or questions that are either factually oriented or value oriented.
     8. Distinction in the instance of theoretically oriented research or of basic research between the purpose, which is often goal-oriented or instrumental in relation to certain pragmatic objectives, and the research problem which is primarily directed toward the findings of relationships, the making of comparisons, or the noting of changes (possible cause and effect relationships) relative to operationally formulated research hypotheses.

---

[1]Michael, W. B. (1967). University of Southern California.

B. Sufficient delimitation of the problem area—narrowing of the scope without becoming concerned with a trivial problem.

C. Review and evaluation of the literature pertinent to problem areas.
1. Adequacy and relevance of the previous investigation cited with reference to the basic difficulty posed, design of the current investigation, procedures followed, and projected analysis of data.
2. Appropriate development of a rationale or theoretical framework from the research studies cited with reference to the current problem under investigation.

D. Clear-cut statement of the conceptions, assumptions, or postulates underlying the problem being investigated.

E. Precise statement of (1) hypotheses or (2) deduced consequences of theories or (3) the objectives of a study (objectives being most common in survey and descriptive research).
1. Hypotheses involving relationships and comparisons.
2. Presentation of deducible consequences or predictions (if any) that are logically consistent with an hypothesis (i.e., antecedent—consequent statement: If A exists, then B follows).

F. Definitions of terms.
1. Clarity in the definitions of key terms and variables (especially constructs).
2. Use of operational definitions whenever possible.

III. Design and methodology (procedures)

A. Logic, structure, and strategy of study carefully delineated.
1. Distinction made between whether the research involves variables manipulated and controlled by the investigator (usually found in experimental research) or whether an *ex post facto* situation exists involving the analysis of data already available or collected as in most field studies and correlational investigations.
2. Appropriate use of paradigms, flow charts, or schematic models.
3. Specification of threats to external and internal validity of the design employed.

B. Clear description of samples studied.
1. Mode of selection of subject cited (e.g., random assignment, matching, voluntary participation, or convenience by being available).
2. Data regarding how representative a sample is relative to a population.
3. Information concerning the possible operation of selective drop-out and survival of the fittest.

C. Adequate information pertaining to the reliability, validity, and standardization properties of instrumentation: psychometric characteristic of scales or tests used.

D. Sufficient description of operational or field procedures followed in the collection of data—where, when, and how data were obtained.

E. Coordination of the specification of the relationship between the null (statistical) hypotheses and the research (problem) hypotheses.

F. Appropriateness of the statistical treatment and data processing procedures.

G. Evidence of a preparatory pilot study having been conducted.

H. Procedure clearly enough described so that other investigators can replicate (repeat) the study performed under essentially comparable conditions in the future.

I. Statement of methodological assumption such as adequacy of reliability and validity of measures, representativeness of samples, fulfillment of appropriate requirements for carrying out statistical tests.

IV. Presentation and analysis of data

A. Logical and orderly exposition in terms of the framework of the hypotheses, deductions, objectives, or questions asked in conjunction with the statement of the problem.
   1. Objective rather than subjective or speculative presentation.
   2. Analysis consistent with and supported by the facts obtained.
   3. Absence of overgeneralizations or sweeping statements that go beyond the data.
   4. Relationships of the findings to previously cited research explicitly shown.
   5. Negative findings relative to the hypotheses as well as positive findings presented with minimal distortion or bias.
   6. Uncontrolled factors influencing data outcomes appropriately cited and discussed.
   7. Weaknesses in the data honestly conceded and discussed with appropriate emphasis.
   8. Lack of confusion between facts and inferences clearly shown—separation of analysis of findings from interpretation and discussion of findings.
   9. Resolution of contradictions, inconsistencies, or misleading elements in the findings.

B. Appropriate and clear use of charts, tables, figures, and graphs.

V. Summary and conclusion

A. Precise and accurate statement of (1) the problem, (2) the methodology followed, and (3) the findings without the introduction of new or irrelevant information.

B. Conclusions at a scope and level of generality justified by the data presented.

C. Appropriate caution exercised and necessary qualifications made in drawing conclusions.

D. Conclusions in a form that other investigators can understand and subsequently verify.

E. Conclusions coordinated with the tentative acceptance or rejection of the research hypotheses presented or with the objectives or questions posed.

F. New questions set forth for possible investigation—recommendations for additional research in the problem area study.

G. Recommendations concerning implementation of the research findings when appropriate relative to the objectives stated in the purpose of the investigation (most frequently encountered in survey studies and action research).

RESEARCH METHODOLOGY—A DISSENTING VIEW

The prerequisite of originality is the art of forgetting, at the proper moment, what we know.

Arthur Koestler

The dominant theme of this Handbook is to be planful and systematic—ideally, to deduce hypotheses from theory and put them to the test or to set objectives, arrange procedures, and intentionally achieve a planned mission.

B. F. Skinner, the psychologist, whose impact on education is only beginning to be felt through such innovations as the modern teaching machine, operant conditioning, and behavior modification, vigorously dissents from any formal view of "the scientific method." In remarks from his book *Cumulative Record*, he discusses what he calls his "unformalized principles of scientific practice."[1]

1. "When you run onto something interesting, drop everything else and study it."
2. "Some ways of doing research are easier than others." [And in searching for an easier way to do something, one may develop more efficient techniques and also discover unforeseen phenomena.]
3. "Some people are lucky." [New ideas and discoveries often are accidental.]
4. "Apparatuses sometimes break down." [And one stumbles upon unexcepted and fruitful consequences.]

Skinner summarizes his point of view in these words:

This account of my scientific behavior . . .is as exact in letter and spirit as I can now make it. The notes, data, and publications which I have examined do not show that I ever behaved in the manner of Man Thinking as described by John Stuart Mill or John Dewey or in reconstructions of scientific behavior by other philosophers of science. I never faced a Problem which was more than the eternal problem of finding order. I never attacked a problem by constructing a Hypothesis. I never deduced Theorems or submitted them to Experimental Check. So far as I can see, I had no preconceived Model of behavior—certainly not a physiological or mentalistic one and, I believe, not a conceptual one.[2]

Another strong argument for the value of an informal approach to scientific research is presented by Arthur Koestler in his scholarly work, *The Act of Creation*[3]—a comprehensive documentation of the thesis that discovery, invention, and originality whether in science, technology, or the arts is remarkably unsystematic, unforeseeable, and "accidental."

All of this is reminiscent of the Persian fairy tale of the Three Princes of the Isle of Serendip (Ceylon) who periodically would sally forth on to the mainland in search of one thing or another. While they never fulfilled any of their intended missions, they always returned with *other* discoveries or experiences even more marvelous. Hence, the term *serendipity*—the finding of valuable or agreeable things not sought for.

---

[1]Skinner, B. F., (1959). *Cumulative record* (pp. 76-100). New York: Appleton-Century-Crofts, Inc.
[2]Ibid, p. 88. Also cited in Gage, N. L. (1963). *Handbook of research on education* (p. 101).Chicago, IL: Rand McNally.
[3]Koestler, A. (1964). *The act of creation*. New York: MacMillan.

REFERENCES

American Psychological Association. (1994). *Publication manual of the American Psychological Association* (4th ed.). Washington, DC: American Psychological Association.

Becker, H. S. (1986). *Writing for social scientists: How to start and finish your thesis, book or article.* Chicago, IL: University of Chicago Press.

Krathwohl, D. R. (1988). *How to prepare a research proposal: Suggestions for conceptualizing implementing, and evaluating research studies* (3rd ed.). Syracuse, NY: Syracuse University Press.

Meloy, J. (1994). *Writing the qualitative dissertation: Understanding by doing.* Hillsdale, NJ: Lawrence Erlbaum.

Pyrczak, F. & Bruce, R. R. (1992). *Writing empirical research reports: A basic guide for students of the social and behavioral sciences.* Los Angeles, CA: Pyrczak Publishing.

Van Til, W. (1986). *Writing for professional publication* (2nd ed.). Boston: Allyn & Bacon.

APPENDIX OF STATISTICAL TABLES

TABLE A[1]

Percent of Total Area under the Normal Curve between Mean Ordinate and
Ordinate at Any Given Sigma-Distance from the Mean

$\frac{\bar{x}}{\sigma}$	.00	.01	.02	.03	.04	.05	.06	.07	.08	.09
0.0	00.00	00.40	00.80	01.20	01.60	01.99	02.39	02.79	03.19	03.59
0.1	03.98	04.38	04.78	05.17	05.57	05.96	06.36	06.75	07.14	07.53
0.2	07.93	08.32	08.71	09.10	09.48	09.87	10.26	10.64	11.03	11.41
0.3	11.79	12.17	12.55	12.93	13.31	13.68	14.06	14.43	14.80	15.17
0.4	15.54	15.91	16.28	16.64	17.00	17.36	17.72	18.08	18.44	18.79
0.5	19.15	19.50	19.85	20.19	20.54	20.88	21.23	21.57	21.90	22.24
0.6	22.57	22.91	23.24	23.57	23.89	24.22	24.54	24.86	25.17	25.49
0.7	25.80	26.11	26.42	26.73	27.04	27.34	27.64	27.94	28.23	28.52
0.8	28.81	29.10	29.39	29.67	29.95	30.23	30.51	30.78	31.06	31·33
0.9	31.59	31.86	32.12	32.38	32.64	32.90	33.15	33.40	33.65	33.89
1.0	34.13	34.38	34.61	34.85	35.08	35.31	35.54	35.77	35.99	36.21
1.1	36.43	36.65	36.86	37.08	37.29	37.49	37.70	37.90	38.10	38.30
1.2	38.49	38.69	38.88	39.07	39.25	39.44	39.62	39.80	39.97	40.15
1.3	40.32	40.49	40.66	40.82	40.99	41.15	41.31	41.47	41.62	41.77
1.4	41.92	42.07	42.22	42.36	42.51	42.65	42.79	42.92	43.06	43.19
1.5	43.32	43.45	43.57	43.70	43.83	43.94	44.06	44.18	44.29	44.41
1.6	44.52	44.63	44.74	44.84	44.95	45.05	45.15	45.25	45.35	45.45
1.7	45.54	45.64	45.73	45.82	45.91	45.99	46.08	46.16	46.25	46.33
1.8	46.41	46.49	46.56	46.64	46.71	46.78	46.86	46.93	46.99	47.06
1.9	47.13	47.19	47.26	47.32	47.38	47.44	47.50	47.56	47.61	47.67
2.0	47.72	47.78	47.83	47.88	47.93	47.98	48.03	48.08	48.12	48.17
2.1	48.21	48.26	48.30	48.34	48.38	48.42	48.46	48.50	48.54	48.57
2.2	48.61	48.64	48.68	48.71	48.75	48.78	48.81	48.84	48.87	48.90
2.3	48.93	48.96	48.98	49.01	49.04	49.06	49.09	49.11	49.13	49.16
2.4	49.18	49.20	49.22	49.25	49.27	49.29	49.31	49.32	49.34	49.36
2.5	49.38	49.40	49.41	49.43	49.45	49.46	49.48	49.49	49.51	49.52
2.6	49.53	49.55	49.56	49.57	49.59	49.60	49.61	49.62	49.63	49.64
2.7	49.65	49.66	49.67	49.68	49.69	49.70	49.71	49.72	49.73	49.74
2.8	49.74	49.75	49.76	49.77	49.77	49.78	49.79	49.79	49.80	49.81
2.9	49.81	49.82	49.82	49.83	49.84	49.84	49.85	49.85	49.86	49.86
3.0	49.87	49.87	49.87	49.88	49.88	49.89	49.89	49.89	49.90	49.90
3.1	49.90	49.91	49.91	49.91	49.92	49.92	49.92	49.92	49.93	49.93
3.2	49.93	49.93	49.94							
3.3	49.95									
3.4	49.97									
3.5	49.98									
3.7	49.99									

---

[1]From Spence, J. T., et al. (1968). *Elementary statistics*. New York: Appleton-Century-Crofts, Inc. In turn, adapted from Lindquist, E. L. *First course in statistics*, Revised, Houghton Mifflin; original source: Pearson, K. (Ed.). Table B. *Tables for Statisticians and Biometricians*. Cambridge University Press.

TABLE B[1]

Values of *t* for One-tailed and Two-tailed Tests at Specified Significance Levels

Degrees of Freedom (*df*)	Test	Significance Level			
	One-tailed:	.050	.025	.010	.005
	Two-tailed:	(.100)	.050	.020	.010
1		6.314	12.706	31.821	63.657
2		2.920	4.303	6.965	9.925
3		2.353	3.182	4.541	5.841
4		2.132	2.776	3.747	4.604
5		2.015	2.571	3.365	4.032
6		1.943	2.447	3.134	3.707
7		1.895	2.365	2.998	3.499
8		1.860	2.306	2.896	3.355
9		1.833	2.262	2.831	3.250
10		1.812	2.228	2.764	3.169
11		1.796	2.201	2.718	3.106
12		1.782	2.179	2.681	3.055
13		1.771	2.160	2.650	3.012
14		1.761	2.145	2.624	2.977
15		1.753	2.131	2.602	2.947
16		1.746	2.120	2.583	2.921
17		1.740	2.110	2.567	2.898
18		1.734	2.101	2.552	2.878
19		1.729	2.093	2.539	2.861
20		1.725	2.086	2.528	2.845
21		1.721	2.080	2.518	2.831
22		1.717	2.074	2.508	2.819
23		1.714	2.069	2.500	2.807
24		1.711	2.064	2.492	2.797
25		1.708	2.060	2.485	2.787
26		1.706	2.056	2.479	2,779
27		1.703	2.052	2.473	2.771
28		1.701	2.048	2.467	2.763
29		1.699	2.045	2.462	2.756
30		1.697	2.042	2.457	2.750

[1]Adapted from Spence, J. T., et al. (1968). *Elementary statistics.* New York: Appleton-Century-Crofts, Inc. In turn, abridged from Fisher & Yates. (1953). Table III. *Statistical tables for biological, agricultural and medical research* (4th Ed.). Edinburgh: Oliver and Boyd, Ltd.

TABLE C[1]

Values of Chi-square (χ^2) for Two-tailed Test at Specified Significance Levels [2]

Degrees Freedom (df) Test:	Significance Level		
	.050	.020	.010
1	3.84	5.41	6.64
2	5.99	7.82	9.21
3	7.82	9.84	11.34
4	9.49	11.67	13.28
5	11.07	13.39	15.09
6	12.59	15.03	16.81
7	14.07	16.62	18.48
8	15.51	18.17	20.09
9	16.92	19.68	21.67
10	18.31	21.16	23.21
11	19.68	22.62	24.72
12	21.03	24.05	26.22
13	22.36	25.47	27.69
14	23.68	26.87	29.14
15	25.00	28.26	30.58
16	26.30	29.63	32.00
17	27.59	31.00	33.41
18	28.87	32.35	34.80
19	30.14	33.69	36.19
20	31.41	35.02	37.57
21	32.67	36.34	38.93
22	33.92	37.66	40.29
23	35.17	38.97	41.64
24	36.42	40.27	42.98
25	37.65	41.57	44.31
26	38.88	42.86	45.64
27	40.11	44.14	46.96
28	41.34	45.42	48.28
29	42.56	46.69	49.59
30	43.77	47.96	50.89

---

[1]Adapted from Spence, J. T., et al. (1968). *Elementary statistics.* New York: Appleton-Century-Crofts, Inc. In turn, abridged from Fisher & Yates. (1953). Table III. *Statistical tables for biological, agricultural and medical research* (4th Ed.). Edinburgh: Oliver and Boyd, Ltd.

[2]When df = 1, the significance level for a *one-tailed test* can be stated as ½ p of a two-tailed test. In that event, the .05 level of significance is 2.71; ½ (.050), or .025, = 3.84; ½ (.020), or .010, = 5.41; and ½ (.010), or .005 = 6.64.

TABLE D[1]

Values of *r* at the 5% and 1% Levels of Significance

Degrees of Freedom (*df*)[2]	Significance .050	Level .010	Degrees of Freedom (*df*)	Significance .050	Level .010
1	.997	1.000	24	.388	.496
2	.950	.990	25	.381	.487
3	.878	.959	26	.374	.478
4	.811	.917	27	.367	.470
5	.754	.874	28	.361	.463
6	.707	.834	29	.355	.456
7	.666	.798	30	.349	.449
8	.632	.765	35	.325	.418
9	.602	.735	40	.304	.393
10	.576	.708	45	.288	.372
11	.553	.684	50	.273	.354
12	.532	.661	60	.250	.325
13	.514	.641	70	.232	.302
14	.497	.623	80	.217	.283
15	.482	.606	90	.205	.267
16	.468	.590	100	.195	.254
17	.456	.575	125	.174	.228
18	.444	.561	150	.159	.208
19	.433	.549	200	.138	.181
20	.423	.537	300	.113	.148
21	.413	.526	400	.098	.128
22	.404	.515	500	.088	.115
23	.396	.505	1000	.062	.081

[1]Spence, J. T., et al. (1968). *Elementary statistics* (2nd ed.) (p. 236). New York: Appleton-Century-Crofts, Inc. In turn, a portion of Table D is abridged from Fisher & Yates. (1953). Table VI. *Statistical tables for biological, agricultural, and medical research* (4th ed.). Edinburgh: Oliver and Boyd, Ltd., by permission. The remainder of the table is from Snedecor, G. W. (1946). *Statistical methods*. Ames, IA: Iowa State College Press. By permission.
[2]*df* = *N* - 2, where *N* is the number of pairs of scores.

TABLE E[1]

Values of p (rank-order correlation coefficient) at the 5% and 1%
Levels of Significance

N (No. of pairs)	.050	.010
5	1.000	—
6	.886	1.000
7	.786	.929
8	.738	.881
9	.683	.833
10	.648	.794
12	.591	.777
14	.544	.714
16	.506	.665
18	.475	.625
20	.450	.591
22	.428	.562
24	.409	.537
26	.392	.515
28	.377	.496
30	.364	.478

[1]Spence, J. T., et al. (1968). Elementary statistics (2nd ed.) (p. 236). New York: Appleton-Century-Crofts, Inc. In turn, computed from Olds, E. G. (1949). Distribution of the sum of squares of rank differences for small numbers of individuals, Ann. Math. Statist., 20, 117-118, the Institute of Mathematical Statistics, by permission.

AUTHOR INDEX

SUBJECT INDEX